TALES FROM THE MASNAVI

TALES FROM THE MASNAVI

Translated by

Arthur J. Arberry

CURZON
PRESS

Published in 1993 by
Curzon Press Ltd.,
St John's Studios
Church Road
Richmond
Surrey TW9 2QA

ISBN 0 7007 0273 3

First published 1961

British Library Cataloguing in Publication Data
A CIP record of this title is available from the British Library

Printed in Great Britain by
Antony Rowe Ltd.

CONTENTS

INTRODUCTION

THE *Masnavi* of Jalal al-Din Rumi (1207-1273), a massive
poem of some 25,000 rhyming couplets divided by its author
into six books, and called by the poet Jami 'the Koran in the
Persian tongue,' by common consent ranks among the world's
greatest masterpieces of religious literature. It must however
be admitted that as it stands the huge work makes very
difficult reading. 'The poem resembles a trackless ocean,'
wrote Professor R. A. Nicholson who devoted many years to
meticulous study and fastidious interpretation. 'There are no
boundaries; no lines of demarcation between the literal
"husk" and the "kernel" of doctrine in which its inner
sense is conveyed and copiously expounded.' Written down
sporadically over a long period of time, without any firm
framework to keep the discourse on orderly lines, it is at
first, and even at repeated reading a disconcertingly diffuse
and confused composition; nevertheless a pattern of a sort
may be seen to knit together the seemingly random topics
and multitudinous digressions, as was shown by G. Richter
in his illuminating monograph *Persiens Mystiker Dschelal-eddin
Rumi* (Breslau, 1933).

The material which makes up the *Masnavi* is divisible into
two different though by no means distinct categories: theoretical discussion of the principal themes of Sufi mystical life
and doctrine, and stories or fables intended to illustrate those
themes as they arise. In presenting the poem for popular
reading, by a public unable to peruse it in the original Persian,
it is of course possible to translate the giant epic word by
word right through from beginning to end. This was done,
for the first and so far the only time, by R. A. Nicholson,
whose eight-volume text-edition, translation and commentary
surely constitutes the greatest single contribution to Islamic
studies of the first half of the twentieth century. Nicholson
himself however would have been the first to concede that
the rich fruits of his single-minded and unremitting labours
were digestible with extreme difficulty, and even then only

by scholars having the same kind of specialist equipment as himself. Yet the poem obviously deserves a far wider circle of readers than that. How can that larger circle be reached and satisfied?

Nicholson made two attempts, in the little leisure left to him by his absorbing preoccupation with the major task. *Tales of Mystic Meaning*, published in 1931, offered in its 170 pages a small but representative selection from the *Masnavi* consisting for the most part of stories scattered through the whole poem. In *Rumi, Poet and Mystic*, which came out posthumously in 1950, an even smaller selection was presented. These two books, meritorious as they are, obviously fall short by a long way of meeting the larger need; yet they point the way to how that need might be met. Their example, and the success which they achieved, have encouraged the present writer to isolate from the *Masnavi* all the illustrative anecdotes as they occur, and to translate them into reasonably idiomatic English. The volume here published, which it is hoped to follow up with another, covers exactly one-half of the original.

The use of the parable in religious teaching has of course a very long history, and Rumi broke no new ground when he decided to lighten the weight of his doctrinal exposition by introducing tales and fables to which he gave an allegorical twist. He was especially indebted, as he freely acknowledges in the course of his poem, to two earlier Persian poets, Sana'i of Ghazna and Farid al-Din 'Attar of Nishapur. More will be said presently of these authors, Rumi's immediate models; but they themselves, though original writers within the boundaries of Persian poetical literature, were not original in an absolute sense. Persian authors, many of whom wrote also or exclusively in Arabic particularly during the earlier history of Islam, leaned heavily upon the traditions established in Arabic writing which preceded the origins of classical Persian literature by some three centuries.

First and foremost, there was the Koran itself to serve as a perfect, because a divinely inspired examplar. As I have endeavoured to demonstrate in my *Koran Interpreted*, that 'incoherency' for which the Suras, making up the corpus of

Muhammad's revelations, have been frequently criticized is apparent rather than real; the criticism arises from a misconception, a failure to notice the unusual but perfectly valid and sound structural pattern of the composition. In the Koran, incidents from the lives of earlier prophets, told with great artistry, are introduced at intervals and episodically as proofs of the eternal verities being enunciated.

In much the same way, anecdotes from the life of Muhammad himself were recited by lawyers, theologians and pastoral preachers to give chapter and verse for their theoretical expositions of Muslim life and doctrine. In the field of statecraft the 'Mirrors for Princes' tradition, taken over from the Sassanian writings of pre-Islamic Persia, was early on supplemented by Indian animal fables to which veiled political meanings were attached. The *Kalila and Dimna*, translated by the Persian Ibn al-Muqaffa' out of the Pahlavi, itself a version from the original Sanskrit, achieved an immediate and lasting popularity though its unlucky author ended his days young in a furnace.

The first mystics in Islam, or rather those of them who were disposed to propagate Sufi teachings in writing as well as by example, followed the lead set by the preachers. Ibn al-Mubarak, al-Muhasibi and al-Kharraz were competent Traditionists and therefore sprinkled acts and sayings of the Prophet, and of his immediate disciples, through the pages of their ascetic manuals. They themselves, and other mystics of their times, furnished the next generation of Sufi writers with supplementary evidence, their own acts and words, to support the rapidly developing doctrine. Abu Talib al-Makki, al-Kalabadhi, al-Sarraj, al-Qushairi and Hujviri (who was the first to write on Sufism in Persian), leading up to the great Muhammad al-Ghazali, all used the same scheme in their methodical statements: first topic, then citation from the Koran, a Tradition or two of the Prophet, followed by appropriate instances from the lives and works of earlier saints and mystics. Biographies of the Sufi masters, such as were compiled by al-Sulami, Abu Nu 'aim al-Isbahani and al-Ansari (the last in Persian), provided rich and varied materials enabling later theorists to enlarge the range of their illustrations.

Meanwhile the allegory, reminiscent of the 'myths' of Plato

13

and the fables of Aesop, established itself as a dramatic alternative method of demonstration. It seems that here the philosophers were first in the field, notably Avicenna who himself had mystical interests; he would have been preceded by the Christian Hunain ibn Ishaq, translator of Greek philosophical texts, if we may accept as authentic the ascription to him of a version 'made from the Greek' of the romance of Salaman and Absal. Among Avicenna's compositions in this genre was the famous legend of Haiy ibn Yaqzan, afterwards elaborated by the Andalusian Ibn Tufail and thought by some, through the medium of Simon Ockley's English translation, to have influenced Daniel Defoe in his *Robinson Crusoe*. Shihab al-Din al-Suhrawardi al-Maqtul, executed for heresy at Aleppo in 1191—only sixteen years before Rumi was born in distant Balkh—combining philosophy with mysticism wrote Sufi allegories in Persian prose, and was apparently the first author to do so; unless indeed we may apply the word allegory to describe the subtle meditations on mystical love composed by Ahmad al-Ghazali, who died in 1126.

Such in brief are the antecedents to Rumi's antecedents. When Sana'i began writing religious and mystical poetry in the early years of the twelfth century, he found the Persian language prepared for his task by Hujviri and Ansari. His greatest and most famous work, the *Garden of Mystical Truth*, completed in 1131 and dedicated to the Ghaznavid ruler Bahram Shah, is best understood as an adaptation in verse of the by now traditional prose manual of Sufism. The first mystical epic in Persian, it is divided into ten chapters, each chapter being subdivided into sections with illustrative stories. It thus gives the superficial impression of a learned treatise in verse; though its affinity to the established pattern of Persian epic is shown by the lengthy exordia devoted to praising Allah, blessing his Prophet, and flattering the reigning Sultan. Rumi in his *Masnavi* quotes or imitates the *Garden* of Sana'i on no fewer than nine occasions. It should be added that Sana'i, like Rumi after him, composed many odes and lyrics of a mystical character; unlike Rumi, he also wrote a number of shorter mystical epics including one, the *Way of Worshippers*, which opens as an allegory and only in its concluding passages, far too extended, turns into a panegyric.

14

Farid al-Din 'Attar, whom Rumi met as a boy and whose long life ended in about 1230, improved and expanded greatly on the foundations laid by Sana'i. Judged solely as a poet he was easily his superior; he also possessed a far more penetrating and creative mind, and few more exciting tasks await the student of Persian literature than the methodical exploration, as yet hardly begun, of his voluminous and highly original writings. His best known poem, paraphrased by Edward FitzGerald as *The Bird-Parliament*, has been summarized by Professor H. Ritter, the leading western authority on 'Attar and a scholar of massive and most varied erudition, as a 'grandiose poetic elaboration of the *Risalat al-Tayr* of Muhammad or Ahmad Ghazali. The birds, led by the hoopoe, set out to seek Simurgh, whom they had elected as their king. All but thirty perish on the path on which they have to traverse seven dangerous valleys. The surviving thirty eventually recognize themselves as being the deity (*si murgh* — *Simurgh*), and then merge in the divine Simurgh.' It is not difficult to apprehend in this elaborate and beautiful allegory, surely among the greatest works of religious literature, the influence of the animal fables of Ibn al-Muqaffa'.

In his *Divine Poem*, which has been edited by Professor Ritter and of which French and English translations are understood to be in preparation, 'Attar takes as the framework of his allegory a legend which might have been lifted bodily out of the *Thousand and One Nights*. 'A king asks his six sons what, of all things in the world, they wish for. They wish in turn for the daughter of the fairy king, the art of witchcraft, the magic cup of Djam, the water of life, Solomon's ring, and the elixir. The royal father tries to draw them away from their worldly desires and to inspire them with higher aims.' The supporting narratives are, like those of *The Bird-Parliament*, told with masterly skill and a great dramatic sense.

For his *Poem of Suffering* Farid al-Din 'Attar drew upon yet another type of folk legend. The story of Muhammad's 'ascension', that miraculous night-journey 'from the Holy Mosque to the Further Mosque' which is hinted at in Sura XVIII of the Koran and was afterwards picturesquely elaborated in the Traditions, had long fascinated Sufi mystics who liked to describe their spiritual raptures in terms of an ascent into heaven. The *Book of Ascension* of al-Qushairi, as yet un-printed, collects together a number of versions of the celestial adventure. In 'Attar's narrative 'a Sufi disciple, in his helpless-ness and despair, is advised by a *pir* to visit successively all mythical and cosmic beings: angel, throne, writing tablet, stilus, heaven and hell, sun, moon, the four elements, mountain, sea, the three realms of nature, Iblis, the spirits, the prophets, senses, phantasy, mind heart and soul (the self). In the sea of the soul, in his own self, he eventually finds the godhead.' It may be remarked in parenthesis that the modern Indian poet Iqbal employed the same allegory in his last great Persian epic, the *Song Immortal*.

Though Rumi was certainly familiar with the first two of these three poems, and probably had recourse to other epics of 'Attar—and his debt to 'Attar's prose *Biographies of the Saints* is manifest—the work which exercised the most immediate and powerful influence upon him was the *Book of Secrets*, a copy of which 'Attar is said to have presented to him. This poem, unlike most of 'Attar's epics, 'has no framework-story, and repeatedly mentions the gnostic motif of the entanglement of the pre-existing soul in the base material world.' Somewhat similar in design to the *Garden* of Sana'i, the *Book of Secrets* is more methodically planned than the *Masnavi* but falls far short of it in size and scope. Professor Nicholson traced seven borrowings from this poem.

The foregoing are but a few of the very many sources on which Rumi drew for his illustrative stories. Professor Nicholson's very learned annotations on the *Masnavi* trace the lineage of most of the anecdotes, and Professor Furuzanfar of Teheran, the leading Persian authority on Rumi, has pub-lished a valuable monograph on this subject. In my *Classical Persian Literature* I have set out the antecedents to the 'Miracle of the Pearls' (Tale 62 in this volume). That story is a good example of how Rumi expanded on his basic materials; 'The Elephant in the Dark' (Tale 71) is a rarer instance of com-pression. The anecdote is told at considerable length by al-Ghazali in his *Revival of Religious Sciences*, and Sana'i gives an elaborate version of it in his *Garden*. Readers may like to look at E. G. Browne's translation and to compare it with Rumi's brief summary.

16

Not far from Ghur once stood a city tall
Whose denizens were sightless one and all.
A certain Sultan once, when passing nigh,
Had pitched his camp upon the plain hard by,
Wherein, to prove his splendour, rank, and state,
Was kept an elephant most huge and great.
Then in the townsmen's minds arose desire
To know the nature of this creature dire.
Blind delegates by blind electorate
Were therefore chosen to investigate
The beast, and each, by feeling trunk or limb,
Strove to acquire an image clear of him.
Thus each conceived a visionary whole,
And to the phantom clung with heart and soul.

When to the city they were come again,
The eager townsmen flocked to them amain.
Each one of them—wrong and misguided all—
Was eager his impressions to recall.
Asked to describe the creature's size and shape,
They spoke, while round about them, all agape,
Stamping impatiently, their comrades swarm
To hear about the monster's shape and form.
Now, for his knowledge each inquiring wight
Must trust to touch, being devoid of sight,
So he who'd only felt the creature's ear,
On being asked: 'How doth its heart appear?'
'Mighty and terrible,' at once replied,
'Like to a carpet, hard and flat and wide!'
Then he who on its trunk had laid his hand
Broke in: 'Nay, nay! I better understand!
'Tis like a water-pipe, I tell you true,
Hollow, yet deadly and destructive too';
While he who'd had but leisure to explore
The sturdy limbs which the great beast upbore,
Exclaimed: 'No, no! To all men be it known
'Tis like a column tapered to a cone!'
Each had but known one part, and no man all;
Hence into deadly error each did fall.
No way to know the All man's heart can find:
Can knowledge e'er accompany the blind?

Further information on the sources of the tales, and the many passages from the Koran to which reference is made in the *Masnavi*, will be found in the notes appended to this volume.

As it is my hope some day to publish a full study of the life, writings and teachings of Rumi, I propose to postpone to that occasion a more extended analysis of the contents, pattern and doctrine of the *Masnavi*. To conclude this short introduction I propose to touch briefly on the prosody and poetic style of this great work, and to explain summarily the method followed in making this translation.

First then as to the prosody: the *Masnavi* is composed throughout—apart from the prose prefaces and headings—in rhyming couplets (which is what its title means) in the metre called *ramal*, the pattern of which consists of three feet, the first two made up of one long syllable, one short, and two longs, the third foot being of one long, one short, one long.

> bishnav az nay chun shikayat mikunad
> v-az juda'iha hikayat mikunad
> k-an nayistan ta mara bibrida and
> az nafiram mard u zan nalida and

This deliberate and somewhat solemn measure, used already by 'Attar in his *Bird-Parliament*, is peculiarly suited to leisurely narrative and lengthy didactic; and Rumi, who in his odes and lyrics proved himself a virtuoso in handling the rarest and most intricate rhythms, controls the more pedestrian metre of the *Masnavi* like the master of melody that he was.

The rhyming couplet had never commended itself as a vehicle of serious poetry to the Arabs, who consequently failed to discover the epic. For the Persians, from Firdausi onwards, the easy flow of poetic discourse essential to epopée was fully secured once the impediment of the Arab monorhyme had been removed. Rhyme then acquired a different function; or perhaps it may rather be said to have resumed its original function as a characteristic feature of elevated or emphatic prose utterance. 'A stitch in time—saves nine'; 'jedes Tierchen—hat sein Plaisirchen': in folk wisdom the rhyme is not meant as an aesthetic embellishment, even less (as in the formal ode of the Arabs and Persians) as a means of displaying linguistic virtuosity. It invests the statement with a kind of magical authority; but being readily contrived in Arabic and Persian, which abound in rhyme, in those languages it carries very little rhetorical weight. It is not a consciously 'poetical' device.

Poets of the 'new style' like Nizami and Khaqani, when they came to employ the rhyming couplet, sought to compensate for its simplicity and informality by loading it with a formidable charge of tropes and figures, and by introducing references so obscure that only the most erudite could fully penetrate their meaning. Rumi for his part, writing not for princes but for the love of God and of his fellow man, was content to eschew artificial ornament almost entirely. The language which he employed was plain and direct, though at times highly idiomatic; this latter feature, which must have appealed immediately to the ordinary folk who heard his verses recited at the nightly 'concerts' of the Mevlevi dervish circle in Konia, presents the modern reader with problems of understanding due not to any original obscurity but to the changes in popular usage which seven centuries have inevitably brought about.

But the major difficulty of interpreting Rumi springs not (as with Nizami and his like) from obscurity of reference, usually to be cleared up by consulting the relevant specialist textbooks, but from obscurity of a doctrine based largely on experiences in their very nature wellnigh incommunicable. Professor Nicholson put this point very well. 'Oriental interpreters expound the *Masnavi* in terms of the pantheistic system associated with Ibn al-'Arabi. Being convinced that the poem was deeply influenced from that quarter, they hold that it cannot be made intelligible without reference to those ideas. So far I agree, though such a mode of explanation is apt to mislead us unless we remember that Rumi is a poet and mystic, not a philosopher and logician. He has no system, he creates an aesthetic atmosphere which defies analysis. As a rule, we apprehend the main drift and broad sense of his words: the precise and definite meanings assigned to them are a makeshift: we can really do no more than indicate parallel lines of thought, call attention to affinities, and suggest clues. Commentators inevitably turn mystical poetry into intellectual prose. Viewed through this medium, what was a fish swimming in its native element becomes a dry dissected specimen on the laboratory table.'

The task confronting interpreters of Rumi who come after Professor Nicholson has been immensely eased by the flood of illumination which his deep study and varied erudition enabled him to throw on the all too frequent shadowy passages of the *Masnavi*. I cannot adequately express my gratitude for his splendid guidance, not only in the printed record available to all, but also during many years of close personal contact. A comparison of the present version with his will disclose very many contexts where I have been unable to suggest any variation of his wording apart from a certain readjustment made for the sake of greater readability. In pure interpretation I have found myself in disagreement with him very rarely indeed. The main differences between my version and his are, first, that I have separated out the stories from the didactic discourses in which they are embedded (and it is in these latter parts of the poem that the major obscurities occur); and secondly, that I have liberated the translation from the somewhat pedantic encumbrances, the brackets signifying a word or a phrase supplied by the translator, the unintelligible literalness mitigated by a sprinkle of footnotes, which are still thought by many scholars to be necessary, as proof of their academic integrity, when translating oriental texts.

My version, like Professor Nicholson's, is in prose. There is in my view no case whatsoever for torturing the fluent verse of the *Masnavi* into formal English metre, much less frozen English rhyme. However, to indicate that the original work was not in prose, I have phrased my version in loose rhythms corresponding very roughly with the rhythmical periods of the Persian. I have sometimes introduced slang expressions where the original seemed to me to compel this treatment; but I have not yielded to the besetting temptation to exaggerate this feature, being conscious that Rumi's style, though simple and at times downright colloquial, is marked by a sustained seriousness and dignity which demand of the translator a corresponding sobriety and self-control.

1

The lament of the reed-flute is a symbol of
the soul's sorrow at being parted from
the Divine Beloved

LISTEN to this reed, how it makes complaint, telling a tale
of separation: 'Ever since I was cut off from my reed-bed,
men and women all have lamented my bewailing. I want a
breast torn asunder by severance, that I may fully declare the
agony of yearning. Every one who is sundered far from his
origin longs to recapture the time when he was united with
it. In every company I have poured forth my lament, I have
consorted alike with the miserable and the happy: each became
my friend out of his own surmise, none sought to discover
the secrets in my heart. My secret indeed is not remote from
my lament, but eye and ear lack the light to perceive it. Body
is not veiled from soul, nor soul from body, yet to no man is
leave given to see the soul.'

This cry of the reed is fire, it is not wind; whoever possesses
not this fire, let him be naught! It is the fire of love that has
set the reed aflame; it is the surge of love that bubbles in the
wine. The reed is the true companion of everyone parted
from a friend: its melodies have rent the veils shrouding our
hearts. Whoever saw poison and antidote in one the like of
the reed? Whoever saw sympathizer and yearner in one the
like of the reed? The reed tells the history of the blood-
bespattered way, it tells the stories of Majnun's hopeless
passion. Only the senseless is intimate with the mysteries of
this Sense; only the heedful ear can buy what the tongue
retails. Untimely the days have grown in our tribulation;
burning sorrows have travelled along with all our days; yet if
our days have all departed, bid them be gone—it matters not;
only do Thou abide, O Thou incomparably holy! Whoever is

not a fish is soon satiated with His water; he who lacks his daily bread, for him the day is very long. None that is inexperienced comprehends the state of the ripe, wherefore my words must be short; and now, farewell!

2

The king and the sick servant-girl, on the redemptive power of love

THERE was a king who lived in former time, and to him belonged power both temporal and spiritual. Now by chance one day he was out riding together with his courtiers upon the chase, when on the highway he beheld a servant-girl; and his soul immediately became enslaved by her beauty—the bird of his soul fluttered within its cage, and he gave money and straightway purchased the maiden. After he had bought her and enjoyed her charms, fate would have it that the girl fell sick. Thereupon the king mustered the physicians from left and right and said to them, 'The life of both of us is in your hands. My life indeed is a thing of no account, but she is the life of my life; I am in agony and sore wounded, she is my cure. Now whoever shall heal her who is my life shall carry off my treasure, my pearls and all my coral.'

All the physicians declared, 'We are ready to risk our lives; we will gather our wits together and pool our intelligence. Every one of us is a Messiah sent to heal his people; the balm for every pain is in our hands.' But in their overweening conceit they forgot to add 'If God wills,' so that God demonstrated to them the incapacity of Man. For all the treatments and cures they tried, her sickness only worsened and her need remained unfulfilled; the distemper reduced the girl till she was as thin as a hair, and the king's eyes flowed with tears of blood like a veritable river.

When the king saw that the physicians were powerless to effect a cure, he ran barefoot to the mosque, hastened to the prayer-niche and drenched the sanctuary with his tears. Coming to himself again out of the deep waters of ecstasy, he loosened his tongue right purposefully to praise and petition God. 'O Thou,' he cried, 'the least of whose gifts is dominion over the world, what shall I say, seeing that Thou knowest all hidden things? O Thou who art ever our refuge in time of need, behold, once again we have lost the way; yet Thou Thyself has said, "Though I know thy secret, yet for all that quickly make it manifest in thy outward act".'

As he raised this loud cry from the midst of his soul, the sea of divine bounty began to surge. Sleep carried him away in the midst of his lamentations, and he saw in a dream an old man appeared to him saying, 'Good news, O king! Your prayers are answered. If a stranger comes to you tomorrow, know that he comes from me; he is the clever physician indeed, and you may take what he says for truth, for he is both truthful and trustworthy. In his treatment you will behold wizardry at its supreme, and in his temper you will perceive the omnipotence of God!'

When the promised hour arrived and it was day, when the sun rose from the east burning up the stars, the king was in the belvedere all expectant to behold that which had been shown to him so mysteriously. He saw a noble and right venerable personage, a sun in splendour in the midst of shadows, who arrived from afar slender as the crescent moon, slim and unsubstantial as a very phantom; that phantasy which the king had beheld in his dream now appeared manifest in the face of the stranger. The king himself in the place of his chamberlains hastened forward to greet the stranger come to him from the unseen world. Both of them were mariners who had learned to swim, the souls of both were knit together without stitching. 'You were my true beloved,' the king cried, 'not she, but in this world one work issues out of another. You are as Mohammed to me, I to you as Omar, and I will gird up my loins to serve you.'

So saying, the king opened wide his arms and took him to his breast, receiving him like love into his heart and soul; he kissed him upon the hands and brow, and enquired after his home and the journey he had made. So questioning him all the while, he drew him to seat of honour saying, 'At last out of my patience I have found a treasure! You are a gift vouchsafed by God to fend off hardship, the meaning of the adage, Patience is the key to deliverance. Welcome to you, chosen one, the heart's approven!'

24

That assembly and bountiful banquet being concluded, the king took him by the hand and led him into the harem; he recited to him the history of the sick girl and her sickness, then seated him down beside the patient. The doctor examined her colour, her pulse and her urine and listened attentively to her symptoms and the causes of her illness. Then he declared, 'Not one of the remedies which they have applied is a true restorative, they have only served to destroy. They were utterly ignorant of her inward state: God preserve me from their concoctions!'

He perceived the nature of her pain, and her secret malady was entirely revealed to him, but he kept it hidden and did not tell the king. It was not the bile, black or yellow, which was the root of her disorder; the smell of every tinderwood becomes apparent in its smoke, and he saw from her sore sorrow that it was her heart that was sore. Her body was well enough, but she was afflicted in her heart; a sure sign of being in love is when the heart is sore—there is no sickness like heart-sickness. The lover's infirmity stands apart from all other infirmities; love is the astrolabe of God's mysteries. So the physician said to the king, 'Empty the house, drive away everyone, kinsfolk and strangers alike. I wish to ask this girl a few questions; let none be listening in the porticos.'

The house stood empty, not one inhabitant remaining apart from the physician and the patient. Then very gently he asked her, 'Where is your home-town? You see, the people of every town require their own treatment. And in that town what relatives have you? With what do you have kinship and connexion? So saying he laid his hand upon her pulse, while he questioned her detail by detail about the injustice of Heaven. When a thorn darts into a man's foot he will put his foot on to his other knee and hunt for the tip of the thorn with the point of a needle; if he cannot find it, he keeps moistening it with his lip. If a thorn in the foot is so hard to find, tell me, what of the thorn that is sticking in the heart? But since that physician was a master at plucking out thorns, he kept laying his hand on one spot after another by way of exploration. As if in conversation he went on asking the girl about her various friends, and she told the doctor all about her home, her former masters, her home-town,

25

her environment. He listened as she told her story, all the time keeping alert to observe the beating of her pulse, knowing that when her pulse began to throb at the mention of a particular name, that person would be her heart's desire in all the world.

First he counted over her friends in her home-town, then he passed on to name another town. 'When you left your home-town,' he asked her, 'in what town did you for the most part dwell?'

She named one town, then passed on to another, without any change of colour or pulse; she enumerated one by one the masters she had served, the towns where she had lived, the houses she had lived in, the hospitality she had enjoyed. She told of town after town, house after house, and still not a vein in her quivered, her cheek did not turn pale; her pulse remained quite normal and unaffected, until the doctor asked her about Samarkand, sweet as sugar-candy. Then suddenly her pulse leaped, she blushed and went pale by turns; for it was from a certain goldsmith of Samarkand that she had been parted.

Having discovered the patient's secret, the physician also found the source of her suffering and affliction. 'Which quarter does he live in as you pass through the town?' he asked. 'Bridge-head,' she replied, 'and his street is Ghatafar Street.' 'Now I know what your illness is,' he told her, 'and straightaway I will demonstrate my magic art to rescue you. Be of good cheer, cast cares aside and rest secure, for I will act on you like the rain on the parched meadow. I will worry for you, so do not worry about yourself; I will be kinder to you than a hundred fathers. Only beware, tell not this secret to any one, not though the king himself make much enquiry about you. Let your heart be the grave of your secret, then you will all the sooner realize your desire.'

Thereupon he rose up and went to see the king. He informed the king of some part of the affair, and then added, 'The best plan would be for us to fetch the man here to cure the girl's sickness. Summon the goldsmith from that distant city; trick him with gold and fine robes.' The king despatched two messengers to those parts, men shrewd, competent and entirely equitable. The two messengers having duly reached Samarkand in quest of the gay and mischievous goldsmith, they addressed him thus: 'Master-goldsmith, fine craftsman and perfect in knowledge, whose quality is famous throughout all cities, behold, King So-and-so has chosen you to be his goldsmith because of your supremacy in the art. Take these fine robes and gold and silver; when you come to his city, you will be his favourite and boon-companion.'

The man, deceived by the sight of so much wealth and fine clothes, forsook his home-town and his children and set off gaily enough on the road, quite unaware that the king had designs on his life. Mounted upon an Arab steed, he galloped along happily, taking for a robe of honour what was in fact his blood-price. When he arrived, a stranger, from the road the physician at once brought him before the king. The king looked upon him with great consideration, and bade him make himself free with his treasure-house of gold.

Then the physician said to the king, 'Mighty monarch, give the girl to this fine fellow. She will be so happy to be reunited with him that the water of their reunion will extinguish the fire of her pining.'

The king gave that moon-faced beauty to the goldsmith and joined together in wedlock that pair so eager for each other's society. For the space of six months they were free to gratify their desire, so that the girl was restored to perfect health. Then the physician prepared a draught for the goldsmith, and as soon as he drank it he began to waste away before the girl's very eyes. His handsome looks did not withstand his sickness, and so the girl's soul no longer remained a victim of his deadly charms. Now that he had become ugly, hideous and hollow-cheeked, little by little her heart cooled towards him.

Love that is for the sake of a fine complexion is no true love; in the end it proves nothing but a disgrace. Would that he had been too a disgrace entirely, for then so evil a judgment would never have come upon him. Blood ran from his eyes like a river, and his good looks proved to be his deadliest enemy: the enemy of the peacock is its fine feathers, and many a king has been the victim of his own splendour. He cried, 'I am the musk-deer for the sake of whose musk-pod that huntsman has shed my innocent blood; I am the

27

fox of the field whose head they have cut off, springing out of ambush, all for the sake of its fur; I am the elephant struck down and slain by its keeper because of its tusks. He that has slain me on account of something other than my true self, does he not know that my blood will not sleep? Today I am the sufferer, but tomorrow it will be he, for shall the blood of one the like of me be shed in vain? Though the wall casts a long shadow, in the end that shadow returns towards the wall. This world is a mountain, and our deeds are a shout echoed back to us.'

So he spoke, and in that same moment passed below the soil. The girl for her part was cleansed of her sickness and her love; for the love of the dead is not enduring, seeing that the departed one never returns to us. But the love of the living is fresher every moment in the spirit and the sight than the bud of a flower. Choose therefore the love of that Living One who is everlasting, the divine saki whose wine outpoured increases life.

3

The greengrocer and the parrot, on the dangers of false analogy

ONCE there was a greengrocer who owned a parrot; it was a green parrot with a fine voice, an excellent talker. Perched outside on the bench, it looked after the shop and exchanged pleasantries with all the tradesmen. One day it sprang off the bench and flew away, spilling the bottles of rose-oil as it went. Its owner, coming out of the house and squatting down on the bench like a true proprietor as if he had not a care in the world, observed that the bench was all oily and his clothes covered with grease. He thereupon struck the parrot on the head, and the blow rendered the bird completely bald.

For a number of days the parrot was silent, and the greengrocer drew deep sighs of regret, plucking out his beard and saying, 'Woe, alas, the sun of my bliss has vanished under the clouds. Would that my hand had been shattered in that moment! How could I ever have struck that sweet-tongued one on the head?'

He gave presents to every passing dervish, in the hope that he might restore the bird's speech. Three days and three nights passed, and he was seated on the bench bewildered and miserable, in utter despair; he kept showing the bird all kinds of wonderful things, still hoping to make him speak again.

Presently there passed by a dervish clad in sackcloth and bareheaded; his head was as innocent of hair as the outside of a bowl or basin. Immediately the parrot started to talk, screeching at the dervish and saying, 'Hullo, you there! How did you, baldpate, come to be mixed up with the bald? Did you perhaps also spill oil from a bottle?'

All the people laughed at the inference the parrot had

29

drawn, supposing the dervish to be in the same case as himself.

The moral is, do not judge holy men's actions by your own standard; the word *shir* in Persian means 'milk' and 'lion', but there the resemblance ends.

4

The Jewish king and the Christians, on the peril of consorting with cunning hypocrites

A KING once reigned in Judea, a worker of oppression, an enemy of Christ and a liquidator of Christians. It was the era of Jesus and his turn to prophesy; he was the soul of Moses, and Moses was his soul, but that squint-eyed king made division on the way of God between those two divine confederates, becoming so squint-eyed in his Jewish malice that one might well cry 'Good Lord, preserve us!' He slaughtered hundreds of thousands of true believers unjustly, proclaiming, 'I am the shelter and shield of the religion of Moses.'

Now the king had a vizier, a sly and artful infidel whose craftiness was such as to tie even water into knots. 'These Christians,' he said, 'are seeking to save their lives by concealing their religion from the king. Spare to slay them, for there is no profit in their slaughter. Religion has no perfume, it cannot be sniffed out like musk or aloeswood; the secret is concealed in a hundred wrappings—outwardly it is on your side, but inwardly it is bitterly opposed to you.'

The king said to him, 'Then tell me what I am to do about it. What is the remedy for that trickery and deception, so that not a single Christian, be he confessing or in secret, may be left in the world?'

'O king,' the vizier answered, 'cut off my ears and hands, slit my nose in bitter judgment, then hale me off to the gallows, where haply one voice may be raised in intercession for me. Let this be done in the place where proclamations are made, upon the highway where four roads meet. Then banish me from your presence to a distant city, that I may cast mischief and confusion among them. For I will say to them, "I am in secret a Christian. O God who knowest all secrets, Thou knowest me! The king, being appraised of the faith I hold, out of fanaticism intended to take my life. I desired to keep my faith hidden from the king and to conform outwardly with his religion; but the king caught a whiff of my inmost secrets, and my words became suspect when I stood before him. He said, 'Your words are like a needle hidden in bread, but there is a window between my heart and yours through which I have seen into your true situation; I have seen your situation, and will not heed your speech.' Had not the spirit of Jesus been my succour, in Jewish rage he would have torn me to pieces. For Jesus' sake I am ready to yield up my very life, to acknowledge the countless graces he has showered upon me. It is not that I grudge Jesus my life; but I am very well versed in the knowledge of his religion, and it troubled me greatly that that holy religion should perish in the midst of those who know it not. Thanks be to God and to Jesus, that I have become a guide to that true faith; so wholly have I escaped from the Jews and Judaism, that lo, I have bound my waist with the Christian girdle. This era is the era of Jesus: men, hearken with your souls to the mysteries of his faith''!'

The king dealt with him exactly as he proposed, and the people stood in amazement at his deed. He banished the vizier to the land of the Christians, and straightway the vizier began to proclaim the faith. Little by little, multitudes of Christian men congregated about him in his dwelling, where he expounded to them in secret the mysteries of the Gospel, the girdle and prayer. Outwardly he was a preacher of the divine ordinances, but inwardly he was the fowler's whistle and snare. All the Christians yielded up their hearts to him, for how great is the power of blind conformity in the common people; they nurtured in their breasts the seeds of love for him, deeming him to be the vicar of Jesus, whereas in secret he was none other than the accursed one-eyed Antichrist—God, hear our prayer, O Thou most excellent helper! Innumerable are the snares and baits that beset us, O God, and we are as greedy birds that are without food. Though we be falcons, or that famed simurgh itself, moment by moment we are caught in a new snare; every moment Thou art delivering us, and again we betake ourselves to a snare, O Thou who wantest not.

That infidel vizier turned religious counsellor had cunningly put garlic in the almond-cake of his preaching. Every man of true intuition felt in his words a sweetness conjoined with a bitterness. Fine things he uttered mingled with things most foul, for he had poured poison into the sugary syrup. Outwardly his words were, 'Be nimble upon the Way'; the effect of his words on the soul were, 'Take things easy!' As for those Christians who were unwary and lacked inward discernment, for them his preaching was as a collar tight on their throats.

For a space of six years in banishment from his king the vizier posed as a refuge for the followers of Jesus. All the people surrendered to him their faith and hearts entirely, being prepared to die at his behest and decree. Meanwhile messages passed between the king and him; secretly he sent comfortable words to his royal master. The king wrote to him, 'My fortunate one, the time has come; be quick, set my heart free from care.' The vizier answered, 'Behold, O king, I am making ready to cast great confusion into the religion of Jesus.'

Now the people of Jesus had in authority over them twelve ameers as rulers; each party followed a single ameer whom they served devotedly, being spurred on by ambition. By now these twelve ameers together with their subjects had become the slaves of that ill-favoured vizier; all relied implicitly upon his words, all followed faithfully the example of his conduct. Each ameer was ready instantly to yield up his life, if the vizier should speak to him the simple word, 'Die!'

The vizier fashioned a scroll addressed to each, but the inscription on each scroll was of a different purport; the ordinances contained in each was of a different kind, this one in contradiction to that from beginning to end. In one he laid down the path of self-discipline and hunger to be the foundation of penitence, the prescription for conversion. In one he said, 'Self-discipline is profitless; upon this Way the only deliverance is by generosity.' In one he said, 'Your hunger and your generosity alike, as coming from yourself, prove you associate other things with Him you worship. Save for the complete trust in God and utter surrender in sorrow and joy alike, all else is a cheat and a snare.' In one he said, 'Your simple duty is to serve God, otherwise the very thought of trusting Him attracts grave suspicion.' In one he said, 'God has revealed certain commandments and prohibitions not for men to act accordingly, but to demonstrate our helplessness, so that we may perceive our own weakness therein and in that hour realize God's omnipotence.' In one he said, 'Regard not your own weakness; beware, that weakness is an act of ingratitude for grace received. Rather regard your own power, for this power comes from Him; know that your power is the grace of Him who alone is.'

In one he said, 'Eschew both of these thoughts; whatever thing holds the gaze becomes an idol.' In one he said, 'Extinguish not this candle, for this gaze is as a candle lighting the gathering. If you give up gaze and phantasy too soon, you will have put out at midnight the candle of union.' In one he said, 'Extinguish, and have no fear, that you may behold multitudinous sights in lieu; for by putting it out the soul's candle will burn more brightly, and because of your fortitude your Laila will become her own mad lover. Whoever abandons the world of his own denial, more and yet more the world comes to wait upon him.' In one he said, 'Whatsoever God has given you, in bringing it into being He made it sweet to you; He made it easy for you, so accept it joyfully, do not cast yourself into agony.' In one he said, 'Give up all that belongs to the self, for such compliance with your nature is evil and wicked.' In one he said, 'That alone is made easy by God which is the life of the heart, the food of the soul.' In one he said, 'You must seek for a master, for you will not find clairvoyance in your ancestry.' In one he said, 'You are yourself a master, inasmuch as you know yourself who is the master. Be a man, be not subject to other men; go, follow your own head, be not one whose head spins round.' In one he said, 'All this that is is one; whoever sees two, why, he is a squinting manikin.' In one he said, 'How can a hundred be one? The man who thinks that is doubtless mad.'

All these sayings are contrary one to the other; they are as much one and the same as poison and sugar, and until you transcend poison and sugar how can you catch even the scent of oneness and unity?

That enemy of the religion of Jesus inscribed twelve documents after this fashion and kind. He had never caught a whiff of the single-colouredness of Jesus, he had not a habit imbued with the tincture of Jesus' dyeing-vat. The vizier was as ignorant and heedless as the king, wrestling as he was with the eternal and inescapable, with a God so mighty that with one breath He brings into being out of nonentity a hundred worlds like ours.

Then the vizier devised in his mind another strategem: he abandoned preaching and sat apart in seclusion, remaining thus forty or fifty days so that he kindled an ardent longing in his disciples' hearts. The people became quite distracted in their yearning for him and because they were parted from his spiritual insight and godly words. 'We have no light without you,' they wailed. 'How does the blind man fare without a leader to guide him? As an act of kindness and for God's sake, pray do not keep us parted from you any longer. We are like children and you are our nurse; spread over our heads the shadow of your protection.'

'My soul,' he replied, 'is never far from those who love me, but it is not permitted me to come out.'

The ameers came to intercede with him, the disciples came to reproach him, saying, 'What a misfortune has come upon us, most generous sir! Without your presence we have been left as orphans bereft of both heart and faith. All the time you are putting forward false excuses, while we heave cold, cold sighs from hearts burning with anguish. We had become accustomed to your sweet discourse, we have imbibed the milk of your wisdom. For God's dear sake do not treat us so cruelly; be kind to us today, not tomorrow and tomorrow. Does your heart really allow it that we, who have surrendered our hearts to you, should lose you forever and be left with nothing to show for our pains? See, your followers are all threshing about like fishes stranded on dry land; unblock the river, let the water flow. There is none the like of you alive anywhere today; for God's dear sake give a helping hand to the people!'

'Beware, you slaves to mere verbiage,' the vizier answered, 'looking only for sermons passing easily from tongue to ear. Stuff cotton-wool in the ears of the lower senses, take the

35

bandage of physical sight off your eyes: the ear of the head is cotton-wool in the ear of the inmost soul, and until the former is deaf the latter will hear nothing. Become without sense, without ear, without thought even, so that you may hear the voice of God calling to the soul to return to Him. So long as you are immersed in the chatter of wakefulness, how can you hope to catch even a whisper of the conversation of sleep? Our physical words and acts are an external journey; the journey internal is above the skies. The material sense, being born of dryness, sees only dryness; the Jesus of the soul sets foot on the waters. The journey of the dry body lies upon dry land; the journey of the soul sets foot on the heart of the sea. Since you have spent all your life travelling on dry land, now climbing mountains, now fording rivers, now faring through deserts, how will you ever discover the true water of Life? How will you ever cleave the waves of the open Sea?'

'O master of evasion,' the disciples cried, 'do not speak to us words so guileful and cruel. Lay on the back of the beast the burden it can endure, assign to the weak in body the task they have strength to perform. Men snare birds with the bait appropriate to each kind: is the date appropriate lure for every bird? If you give a baby bread in place of milk you can be sure that the poor child will choke on the bread and die, but as soon as it has cut its teeth the child will ask for bread of its own accord. How can a bird fly when its feathers have not yet sprouted? Why, it will be a morsel for any marauding cat; but once its feathers are grown it will fly of its own without any trouble at all, not needing the whistle of good or evil to call it. Your speech silences the Devil and fills our ears with understanding. With you in our midst, earth is better for us than heaven; without you, darkness is over all our heaven. The heavens are clothed in the outward form of sublimity, but the true essence of sublimity belongs to the pure spirit; the outward form of sublimity is tailored to fit bodies, but bodies are nothing but names in the presence of reality.'

'Cut short your arguments,' replied the vizier, 'and let my good counsel seep into your souls and hearts. If I am worthy of trust, the trustworthy is above suspicion, even

36

though I should call the heaven earth. If I am perfect, why do you disbelieve in my perfection, and if I am not perfect then why bother and plague me as you do? I simply will not come out of my seclusion, for here I am occupied with the interior life.'

'It is not a question of disbelief, vizier,' they all protested. 'Our words are not like the observations of outsiders. See, the tears we shed are because of our separation from you, the sighs we heave come from the midst of our souls. An infant does not quarrel with its nurse; it weeps, though it knows nothing of good or evil. We are as a harp, and you pluck on our strings; if the tune is a lament, the lament is not of our making but yours. We are like a flute; the music within us is from you; we are like a mountain; the echo in us is from you. We are as chessmen moving to victory or defeat; our mating and being mated are of you, O most admirable player. Who are we, the soul of whose souls you are, that we should continue to be when you are amongst us? We and our entities are in truth nonentities; you are the absolute Being displaying the perishable. We are all lions, but lions emblazoned on banners which charge only as the wind waves them moment by moment; they charge visibly, and the wind is invisible—may that which is invisible not fail us ever! Look not upon us, fix not on us your gaze, but consider your own grace and generosity. We were not, and we made no demand that we should be; your loving kindness heard our unspoken petition.'

'Disciples,' the vizier cried from within his cell, 'now let this thing be known to you from me, that Jesus himself sent to me such a message: "Dwell apart from all your friends and kinsfolk, turn your face to the wall, sit alone, seek seclusion even from your very own being." After this charge I have no leave to speak; after this commandment I have no truck with talk. Farewell, friends; I am a dead man, I have transported my baggage up to the fourth heaven that I may burn like brushwood under the fiery sphere, consumed in weariness and destruction. Henceforward I shall be seated beside Jesus, enthroned on the topmost reach of the fourth heaven.'

Then one by one he summoned those ameers to him and

37

spoke to each one of them words apart. To each one of them in turn he said, 'You are God's vicar and my vicegerent in the religion of Jesus, and those other ameers are your followers; Jesus has designated all of them to be your partisans. If any ameer stretches up his neck to rebel against you, seize him and either slay him, or keep him your prisoner. Only do not declare this so long as I am alive, do not seek this sovereignty until I die. See, here is the scroll and the ordinances of Christ; recite them one by one in a clear voice to the community.'

So he spoke to each ameer separately: 'There is no vicar but you in the religion of God.' Each one he honoured thus severally, and all that he said to that one he said too to this one; to each of them he gave one scroll, each contrary to the other, for so he had planned, so that all the scrolls were at difference one with the other just as the shapes of the letters differ, from A to Z. After that he shut the door for another forty days; then he killed himself, and so escaped from this earthly life.

When the people learned the news of his death, the scenes enacted at the grave were like what shall come to pass on the Last Day. So great a congregation gathered about his tomb, plucking out their hair and rending their clothes in the agitation of their grief, that God alone knows the reckoning of their numbers, Arabs, Turks, Greeks and Kurds. They scattered his dust over their heads, deeming grief for him to be the surest remedy for their own sorrow. For a whole month those people shed their tears of blood upon his grave.

When a month had passed the people said, 'Elders, who among the ameers is designated to take his place? For we would recognize him as our leader in his stead, put our hands into his and surrender ourselves to his guidance. Now that the sun has vanished, leaving the brand of sorrow in our hearts, we must needs have recourse to a lamp in lieu thereof; since the prospect of union with our dear one has disappeared, we must needs have a vicar to remind us of him; since the rose is over and the garden all laid to waste, whence shall we find us the scent of the rose? From the rosewater.'

Then stepped forward one of those ameers and stood before that loyal-minded people. 'Lo, I am that man's vicar,' he declared. 'I am the vicar of Jesus in this present time. See, this scroll is my proof that the vicarate is mine after him.'

Another ameer came out of his lurking-hole and put forward the same claim to be the appointed vicegerent; he also displayed a scroll from under his arm, so that a true Jewish fury rose up in both of them. The rest of the ameers, one following the other, drawing swords of fine temper, each holding a sword and a scroll, fell upon one another like elephants enraged. Hundreds of thousands of Christian men were slaughtered; veritable hillocks rose from their struck-off heads. Blood flowed to left and right like a river in spate, the dust of battle soared like mountains into the air. The seeds of dissension which the vizier had sown thus turned into a terrible calamity for them all.

5

The lion and the beasts, on the
true nature of trust in God

A GROUP of beasts of the chase inhabiting a delightful valley were always being worried by a lion; it was enough for the lion to pounce out of his covert for the green pasture to turn sour on them all. They therefore plotted together and came to the lion with the following proposal: 'We will keep you well fed by means of a regular allowance. Do not come after any prey over and above your allowance, so that this grass may not become bitter for us.'

'Very well, if I find you are faithful to your engagement and do not cheat me,' the lion replied. 'I have had enough tricks played on me by Tom, Dick and Harry. I am utterly destroyed by men's treacherous deeds; I have tasted the bite of snake and scorpion too. But worse in guile and spite than all men put together is the old Adam lurking in ambush within me. I have heard the Prophet's saying, ''Believers will not be bitten twice,'' and I have adopted it with all my heart and soul.'

'Wise and well-informed lion,' the beasts all said, 'Remember the Prophet also bade us put all precaution aside, for it is impotent against the decree of God. Caution leads to endless trouble and turmoil: come, put your trust in God, that is the better course. Do not wrestle with destiny, fierce and ferocious beast, lest destiny on its part picks a quarrel with you. We must all be dead things before the doom of God, lest we be smitten down by the Lord of the Daybreak.'

'Very true,' commented the lion. 'Yet if trust in God be the guide, nevertheless the Prophet has taught us also to fend for ourselves. Did he not proclaim in a loud voice, ''Trust in God, and hobble your camel''? ''God loves the honest workman"—give heed to that hint; do not let trust in God make you lazy about ways and means.'

'To earn at the expense of God's weaker creatures,' they retorted, 'is a mouthful of pure hypocrisy—the larger the gullet, the bigger the mouthful. There is no trade better than trust in God: what is dearer to God than the heart resigned? Many a one runs away from misery only to encounter a greater misery; many a one starts back from a snake to be stung by a scorpion. The man plotted a plot, and his plot proved a trap to ensnare him; what he supposed would save his life drained his blood instead. He secured the door, while the enemy was within the house; the plot devised by Pharaoh was a good example of this. That rageful man slew hundreds of thousands of babies, but the very one he was seeking out was in his own house. Since our sight is riddled with many infirmities, annihilate your own sight in the sight of the Friend. His eyes for ours—that is indeed a fair recompense; in His sight you will discover all your heart's desire. So long as the child cannot catch for itself and cannot run, the only thing it can ride on is its daddy's neck; but when it can get up to mischief and tries to show off its paces it very soon falls into plenty of trouble and misery. Before hands and feet were created the spirits of God's creation soared serenely in the realms of purity, faithful to God; but when the command, "Get you down from Eden," was made binding on them they became the prisoners of rage and greed and self-satisfaction. We are the children of God, babes craving for milk; did not the Prophet say, Men are the children of God? He who sends down the rain out of heaven is also able of His mercy to give us bread.'

'True,' said the lion. 'But the Lord of mankind has set a ladder before our feet. Step by step we must climb to the rooftop; to fold one's hands and to say "What will be will be" is the rawest of hopefulness. You have feet, so why do you make out you are lame? You have hands, so why do you hide your clutch? When a master puts a spade in the slave's hands, the slave knows what he requires without needing to be told. The hand and the spade are alike hints from God; He expresses His will through our power to reflect on our end. When you take His hints to heart and devote your life to fulfilling that hint, then He will give you many hints to His mysteries, relieve you of your burden and give you your true work. Bear His burden, and He will cause yourself to be borne; accept His will, and He will make you acceptable. Accept His commandment, and you shall declare it; seek union with Him, and you shall thereafter be united. Free will is the striving to thank God for His favour; determinism on your part is a denial of that favour. Thanksgiving for free will increases your free will; determinism snatches God's favour from your hand. Your determinism is like sleeping on the road; till you see that door and threshold, do not sleep. Heedless determinist, do not sleep save in the shadow of that fruitful tree, that every moment the wind shaking its branches may scatter on the head of the sleeper sweetmeats and food for the way. Determinism is sleeping in the midst of highwaymen; the cock that crows untimely, how shall it be spared? And if you thumb your nose at His hints you may think yourself a proper man, but look closer—you are a silly woman! You are losing the little intelligence you possess; when sense flies out of the head, that head becomes a tail. Ingratitude being a shame and a scandal, it bears the ungrateful to the bottom of Hell. If you put trust in God, trust Him in your work; sow your seed, then rely on the Almighty.'

They shouted at him with one voice, 'Those greedy ones who have sowed the seeds of material means, those countless multitudes of men and women, why did they remain denied their fortune? Generations without number since the world began, their hundred mouths open like ravening dragons; such plots they plotted, that cunning crowd, rooting up mountains from their foundations, yet except that portion predestined in eternity nothing accrued from their hunting and toil; all failed in their planning and doing, only the doing and dooming of the Creator remained. To earn is nothing but a name, illustrious one; think not, crafty one, that exertion is aught but a fancy.'

'True,' said the lion. 'All the same, consider the exertions of the prophets and of true believers. Almighty God prospered their exertion, the oppression and afflictions they endured. All that they devised always turned out excellent; whatever the subtle man does is subtle. The snares they laid caught the Bird of Heaven, and all their wants turned to super-abundance. To endeavour is not to wrestle with Destiny, since Destiny itself laid this labour upon us. Your head is not broken, so do not bandage it; toil this day or two, then laugh to eternity! Exertion is a fact, sickness and remedy are facts; the sceptic even in denying exertion exerts himself!'

Many proofs of this kind the lion put forward till the determinists became tired of answering him. The fox, the deer, the hare and the jackal deserted determinism and argumentation and made solemn compact with the raging lion, so that he should not lose anything by the bargain; his daily portion of food should come to him without toil or trouble, and consequently he would not need to make any further demands. They all cast lots, and day by day on whomsoever the lot fell, that creature would run to the lion as swift as a cheetah.

When it came to the hare's turn to quaff this bitter cup he cried out in a loud voice, 'How long shall we bear this injustice?'

The other beasts answered him, 'All this while we have sacrificed our lives to be true to our covenant. Rebel, do not seek to give us a bad name. Go, go quickly, so that the lion may not be upset.'

'Give me a little respite, friends,' pleaded the hare, 'and you shall all escape from calamity by my cunning. By my cunning your souls will find security, and this will remain an inheritance for your children.'

'Donkey!' they all shouted at him. 'Now just you listen. Keep yourself within your proper limits as a hare. Say, what are you boasting about, of such notions that never came into the heads of your betters? Either you are puffed up with conceit, or Destiny is snapping at your heels—how otherwise can such words be thought appropriate to you?'

'Friends,' he replied, 'it was God Himself who inspired me; the weak has been suddenly given a powerful judgment: That which God has taught to the bee belongs not to the lion and the onager; the bee builds houses full of juicy sweet-meat, and it was God who opened to it the door to that science. What God has taught the silkworm, does any elephant know such a trick?'

43

Then they said, 'O fleet-footed hare, reveal the idea you have in mind. You have wrestled with a lion, so declare the plan which you have meditated. Counsel bestows perception and understanding; one mind is assisted by many.'

'It is not wise to blab out every secret,' the hare said. 'Pairs sometimes turn into singlets, and vice versa. Tell your secret to just one or two, and you can kiss it goodbye; a secret shared by more than two is soon public property.'

After a short delay he then set off to confront the sharp-clawed lion. The latter, because the hare was so late in coming, was tearing up the earth and roaring terribly.

'I always said the promise of those dirty beasts would prove worthless and futile and would come to nothing. Their fine phrases have made a proper monkey of me; how long, how long am I to be the dupe of this treacherous world? While my ears were occupied with listening, the enemy blindfolded me. The tricks of those determinists have bound me hand and foot; they have slashed me all over with their wooden sword. After this I will not listen to all their gabble, mutterings of devils and gibbering ghouls, the whole lot of it. Now my heart, stay no longer but tear them to pieces; flay off their skins—they are nothing but skin.'

All on fire and in furious rage, at last the lion sighted the hare far off bounding along undismayed and bold as brass, looking angry and sharp indeed and in a sour temper. For the hare thought, 'If I come contritely, he will suspect me; put on a bold front, and every doubt will vanish.'

When he had come further on and was approaching the threshold, the lion shouted at him, 'Now then, villain! I who have torn great oxen asunder, I who have boxed the ears of rogue elephants—what is this bit of a hare, to venture to stamp my orders into the dust?'

'Mercy!' the hare cried. 'I have a good excuse, if your lordship's indulgence will only lend me a hand.'

'What sort of excuse?' said the lion. 'How shortsighted can fools be? Do they come at this time into the presence of kings? You are an unseasonable bird, so your head must be chopped off. It is not right to listen to the excuse of a fool; a fool's excuse is even worse than his crime, and the excuse of an ignoramus is a poison slaying wisdom. Your excuse, my hare, is utterly empty of wisdom; what, am I a hare then, for you to pour it into my ears?'

'Truly I am worthless, king, yet reckon me as worthy, and lend an ear to the plea of one who has suffered oppression.' The hare continued, 'Do so especially as a thank-offering for your high estate, and do not drive from your path one who has lost the way. The ocean, that gives some water to every river, suffers all kinds of rubbish to float upon its surface, and will never diminish for all this munificence; the ocean is neither augmented nor diminished by its bounty.'

The lion said, 'I keep my bounty for the appropriate occasion; I cut clothes for everyone according to his height.'

'Listen now,' said the hare. 'If I am not appropriate to your goodness I put my head into the jaws of the dragon of your wrath. It was at breakfast time that I set out upon the way, going along with my companion to come to the royal presence. The beasts assembled had delegated another hare for your sake to travel along the road with me so that we should make a pair. Upon the way a lion attacked your humble servant, indeed he attacked the both of us as we journeyed together. I told him, "We are the slaves of the Emperor himself, we are the poor fellow-servants of the imperial court." "Who is the Emperor?" the lion cried. "Are you not ashamed? Do not mention in my presence every worthless creature. I will tear to pieces both you and your king, if you and your friend dare to turn aside from my door." I answered him, "Only suffer me once more to behold the face of my king and to carry him tidings of you." "Then leave your fellow-traveller as a pawn with me," he replied. "Else you yourself shall be a sacrifice in accordance with my sacred law." For all that we pleaded with him our prayers were unprofitable; he pounced upon my comrade and left me to go alone. My friend, I may add, in plumpness made three of me—such a handsome hare he was, so beautiful and so fat. Henceforward that other lion has barred the road; the thread of our covenant is snapped. Give up hope hereafter of your regular allowance; I tell you the simple truth, and truth, alas, is bitter. If you want your regular allowance you will have to clear the way. Come along, then, and drive that impudent brute away.'

45

'In the name of God, come on then; let us see where he is,' said the lion. 'You go ahead in front, if you are telling the truth, and I will give him his deserts, aye, and a hundred like him. But if you are lying, I will give you what you deserve.'

The hare set out ahead like a guide, to lead him to his snare, even to the well which he had himself had waymarked, the deep, deep well he had laid as a snare for the lion's life. When the lion drew near the well he observed that the hare had dawdled and lagged behind on the way.

'Why have you drawn your foot back?' he demanded. 'Do not draw back, come on!'

'Why now, where is my foot?' exclaimed the hare. 'I swear my hands and my feet have deserted me. See, my soul is a-tremble, my heart has leapt from my breast. Do you not see my colour? My face is as pale as gold, giving precise information about my internal state.'

'What ails you, hare?' cried the lion. 'Of all the causes of your sickness tell me the one most particular, that is what I want to know.'

'The lion I mentioned inhabits this well,' the hare replied. 'He dwells in this fortress, secure from all harm.'

'Come on,' said the lion. 'One blow from me will subdue him. You go and see if the lion is now in the well.'

'I am consumed by that terrible fieriness. Perhaps you will draw me along in your shadow,' said the hare. 'With you to back me, O mine of bounty, I can open my eyes and peep in the well.'

The lion drew the hare close to his side, and under his protection he ran off to the well. As soon as they looked in the well together there shone in the water the gleam of them both. The lion perceived his own reflexion; there shone from the water the shape of a lion with a plump hare beside him. Seeing his adversary in the water, he left the hare and leapt into the well; he fell into the well he himself had dug, for his evildoing was recoiling on his own head.

The hare, rejoicing at this deliverance, scampered off to the desert to rejoin the beasts; he had seen the lion slain miserably in the well, so he whirled with joy all the way to the meadow, clapping his hands at having escaped from death, green and dancing in the air like a leafy bough.

46

Then all the wild creatures assembled together, happy and laughing gaily, beside themselves with excitement. They made a ring with the hare in the middle like a candle; all those desert-dwellers bowed down before him.

'Are you a heavenly angel, or a fairy?' they cried. 'No, you are the Azrael of ravening lions. Whatever you may be, our souls are your sacrifice. You have won the day: all power to your elbow! Declare to us now how you plotted so guilefully, how you guilefully wiped out that horrible brute. Declare, that your story may cure our ills; declare, that your story may be balm to our souls.'

'It was with God's assistance, my masters; else, what in the world is a hare to accomplish such a thing? God,' the hare replied, 'vouchsafed the power to me and gave light to my heart; the light in my heart lent strength to my hands and feet.'

6

Solomon and the Angel of Death

ONE day in mid-morning a nobleman ran into Solomon's judgment-hall, his face pale with anguish, his two lips blue. Solomon said to him, 'Sir, what has happened?'

'Azrael, the angel of death,' said the man, 'has looked upon me so angry and baleful.'

'Well, what is your wish?' asked Solomon. 'Declare it.'

Said the man, 'Command the wind, O lord-protector, to transport me hence unto Hindustan; it may be that coming there, your slave will save his soul alive.'

Solomon ordered the wind to bear him swiftly over the waters to the depths of Indis.

The following day, when his court was in session, Solomon spoke to Azrael thus: 'Did you look on that true believer so balefully to drive him a wanderer far from home?'

Said Azrael, 'When did I look on him balefully? I beheld him with astonishment as I passed by, for God had commanded me, saying, "This very day seize you his spirit in Hindustan!" I said to myself in wonder, "Even though he had a hundred wings, for him to be in India this day is a far journey".'

From whom shall we flee? From ourselves? Impossible!
From whom shall we snatch ourselves? From God? How
    impious!

48

7

The merchant and his parrot,
on dying to live again

THERE once was a merchant who had a parrot, a pretty poll-parrot shut up in a cage. Now the merchant, intending to travel to India, on the point of departure generously asked every man-slave and slave-girl, 'Tell me quickly what I shall bring for you.'

Each of them asked for a thing much desired, and that good man gave his promise to all.

Then he said to his parrot, 'What present would you like for me to bring you from the confines of India?'

The parrot answered, 'When you see the parrots there, tell them all about my situation, that "So-and-so parrot is yearning after you, but by heaven's decree he is my prisoner. He sends you greetings, and begs for justice, and craves of you help and the way to right guidance. He says, 'Is it right that I should perish of yearning here, give up the ghost and die in separation? Is it fair that I should remain in vile bondage while you disport yourselves on herbage and tree? Is it so that friends keep faith—I in my prison and you in your rose-garden? My masters, remember this miserable bird; drink a cup at morning in the midst of the mead. A friend is happy to be remembered by his friends, as witness in particular Majnun and Laila. You who consort with your graceful beloved, the cups I am quaffing are charged with blood. And you, best beloved, drink one cup in remembrance of me, if you desire to grant me justice; or at least, in remembrance of this poor wretch, fallen to the ground and sifting the dust, when you have drunk, spill one draught on the dust. Where now, I wonder, is that covenant, that oath? Where are the promises of that sugar-sweet lip? If you have parted with your slave because he served you ill—if you do evil to the evildoer, wherein lies the difference between him and you? Yet the evil you do in anger and battle is more delightful than music and lute-song; your cruelty is better than the best of good fortune, your vengeance is dearer to me than my life. If this is your fire, why, what must your light be? If this is your mourning, how is your festival? No one can fathom the depths of the sweetnesses possessed by your cruelty, the depths of your charm.' I lament, and yet I fear that he may believe me and out of his bounty diminish that cruelty. I love exceedingly both his violence and his tenderness; it is marvellous how I adore these two opposites. By Allah, if I escape from this thorn, and enter the garden, for this cause I shall make lament like the nightingale. O wonderful nightingale, that opens his mouth to eat the thorns with the roses! What nightingale is this? Say rather, a fiery dragon; on account of his love all unsweet things to him are sweetness. He adores the All, and himself is the All; he loves himself, and seeks after his own love".'

The merchant accepted this message, and promised to convey the bird's greetings to its fellow-parrots.

When he reached the remotest regions of India he espied in a plain a number of parrots. He halted his beast, then he called aloud, conveying the greeting and discharging thus his trust. One of those parrots trembled exceedingly, fell down, and died; its breath stopped dead. The merchant repented of having told the news saying, 'I have encompassed the destruction of the poor creature. This one must have been a kinsman of my little parrot, it must have been a case of two bodies and one soul. What made me do this? Why did I deliver the message? I have burnt up the wretched creature by my raw words.'

The merchant completed his trading-mission and returned home well content. He brought a present for every man-slave, he bestowed a token upon every slave-girl.

Up spoke the parrot, 'Where is my present? Tell me all you said and everything you saw.'

'No,' said the merchant. 'I repent that bitterly, gnawing my hand and biting my fingers. Why did I in my ignorance and thoughtlessness idly convey such a crude message?'

'What do you repent of, master?' said the parrot. 'What is it that occasions such anger and remorse?'

The merchant said, 'I recounted all your complaints to an assembly of parrots like yourself. That one parrot scented out your pain; her heart broke, and she trembled and died. Then I repented and thought, "Why did I say that?" but what was the use of repenting once I had spoken?'

When that bird heard what the other parrot had done he trembled exceedingly, fell down and turned cold. The merchant, seeing the bird thus prostrate, jumped up and flung his cap upon the ground; seeing his pet so pale and in such a case, the merchant dashed forward and rent his collar.

'Pretty poll,' he cried, 'with your sweet affection, what has happened to you? Why have you become so? Alas and alack for my sweet-voiced bird, alas and alack for my comrade and confidant! Alas and alack for my bird of sweet melodies, wine of my spirit, my garden and sweet herbs! Had King Solomon possessed such a bird, how would he have occupied himself with the other birds? Alas and alack for the bird I found so cheap and so swiftly turned away my face from his face! Ah, tongue, what tons of trouble you are to me! Yet since you yourself are speaking, what shall I say to you? Ah, tongue, you are both the fire and the corn-stack; how long will you dart this fire into this stack? In secret my soul is lamenting on account of you, though it is doing whatsoever you tell it. Ah, tongue, you are at once an inexhaustible treasure and at the same time a sickness incurable; you are at once a whistle and a decoy for birds and at the same time a consoler in the loneliness of banishment. Behold, you have caused my bird to fly away from me; browse no longer in the pasture of oppression.'

The merchant in the fire of agony and yearning was uttering a hundred such distracted phrases; the drowning man clutches at every straw in his soul's anguish. When he had done speaking, he flung the bird out of its cage. Thereupon the little parrot flew up to a lofty bough; the dead bird flew up as swiftly as the sun in the east charges upon the sky. Amazed at the action of the bird the merchant uncomprehending suddenly beheld the bird's secret.

'Sweet nightingale,' he cried, lifting up his face, 'enrich

me by explaining the mystery of your case. What did that Indian bird, that you learned to devise so cunning a trick and so consumed me?'

'By her action she gave me good counsel,' the parrot answered. 'She bade me yield up my charming voice and my affection for my master, since it was my voice that had put me in bondage. By "dying" herself she intended so to advise me: "You who have become a minstrel to entertain both high and low, become dead as I am dead, that you may find deliverance".'

'In God's protection depart!' the merchant cried. 'Now you have shown me a new way to go.'

8

The Bedouin and his wife, on the conflict between reason and passion

ONCE upon a time there was a caliph who outrivalled Hatim in generosity; having hoisted the banner of bounty and munificence, he had eliminated poverty and want from the world; the oceans were emptied of pearls by his largesse, his dower extended from Qaf to Qaf. In a world of dust he was cloud and water; in him the bounty of God the All-giver displayed itself. Pearl-bearing sea and gem-bearing mine quaked at his munificence, caravan upon caravan hastened to his liberality; his gate and portal was the kiblah of want, the fame of his openhandedness had gone through all the world. Persians and Greeks, Turks and Arabs stood in amazement at his bounty and generosity. He was the Water of Life, the Ocean of liberality; Arabs and non-Arabs alike were revived by him.

One night a Bedouin woman spoke thus to her husband, carrying her chatter beyond all limits: 'We are enduring all this poverty and hardship; all the world is happy, we alone are miserable. No bread have we, and our relish is anguish and envy; no pitcher have we, and our water is the tears of our eyes. Our raiment by day is the burning sun; by night the moonshine is our mattress and coverlet. We imagine the crescent moon to be a croissant, and lift up our hands towards the sky. The beggars themselves are ashamed of our beggary; day is turned to night by our worry over our daily bread. Kinsfolk and strangers alike start away from us like the Samaritan who was outcast from men. If I beg from anyone a handful of lentils he says to me, "Silence, you death and you plague!" The pride of the Arab is in fighting and giving; you are a blot on the Arabs, like a blunder in fine writing. What fighting can we do? We are slain without fighting, set spinning by the sword of our utter indigence. What giving can we do? We are wrapped up in beggary, tapping the vein of the gnat in the air. If ever a guest comes, as sure as I stand while he sleeps in the night I will make steps for his coat! Such is our state in our poverty and suffering; I pray that no guest may be deluded by us! If you have never seen a ten-year famine in pictures, open your eyes now and look at ourselves. Our outward guise is like the heart of the impostor—all darkness within, while his tongue flashes finely. The impostor has a famine of soul inside of him, whereas outside of us is a famine of bread. Why should we hide the truth like the impostor, suffering agonies for the sake of sham fame?'

'How long will you always hunt for income and harvest?' her husband said to her. 'What remains of our life? The greater part is past. The intelligent man looks not at surplus or shortage since both pass away as swift as a torrent. Whether life be limpid or a muddy torrent, since it lasts not a moment forbear to speak of it. Thousands of animals in this world live happy, contented lives, not tossing up and down. The ringdove on the tree coos thanks unto God, even though her food for the night is not secured; the nightingale trills praise be to God saying, "On Thee I rely for my livelihood, Thou who answerest prayer." The falcon takes joy in the hand of the king and has turned his back on all manner of carrion. Even so take every creature, from gnat to elephant, all are children of God, who is an excellent provider. All these griefs that inhabit our breasts spring from the vapour and dust of our being and our passion. These uprooting griefs are a scythe cutting us down; it is the Devil himself who puts such dark thoughts in our minds. Know that every anguish is a little death; expel that little death from you, if you have the means to do so! Know too, that since you cannot flee from the little death, death whole and complete will be poured over your head; yet if the little death has become sweet to you, know that God will make sweet death whole and complete. Pains are a messenger coming from death; foolish one, turn not your face away from his messenger. Those who live in sweetness die in bitterness; he who pampers the body does not save the soul. Men drive sheep

54

from the plain into the city; the fatter they are, the speedier they are slain. See, the night is past and dawn has come; how long, my pippin, will you repeat your tale of gold over from the beginning? When you were young you were more content; once you were precious as gold, now you have become a hunter for gold. Once you were a fruitful vine; how is it you have turned worthless? How have you turned rotten with your fruit still ripening? Your fruit should grow sweeter, not turn sour again, going ever more backwards like a man twisting rope. You are my mate, and a mate should be of like quality if the business of matrimony is to prosper. A married couple ought to match one another; consider a pair of shoes or of boots, if one of the pair is too tight for the foot both of them are utterly useless to you. Have you ever seen a pair of doors, one small and one big? Or a jungle-lion mated to a wolf? A pair of bags do not sit right on a camel when one is little and the other full size. I am marching to contentment with a stout heart; why are you marching towards cantankerousness?'

After this fashion that well-contented man in all sincerity and earnestness argued with his wife till daybreak.

His wife screamed at him, 'Reputation is your God! I will not swallow your spellbinding words any more. Do not speak such presumptuous and pretentious rubbish! Off with you, do not utter such words of pride and arrogance! How long must I listen to your blather and bombast? Look at your deeds and condition and be a bit ashamed! Pride is always ugly; it is uglier in beggars—like getting into a wet bed on a wintry day. You with your house as fragile as a spider's, how long will you bluster and blow out your beard? When have you lit up your soul with contentment? All you have learned of contentment is its fine name. "What is contentment? A treasure that perishes not," said the Prophet. You do not know the difference between true gain and pain. The contentment he spoke of is the soul's treasure; boast not that you possess it, you grief and pain to the soul. Do not call me your mate, do not hug yourself; I am the mate of justice, not the mate of imposture. I like the way you hobnob with beys and bashas, you who tap the vein of the locust in the air. You battle with dogs to get hold of a bone; you weep

55

and wail like an empty-bellied reed. Do not look at me so aloofly and contemptuously or I will tell you what blood you have in your veins. You consider you have a superior brain to me; yes, I am a pinch-brained woman, but have you looked at me fairly? Do not leap upon me like an incautious wolf! Better no brain than a shame of a brain like yours. May God be the adversary of your wrongdoing and cheating! May your superior intelligence never reach to undo me! You are a snake and a snakecharmer rolled up in one; marvellous! snake and snake-catcher both together, you disgrace to the Arabs! If the crow only knew its own hideousness, it would melt away of anguish and grief like the snow. The charmer chants his spell like a foeman; he binds his spell on the snake, while the snake binds its spell on him—if the snake's spell were not a trap set to ensnare him, how would he have become a prey to the spell of the snake? The charmer out of his greed for gain and for making money is not aware at the time of the snake's spell. The snake says, "Charmer, beware and beware! You have seen your own spell work; now see mine. You beguile me with God's name so as to confuse me and put me to shame; it was God's name, not your design, that trapped me. Woe to you, to have made the name of God a snare; God's name will take vengeance on you for me—I have yielded myself, soul and body, to the name of God. Either by my stroke God's name will cut your life's vein, or it will cast you, like me, into a prison vile".'

Many rough sayings like these, whole books of them, the wife recited to her young husband.

'Woman,' he cried, 'are you a woman, or the father of all sorrow? I take pride in poverty; do not beat me on the head. Wealth and gold are like the cap a man puts on his head; it is only the bald man who makes a refuge out of his cap, the man with curly and handsome locks is all the happier when his cap is off. The man of God is like the eye; his sight is better naked than covered. When a slavedealer offers a slave for sale he strips off the garment that hides defects; but if there is a defect, will he strip that slave? No indeed, he tricks the purchaser by means of the garment saying, "This one is shy of both good and bad; strip him naked and he will run away from you." The merchant is plunged up to his ears in vice, but the merchant has money, and that covers up his vice, for the covetous man sees not his vice through cupidity—cupidity is a powerful conjoiner of hearts. But let the poor man speak words of pure gold, his ware will not find its way into any shop. The business of beggary transcends your understanding; do not look upon beggary so disdainfully, for beggars transcend both property and wealth, they have a copious portion from the Almighty. The High God is just, and do the just act tyrannously towards the dejected? Do they give affluence and much goods to the one and cast the other upon the fire? If any man entertains such thoughts of God who created both worlds, may he burn in Hell! Are the words "I take pride in poverty" an empty boast? No indeed; hidden in them is boundless pomp and glory. In your anger you have called me many fine names—friend-catcher, snake-catcher, that is what you have called me. If I catch snakes, yet I pluck out their fangs so as to save them from having their heads crushed; the fangs of the snake are the enemy of its life, and by my skill I make the enemy a friend. Never out of covetousness do I chant my spell; indeed, I have utterly overthrown covetousness. God forbid! I covet nothing of any man; a whole world of contentment inhabits my heart. That is what you see things like, sitting up in your pear-tree; come on down out of it and your ideas will soon change. You spin round and round and of course you become giddy, then you see the house spinning round, but it is really yourself. Woman, if you consider me very covetous, I beg you, rise above such feminine confusion; I grant it looks like covetousness, but in fact it is a Divine mercy—what room is there for covetousness when God's grace is present? Make trial of poverty just for a day or two, and you will see in poverty twofold riches; bear with poverty steadfastly and give up this disgust, for in poverty dwells the light of the Almighty. Be not a vinegar-purveyor; behold the thousands of souls immersed through contentment in a sea of honey; look at the multitudinous souls suffering bitterly, yet steeped in rose-syrup like so many roses. Ah, if you but had the comprehension, then would be revealed to you the whole story of my heart from my very soul. This speech is as milk held in the breast of the soul, it will not flow well without someone to draw it; when the listener is thirsty and craves to be quenched, then the preacher, though he be dead, suddenly becomes eloquent, yea, let the listener be fresh and unwearied, even the man dumb and mute discovers a thousand tongues. When a stranger enters my door the women of the harem veil themselves, but if an innocent kinsman enters those covered ones raise their veils. Everything that is fashioned fair and lovely and beautiful is so fashioned for the sake of the eye of the beholder; how should the voice of the lute, the high notes and the low, speak for the sake of the ear insentient of one who is deaf? God did not make musk fragrant to no purpose, He made it for the living sense, not for the stopped-up nostril. God has fashioned earth and sky, and raised in the midst of them much fire and light, earth for the sake of the things of clay, heaven to be the dwelling-place of celestial beings. The base man is the foe of the lofty; the purchaser of either place is declared by his works. Chaste woman, have you ever risen up and adorned yourself for the sake of a blind man? If I should fill all the world with hidden pearls, what would it profit me, since they are not your portion? Have done then, wife, with this warfare and waylaying, or if you will not have done with it, then have done with me! What place have I to make war whether on good or bad, seeing that my quiet heart recoils even from peacemaking? Now, whether you keep silence, well; if not, I will procure it, for at this very moment I will quit my hearth and home.'

When the woman beheld her husband so fierce and ungovernable she fell to weeping; tears indeed are the lure of women.

'When did I ever dream to hear such words from you?' she cried. 'What I hoped of you was something quite different. I am your dust,' she whined in abasement, 'unworthy to be called your lady. I am yours entirely, body and soul; your authority is absolute. If my heart lost patience on account of poverty, that was not for my sake but for yours. You have been my cure in every sickness, and I cannot endure to see you penniless. By your life I swear, this is not on my own behalf; this weeping and wailing is all because of you. By Allah I swear, every breath I draw my self is fain to die for

58

your self here before you. Ah, that your soul, for which my soul would be a sacrifice, were only apprised of the thoughts in my soul! Since you have entertained such an opinion of me, I have become aweary of both soul and body. I cast dust on all silver and gold, since you so entreat me, O comfort of my soul. You who inhabit my very soul and heart, will you have done with me for so little offence? Have done with me then; the power is in your hands; yet my soul entreats you against so cruel a verdict. Bring back to mind the time when I was fair as an idol and you worshipped me, my own idolater. Your slave has kindled her heart to accord with you; whatever you call "well-cooked" your slave pronounces "to a frazzle"! I am your spinach, whatever you cook me with; whether you are sour broth or sweet, you suit me perfectly. I have spoken infidelity; behold, now I have come back to the faith, ready with all my soul to obey your command. I was not aware of your royal nature, rudely I galloped my ass into your presence; now, having made a lamp of your pardon to light me, I am truly penitent, I put opposition from me. See, I set before you both sword and winding-sheet; I stretch my neck before you; smite! You speak words of bitter separation; do whatsoever you will, only do not this. Your inmost spirit pleads for me within you, interceding perpetually with you without me; my pleader within you is your noble nature, relying on which my heart made bold to sin. Wrathful one, have mercy unbeknownst to yourself, you whose nature is sweeter than a mountain of honey.'

After this fashion she was speaking, tenderly and without reserve, when she was overcome by a fit of weeping. When her tears and sobbings passed beyond all bounds—and even without tears she was ravishing enough—out of that rain-cloud darted a lightning-flash that struck a spark into the heart of that lonely man. God created woman that man might repose in her; how then can Adam be parted from Eve? Water overcomes fire when it dashes furiously against it, but fire makes it to seethe when it is screened in the pot; when a cauldron intervenes between the two, fire annihilates water and turns it into air. If in outward appearance, like the water, you dominate your wife, inwardly you are dominated, a petitioner of your wife. This is a property peculiar to Man; in beasts love is inferior, owing to their inferiority. The Prophet himself declared that woman prevails exceedingly over the intelligent, over the perceptive, whereas ignorant men prevail over woman inasmuch as within them is the brutality of animals. Such men lack tenderness, gentleness, affection because animality prevails over their humanity; love and tenderness are human qualities; passion and lust are animal qualities. Woman is God's radiance, not that mortal beloved; she is creative, you might say she is not created.

The husband felt sorry for what he had said, as sorry as a little tyrant in the hour of his death.

'How did I ever become the adversary of the life of my soul?' he cried. 'How did I come to aim kicks at the head of my soul? Wife, I am penitent; if I have been an infidel, now I become a Moslem. I have sinned against you; have mercy on me, do not pluck me by the roots and destroy me entirely. Now I have given up opposing you; you have the authority; unsheathe the sword! Whatever you command me, that I will do, I will not consider the issue, be it good or ill. I will become wholly naughted into your being since I am in love with you; love makes blind and deaf.'

'Are you truly my friend, I wonder,' said the wife, 'or would you reveal my secret by a trick?'

The husband answered, 'No, by Allah who knows the secret thought most hidden, and out of dust created Adam, His chosen one, in the three cubits of bodily form that He gave him showing forth all that was in the tablets and the world of spirits. God taught Adam the Names, by virtue of which at the beginning he rehearsed all that shall come to pass to eternity, so that the angels listening were amazed at his instruction, and from his sanctifying God discovered a new sanctity. Not in the wide expanse of their heavens was contained that revelation which then appeared to them from Adam; compared with the spaciousness of the range of that pure spirit the expanse of the seven heavens became narrow indeed. God's decree spread for us the carpet of indulgence: "Speak to Me without reserve, without fear all that comes upon your tongues, as only children speak with their father. For what matters it if your words be unseemly? My mercy likewise outruns My wrath. A hundred fathers and mothers are every moment born and die within My clemency; their clemency is but the foam of the sea of My clemency—the foam comes and goes, but the sea continues forever.'' What shall I say indeed? Compared with that pearl, this oyster-shell is nothing but the foam of the foam of the foam of the foam. By the truth of that foam, by the truth of that pure sea, these words I have spoken are not to make trial or to boast, they are spoken out of love and sincerity and humility, that I swear by the truth of Him to whom I return. If my affection seems to you but a trial to try you, just for one moment put the trial to the test. Hide not your secret, that mine may become manifest; command anything whatsoever I am able to perform. Hide not your heart, that my heart may become manifest and that I may accept whatsoever I am capable of. What I am to do? What remedy is in my hands? Consider into what plight my soul is plunged.'

The wife, said, 'Lo, a sun has shone forth in splendour, from whom a world entire has received light; namely, the vicar of the All-merciful, the Creator's vicegerent, through whom the city of Baghdad is as happy as the spring. If you attain to that king, you yourself will become a king; how long will you go in quest of every kind of disaster?'

'How should I be acceptable to the king?' the husband demanded. 'How should I go to him without any pretext? I must have some reference, some device or other; can a man ply any trade properly without tools?'

'When the king of generosity enters the field,' the wife replied, 'the very lack of a tool becomes a tool most powerful. The tool is the proof of imposture and self-existence; God's work is done without such a tool, in all abasement.'

The husband said, 'How shall I do business without a tool, unless I make it clear that I really have no tool? I must have some testimony to my bankruptcy, that the king in his great wealth may have compassion on me. Produce some testimony other than your empty chatter; show it forth, so that the handsome king may take compassion. Testimony that consists merely of empty chatter is soon invalidated before that judge supreme. He requires truth as testimony to a man's condition, so that his inward light may shine forth without his speaking.'

61

'Truthfulness,' commented the wife, 'is when people by all their effort rise clean out of their personal existence. Now we have some rain-water in our pitcher; it is your own property, your capital and your means. Take this pitcher of water and be off with you. offer it as a present to the king of kings. Tell him, "We have not any means but this; in the desert there is nothing better than water." Though his treasury is full of gold and jewels, he never gets water like this; it is very rare.'

'Who ever had a present the like of it?' said her husband, blowing out his moustaches. 'Truly this is worthy of such a king. Yes,' he continued, 'plug the mouth of the pitcher; take very good care, for this gift will be very profitable to us. Sew up the pitcher in felt, and let the king break his fast with our offering. Such water is not to be found in all the world; no other water is half so pure.'

Thereupon that Bedouin picked up the pitcher and set forth on the road, carrying it with him day and night, trembling for his pitcher lest some accident befall it, carrying it all the way from the desert to the city.

His wife meanwhile unrolled her prayer-rug and petitioned the good Lord to preserve her husband and his load. 'Guard our water from good-for-nothing rascals,' she prayed over and over. 'Bring our pearl, Lord, to that sea. Though my husband is wary and artful, yet the pearl has many thousands of enemies. Pearl, did I call it? Nay, it is the water of Paradise-river; a single drop of this is the origin of the pearl.'

Thanks to the wife's prayers and supplications, thanks too to the husband's carefulness and endurance he bore it, safe from thieves and undamaged by stones, without delay to the abode of the caliphate. There he beheld a court replete with bounties where all those in need had spread out their nets; every moment, on every side, some needy petitioner bore away from that door a gift and a robe of honour—like the sun and rain it was, free alike to infidel and believer, goodly folk and evil, nay, it was like Paradise. Some he beheld already arrayed in their finery, others risen to their feet awaiting the caliph's good pleasure.

'Come hither, you who seek!' he heard a voice cry.

Bounty is in need of beggars, needy as any beggar. Bounty is seeking the beggars and the indigent, even as the beautiful who seek for a clear mirror; the face of the beautiful through the mirror is made lovely, the face of beneficence through the beggar is made visible. Therefore God charged the Prophet, in the Sura of the Forenoon, "And as for the beggar, scold him not".'

When that Bedouin from the far desert arrived at the gate of the abode of the caliphate the officers went to meet him. They sprinkled much of the rosewater of gentleness on his breast; they understood his need without need of speech, for it was their business to give before being asked.

'Honourable Arab,' they addressed him, 'whence have you come? How do you do, after such a weary journey?'

'Honourable I am,' he replied, 'only if you do me honour; what sort of face is mine if you put me behind your backs? Sirs, you who behold all by the light of God and have come from God for the sake of charity that by the alchemy of your regard you may transmute the dross of humanity into the gold Divine, I am a stranger come out of the desert, come in the hope of the Sultan's good grace. The scent of his grace seized all the desert; the grains of sand even sprang to life thereby. All this way I came for the sake of gold; now I am come here, I am entranced by what I behold. I came to this door seeking after pelf; as soon as I entered the portico I was promoted to the seat of honour. I brought water as a present, hoping to win bread; hoping for bread brought me to the heights of Paradise. It was bread that drove Adam out of Paradise; it is bread that has commingled me now with the dwellers in Paradise. I have been delivered from water and bread like the angels; freed from desire, I spin like heaven's sphere about this door.'

Then he presented his pitcher of water; he sowed the seed of service in that high presence. 'Convey this offering to the Sultan,' he said. 'Redeem the king's petitioner from his need. See, it is sweet water, and a new, green pitcher— some of the rain-water that collected in our dyke.'

The officers smiled at his words, but they accepted his gift as if it were priceless as life; for the loving kindness of that good and knowing king had made its mark upon all his courtiers. When the king saw the offering and heard the Bedouin's story he filled the pitcher with gold and added other gifts, delivering the Arab out of his poverty with many charities and robes of honour.

'Give into his hand this pitcher full of gold,' he said. 'When he turns for home again, lead him to the Tigris. He has come hither by way of the dry land and wayfaring; by way of the water his journey back will be nearer.'

When the Bedouin embarked in the ship and saw the Tigris he bowed his head in shame, prostrating himself. 'Marvellous is the loving kindness of that bountiful king,' he cried. 'Even more marvellous it is that he took my water. How did it come to pass that that ocean of generosity so quickly accepted from me such spurious coin?'

Know, my son, that this whole world is a pitcher filled to the brim with wisdom and beauty. The world is a single drop of the Tigris of God's beauty which on account of its fullness cannot be contained within any vessel.

9

The grammarian and the boatman

A GRAMMARIAN once embarked in a boat. Turning to the boatman with a self-satisfied air he asked him:

'Have you ever studied grammar?'

'No,' replied the boatman.

'Then half your life has gone to waste,' the grammarian said.

The boatman thereupon felt very depressed, but he answered him nothing for the moment. Presently the wind tossed the boat into a whirlpool. The boatman shouted to the grammarian:

'Do you know how to swim?'

'No,' the grammarian replied, 'my well-spoken, handsome fellow.'

'In that case, grammarian,' the boatman remarked, 'the whole of your life has gone to waste, for the boat is sinking in these whirlpools.'

You may be the greatest scholar in the world in your time, but consider, my friend, how the world passes away—and time!

10

The man who wanted to be tattooed, on the necessity of self-discipline

IT is the custom of the people of Qazvin to tattoo themselves blue on their bodies, hands and shoulders with the point of a needle, so that they suffer no hurt at all. Now one day a man of that city went to a barber and said to him, 'Do me a favour, kindly tattoo me.'

'What figure do you want me to tattoo, my brave?' asked the barber.

'Tattoo the figure of a raging lion,' the man directed. 'I was born under Leo, so prick out the picture of a lion. Put your back into it, prick in plenty of blue.'

'Where shall I prick the figure?' asked the barber.

'Prick the pretty picture on my shoulder-blade,' said the man.

As soon as he started to stick the needle in the customer, feeling the sharp pain in his shoulder-blade, squealed right bravely:

'Noble sir, I declare you have slain me! What sort of figure are you tattooing?'

'Why, a lion, just as you ordered.'

'With which part of it did you begin?'

'I started at the tail,' the barber answered.

'Omit the tail, my dear fellow,' said the man. 'The lion's tail and rump fair took my breath away; its rump has completely choked my windpipe. Let the lion lack for a tail, lion-maker; the prick of the needle has made my heart faint.'

The barber began to prick in another place, without fear, without favour, without compassion.

'Which part of his body is this now?' the man yelled.

'This is the ear, my good man,' said the barber.

'Let him be without ears, wise physician. Omit the ears, and cut the cloth short!'

The barber stuck his needle in yet another spot, and once again the man started to howl.

'Which part of his body is this in the third place?'

'This is the belly of the lion, your honour.'

'Let him lack for a belly,' the man entreated. 'The picture is full enough already; what need for a belly?'

The barber was reduced to complete bewilderment and stood for a long time finger in mouth. Finally the maestro flung the needle to the ground.

'Did ever the like of it happen to anyone?' he cried. 'Who ever saw a lion without a tail, a head and a belly? God himself never created such a lion!'

Bear with fortitude, brother, the pain of the lancet, that you may escape from the poison of your infidel self. People who have escaped out of self-existence—sun, moon and stars bow down before them.

11

*The lion, the wolf and the fox,
on the three faculties of man*

A LION, a wolf and a fox went out to hunt for food in
the mountains, thinking that by supporting one another they
would the more firmly bind and fetter their prey; the three
of them together would secure abundant game in that wilderness profound. Though the ferocious lion in truth was
ashamed of their company, yet he showed them due courtesy
and took them along with him on the way; for such a
monarch, common soldiery is a troublesome nuisance, yet
he went along with them—union is a Divine mercy; such a
resplendent moon is disgraced by the stars, and travels among
them out of pure generosity. God commanded His Prophet,
'Take counsel with them,' for all that no counsel is to be
compared with his own. In the measuring-scales barley and
gold sit side by side, but this does not mean that barley has
thus acquired the substance of gold. Now the spirit has
become the body's fellow-traveller; for a while the dog
has become the guardian of the palace-gate.

When the wolf and the fox, frisking at the stirrup of the
majestic lion, had come to the mountains they discovered
there a mountain-ox, a goat and a fat hare; so their business
prospered, for whoever follows in the tracks of a furious
lion, roast-meat fails him not whether by day or night.
Having brought their catch down from the mountain into
the thicket, slain and lacerated and wallowing in gore, the
wolf and the fox had high hopes that, after the justice of
monarchs, the fruits of their hunting would be fairly divided
between them. The reflexion of the hope of that hungry pair
struck the lion, and he knew at once the foundation of their
hopes; one who is a lion and prince of spiritual mysteries
knows whatever thought passes in the minds of his following.

Right well he knows, and goes on silently; he smiles in your face to conceal his understanding.

The lion knew well the whisperings in their breasts; yet he said not a word, and for the while showed them all courtesy. But within himself he said, 'I will show you your deserts, rascally beggars! Was not my judgment sufficient to satisfy you? Is this the opinion you have of my munificence, you whose very minds and judgment are derived from my judgment, from my gifts that adorn the whole world? What other than good should the picture think of the painter, seeing that he bestowed of his thought and experience upon it? Did you entertain such a base opinion of me, you who are a disgrace to this earth? Those who think evil thoughts of God—I will strike off their heads, like the hypocrites they are. I will deliver heaven's sphere of your disgrace, that this tale may remain in the world for ever.'

So the lion meditated, while outwardly he went on smiling: my friend, do not trust the smiles of the lion! Worldly possessions are the smiles of God, making us drunken and deluded and threadbare. Poverty and suffering are better for you, my master, for then that smile will uproot its snare.

The lion said, 'Wolf, assign this catch; ancient wolf, make a new dispensation of justice. Act as my deputy in the distribution, then we shall see of what sort of stuff you are made.'

'King,' said the wolf, 'the wild ox is your share. It is big, and you are big and stout and nimble. I shall have the goat, because the goat is middling and intermediate. Fox, you take the hare. There, that is all fair and above board.'

'Wolf, how could you speak like that?' the lion demanded. 'What, with me present, do you speak of "me" and "you"? Why, what a mongrel the wolf must be, to regard himself in the presence of a lion like me, peerless and incomparable! Come here, you self-opinionated ass!'

The wolf approached, and the lion fell on him with his claws and tore him asunder, flaying off his skin because he saw him lacking the core of right behaviour.

'Since the very sight of me did not transport you out of yourself,' he said, 'a spirit like yours must perforce die miserably. Since you were not passing away from yourself in my presence, it was an act of grace to behead you.'

The headstrong lion tore off the head of the wolf so that two-headedness and distinction might not remain. Then the lion turned his attention to the fox.

'Divide the catch, and let us breakfast,' he ordered.

'Choicest of kings, this fat ox shall be your breakfast,' said the fox, bowing low. 'This goat shall be laid aside for the victorious king's midday meal. Lastly the hare—that will be a titbit for supper for a king so gracious and bountiful.'

'Fox,' said the lion, 'you have lit a torch of justice. Who taught you such an admirable division? Where did you learn it from, my great fellow?'

'King of the world,' replied the fox, 'from what happened to the wolf.'

'Since you have pledged yourself entirely to the love of me,' the lion said, 'pick up all three, and take them with you. Fox, since you have become altogether mine how should I hurt you, seeing you have become myself? I am yours, and all the beasts of the chase are yours; set your foot on the seventh heaven, and mount on high! Since you took warning by the miserable wolf, you are no more a fox; you are my very own lion.'

'Thanks a hundredfold to the lion,' the fox remarked, 'in that he summoned me after the wolf. If he had bidden me to divide the catch first, who then would have escaped from him with his life?'

Thanks also be to Him who put us into the world after the peoples of old, so that we heard of the punishments God visited upon past generations of men who lived in former times, that we, knowing what befell those wolves of long ago, like the fox may keep more vigilant watch over ourselves.

12

The man who said, 'It is I'

A CERTAIN man once came and knocked on the door of a friend.

'Who are you, faithful one?' his friend asked.

'I,' he answered.

'Go away,' the friend said. 'It is not the proper time. There is no place for such a raw fellow at a table like mine.'

What shall cook the raw, but the fire of banishment and separation? What shall deliver him out of hypocrisy?

That wretched man departed and wandered abroad for a year, burned as with sparks of fire in separation from his friend. So, scorched, he was cooked; then he returned and once more circled about the house of his companion. Fearful a hundredfold, he gently knocked at the door, anxious lest any unmannerly word should escape his lips.

His friend called, 'Who is that at the door?'

He answered, 'You also are at the door, heart-ravisher!'

'Now,' the friend cried, 'since you are I, come in, O I! There is not room in the house for two I's.'

13

Joseph and the mirror

A LOVING friend came from the far ends of the earth and became the guest of Joseph the veracious, for they had been well acquainted in the days of childhood, reclining together against the pillow of good acquaintanceship. The friend recalled to Joseph the malevolence and envy of his brethren.

'Yes,' said Joseph, 'that was like a chain, and I was the lion. The lion is not shamed by the chain; I make no complaint against the destiny of God. If the lion had a chain on his neck, yet he was prince over all the chain-makers.'

'How was it with you,' asked the friend, 'in the prison and the well?'

'Like the moon in her occlusion, when she is on the wane. If in her occlusion the moon is bent double, yet at the last does she not become the full moon in heaven? And now, my friend,' Joseph said, having told his story, 'what traveller's present have you brought me? Come, give me my present.'

The friend, put to shame by this demand, cried alas.

'How many presents I have sought out for you, but I saw nothing worthy to offer. Should I bring a grain of gold to the mine? Should I bring a drop of water to the Sea of Oman? I should bring cumin-seed to Kirman, if I brought you even my heart and soul as an offering. There is no seed on earth that is not in this stack, save only your beauty which has no rival. Therefore I thought it suitable that I should being you a mirror, like the light dwelling within an innocent breast, so that you may see in it your lovely face, you who are like the sun, the candle of heaven. I have brought you a mirror, light of my eyes, so that when you see your face in it you may remember me.'

What is the mirror of Being? Not-being. If you are not a fool, bring not-being as your offering.

14

Harut and Marut reproved

HARUT and Marut, angels, famed for their arrogance were pierced by the poisoned arrow of God's anger. They put their reliance in their own sanctity, but what boots it for the buffalo to rely on the lion? Though he devises a hundred shifts with his horn, the furious lion will tear him to pieces limb by limb; though his horns be as numerous as the hedgehog's bristles, the buffalo will certainly be slain by the lion.

Though the fierce Sarsar wind plucks out many trees, it makes every green blade shine more freshly, for that blustering gale pities the infirmity of the grass: boast not vainly, my heart, of your strength. How should the axe fear the spissitude of the branches? It cuts them to pieces; yet it beats not itself against a leaf, it beats not its edge save against an edge. What cares the flame for the multitude of firewood? Shall the butcher flee from the multitude of the sheep?

What is the form compared with the reality? Very infirm. It is its reality that keeps the sky inverted like a bowl. Take your analogy from the heavenly wheel: from whom comes its circular motion? From counselling Reason; the motion of this body round as a shield derives from the veiled Spirit, my son. The motion of the wind springs from its reality, like the wheel that is prisoner of the water of the stream.

All the tiers of earth and heaven are but as straws in that flowing sea; the rushing and dancing of the straws in the water spring from the water when it is tossed. When the sea wishes to still their struggling it casts the straws towards the shore; when it draws them from the shore into the surging main it does with them as the Sarsar wind with the grass.

When Harut and Marut espied from their heavenly lattice the sin and wickedness of the people of earth they began to

73

bite their hands in anger; yet they lacked eyes to behold their own fault.

An ugly man saw himself in the glass; he turned his face away from that image, and was furious.

Whenever the self-opinionated man sees a sin committed by another, a fire blazes up in him straight out of Hell; he calls that pride the defence of the faith, not seeing in himself the spirit of arrogance. But defence of the faith has a different token, for out of that fire a whole world becomes green.

God said to Harut and Marut, 'If you are true furbishers, regard not contemptuously the doers of black deeds. Rather utter thanks, you heavenly host and servitors, that you are freed from lust and the itch of the loins. If I impose upon you that kind of nature Heaven will no longer receive you. That preservation from sin you have in your bodies springs from the reflexion of My preservation and guardianship; regard it therefore, I charge you, as of Me, lest the accursed Devil prevail against you.'

15

The deaf man who visited a sick neighbour

AN affluent man once said to one who was deaf, 'Do you know one of your neighbours has been taken ill?'

The deaf man said to himself, 'With my hardness of hearing what shall I understand of the words uttered by that young man, particularly as he is ill and his voice is weak? However, I must go there, I cannot escape. When I see his lips moving, I will guess what he is saying out of my own initiative. When I say, "How are you, my poor suffering friend?" he will answer, "I am fine," or "Quite well, thank you." Then I will say, "Thank God! What have you had to drink?" He will answer, "A sherbet," or "Some bean-soup." Then I will say, "Good health! Which doctor is attending you?" He will answer, "So-and-so." I will say, "He has a lucky foot; since he has called, all will go well with you. I have made trial of his foot myself; wherever he goes, every want is granted".'

Having prepared in advance these guesswork answers, the good fellow went to call on the invalid.

'How are you?' he asked.

'Dying,' the sick man said.

'Thank God!' cried the deaf man.

Thereupon the invalid became vexed and indignant.

'What sort of thank God is this?' he thought. 'He must have been my enemy.'

The deaf man had made his guess, but it had turned out wrong.

'What have you had to drink?' he asked next.

'Poison,' said the sick man.

'Good health!' cried the visitor, making the patient still more angry.

'Which doctor is attending you?' the deaf man went on.

75

'The Angel of Death. Get out!' the sufferer shouted.

'Cheer up, he has a lucky foot,' said the deaf man, and took his departure. 'Thank God!' he repeated gaily. 'Now I will be off.'

'This man is the enemy of my life,' cried the invalid. 'I never realized he was so malicious.'

Many there are who perform works of devotion, and set their hearts on being approved and rewarded, yet those very works are in reality secret sin against God; what was thought to be pure is in fact most foul.

16

The Greek and the Chinese artists, on the difference between theologians and mystics

IF you desire a parable of the hidden knowledge, tell the story of the Greeks and the Chinese.

'We are the better artists,' the Chinese declared.

'We have the edge on you,' the Greeks countered.

'I will put you to the test,' said the Sultan. 'Then we shall see which of you makes good your claim.'

'Assign to us one particular room, and you Greeks another,' said the Chinese.

The two rooms faced each other, door to door, the Chinese taking one and the Greeks the other. The Chinese demanded of the king a hundred colours, so that worthy monarch opened up his treasury and every morning the Chinese received of his bounty their ration of colours from the treasury.

'No hues or colours are suitable for our work,' said the Greeks. 'All we require is to get rid of the rust.'

So saying, they shut their door and set to work polishing; smooth and unsullied as the sky they became.

There is a way from multicolority to colourlessness; colour is like the clouds, colourlessness is a moon. Whatever radiance and splendour you see in the clouds, be sure that it comes from the stars, the moon and the sun.

When the Chinese had completed their work they began drumming for joy. The king came in and saw the pictures there; the moment he encountered that sight, it stole away his wits. Then he advanced towards the Greeks, who thereupon removed the intervening curtain so that the reflexion of the Chinese masterpieces struck upon the walls they had scoured clean of rust. All that the king had seen in the Chinese room showed lovelier here, so that his very eyes were snatched out of their sockets.

The Greeks, my father, are the Sufis; without repetition and books and learning, yet they have scoured their breasts clean of greed and covetousness, avarice and malice. The purity of the mirror without doubt is the heart, which receives images innumerable. The reflexion of every image, whether numbered or without number, shines forth for ever from the heart alone, and for ever every new image that enters upon the heart shows forth within it free of all imperfection. They who have burnished their hearts have escaped from scent and colour; every moment, instantly, they behold Beauty.

17

Muhammad and the vision of Zaid, on concealing the secrets of God

ONE morning the Prophet said to Zaid, 'How are you this morning, my sincere Companion?'

'God's faithful servant,' Zaid replied.

'Where is the token of the garden of faith, if it has truly bloomed?' again asked the Prophet.

'I have thirsted by day,' said Zaid. 'At night I have not slept out of passion and burning anguish. So I have passed beyond day and night, even as the lance-point passes through the shield. For in the beyond all nations are one; a hundred thousand years are the same as an hour. Post-eternity and pre-eternity are there united. Reason by inquiry has no way thither.'

'Where is your traveller's present from this way?' asked the Prophet. 'Produce it! Where is the token genuine of that fair land?'

'When other men behold the sky,' Zaid replied, 'I behold the Throne with those that dwell there. The eight Paradises and seven Hells are as plain to me as the idol to the idolater. I tell apart the people of earth one by one as wheat is told from barley in the mill, so that it is as clear to me as snake and fish who is marked for Paradise and who is excluded. I see them all plainly as on the Resurrection Day as living multitudes, men and women. Say, shall I tell it forth, or shall I hold my tongue?'

The Prophet bit his lip at him, as though to say, 'Enough!'

'Prophet of God,' Zaid continued, 'shall I tell the secret of the Mustering? Shall I make manifest in the world today the Resurrection? Suffer me to rend asunder the curtains, so that my spirituality may shine forth like a sun; so that the sun may be eclipsed by my light, and that I may show

79

forth the date-tree and the willow. I will show forth the mystery of the Resurrection, I will show forth the true coin and the base alloy, the Companions of the Left with their hands severed; I will show forth the colour of unbelief, the colour of fraud. I will reveal the seven orifices of hypocrisy in the light of the moon that suffers neither eclipse nor waning. I will show forth the sackcloth of the damned, I will cause to be heard the drums and kettledrums of the prophets. I will bring forth manifest before the eyes of the infidels Hell and Paradise and Purgatory. I will show forth the Pool of Kauthar bubbling, sprinkling water on the faces of the blest, the gurgle ringing in their ears; and as for those who run about Kauthar athirst, I will name them one by one and tell who they are; their shoulders are rubbing against my shoulders, their ululations are piercing my ears. Before my very eyes the people of Paradise, choosing freely, clasp one another to their bosoms, visiting one another in their establishments and snatching kisses from the lips of the houris. My ear has become deafened by the shouts of "Woe, woe!" uttered by the damned in their misery, the cries of "Alas!" These are but hints; I would speak out of the depths, but that I fear to vex the Messenger of God.'

After this fashion he was speaking, intoxicated and beside himself. The Prophet suddenly twisted his collar

'Careful!' cried the Prophet. 'Pull up, your horse is too hot. When the reflexion of "God is not ashamed before the truth" strikes, shame departs. Your mirror has slipped out of its covering: how should the mirror and the balance tell untruth? How should the mirror and the balance hold their breath for fear of vexing and shaming anyone? Mirror and balance are noble touchstones; though you should woo them two hundred years, saying, "For my sake conceal the truth, indicate the surplus, do not indicate the shortcoming," yet they will answer you, "Mock not your beard and moustache! When shall mirror and balance trick and deceive? Since God has exalted us that the truth through us may be known, if we show not the truth what worth are we, my lad? How shall we become a norm for the faces of the fair?" Yet for all that, slip the mirror back into its cloth, if revelation has made of your breast a Mount Sinai.'

'What then?' said Zaid. 'Shall the Sun of the Truth and Orb of Eternity be contained under the armpit? It bursts asunder both armpit and fraud; neither madness nor reason remains in its presence.'

'Lay one finger upon one eye,' said the Prophet, 'and you see the world empty of the sun. One finger-tip becomes a veil over the moon, which is a symbol of God the Concealer. A single point suffices to cover the world, a single slip causes the sun to be eclipsed. Rise up, Zaid, shackle the heavenly Buraq of your utterance. Since the power of speech exposes faults, so now it is rending the veils of concealment. God desires concealment for a season: drive off this drummer, and bar the way! Gallop not so; draw your rein; it is better that the mystery should be hidden; it is better that every man should rejoice in his own presumption. God desires that even His creatures who despair should not turn their faces away from the worship of Him; even because of a hope they acquire nobility and for a few days run at its stirrup. God desires that that mercy should shine upon all, upon the evil and the good, out of the universality of His compassion. God desires that every man, be he prince or prisoner, should live in hope and fear and walk with caution. Hope and fear are within the veil that they may be nurtured behind this veil; if you could rend the veil, where then are fear and hope? Earthly trial and probation depend upon things unseen.'

18

The fire that consumed Medina,
on quenching lust

A GREAT fire broke out in the time of Omar, devouring even stones as if they were dry wood; it fell upon edifices and houses, darted even into the wings and nests of the birds. Half the city caught fire from the flames; the water wondered at the fire, and was afraid of it. Certain prudent persons were throwing skins of water and vinegar upon the fire, but out of contentiousness the fire went on increasing, receiving reinforcement from the Infinite.

The people hastened to Omar, saying, 'Our fire will not at all be quenched by water.'

'That fire,' said Omar, 'is a sign from God. It is a flame from the fire of your iniquity. Abandon water, and distribute bread; abandon avarice, if you are my people.'

'We have opened our doors,' the people replied. 'We have always been openhanded and charitable.'

'You have given bread,' he answered, 'out of wont and habit. You have not opened your hands for God's sake, but only for glory, proudly and ostentatiously, not because of godly fear and humble supplication.'

The outward fire may be quenched with water, but the fire of lust transports a man to Hell. The fire of lust is not assuaged by water, for it has the nature of Hell to torment eternally. What extinguishes the fire of lust? The light of religion: your light shall put out the fire of the unbelievers.

19

Ali and the infidel who spat in his face, an example of chivalry

LEARN from Ali true sincerity in action; know that the Lion of God was cleansed of all imposture.

In battling for the faith he overcame a certain knight, quickly drew his sword and made haste to slay him. Thereupon that man spat in Ali's face, the face of him who was the pride of every prophet and saint; he spat on the cheek before which the face of the moon itself bows low. Forthwith Ali cast his sword aside and relaxed his vigour in fighting him. The enemy champion was amazed by this deed, by his showing forgiveness and mercy without any occasion.

'You lifted up your sharp sword against me,' he said. 'Why have you now flung it aside and let me be? What did you see better than battling against me, that you have become so dilatory in hunting me down? What did you see, that so fierce a wrath as yours subsided, that such a lightning flashed and then recoiled? What did you see, that from the reflexion of your vision a flame burst forth in my heart and soul? What did you see loftier than all being and space that was better than life itself, so that you gave me life? In courage indeed you are the Lion of the Lord; in chivalry who can say what name to call you? In chivalry you are like the cloud of Moses in the desert, out of which came that banquet and bread incomparable. Ali, you who are mind and eye entirely, declare a little portion of what you have seen. The blade of your clemency has split my heart, the water of your knowledge has purified my earth. Declare it! I know well that these are the mysteries of God, for it is His work to slay without a sword; He is the Artificer without tools and limbs, the Bestower of these profitable gifts; He causes the mind to taste innumerable wines whereof the eyes and ears have no intelligence. Declare, falcon of the heavenly heights hunting goodly prey, what thing you saw at this time from the Creator. Your eye has learned to perceive the very Unseen, such things as the eyes of those present with God are stopped against. Unfold the mystery, Ali, well-pleasing to God, you who are such goodly ease after a malignant fate; either do you declare what your reason has discovered, or I will tell that which has shone forth upon me. It has shone forth upon me from you; how shall you conceal it? Without speech of tongue, like the moon you are darting forth rays; yet if the moon's orb found the faculty of speech, more swiftly would it bring night-travellers to the right way so that they are secure from error and inadvertency, the voice of the moon prevailing over the voice of the ghoul. Since the moon points the way even without speaking, when it speaks it becomes radiance upon radiance. Since you are the gate of that city of knowledge, since you are the ray of the sun of clemency, be open, O gate, to him who seeks the gate, so that through you the lifeless husks may come to the living core; be open to everlasting, O gate of mercy, O entrance-hall unto Him like to whom is not any one. Speak, Prince of the Faithful, that my soul may stir in my body like an embryo in the womb. Declare, falcon of the shining wings schooled to the king and his forearm, declare, royal falcon seizing the fabulous simurgh, by your own arm without army shattering an army. You are a community in yourself, at once one and a hundred thousand: declare, you to whose falcon your humble servant is a prey. Wherefore this mercy in the place of fury? Whose way is it to give the hand to the dragon?'

'It is for God's sake that I wield the blade,' replied Ali. 'I am the servant of God, not the commissary of the body. I am the Lion of God, not the lion of passion; my deed testifies to my religion. "When thou threwest, it was not thyself that threw''—God's words are true of me in the war; I am as a sunbeam cast by God, the Sun. I have cleared the baggage of self out of the way, reckoning all but God to be non-existent. I am a shadow, and my Lord is the sun; I am the chamberlain, I am not the curtain forbidding Him. I am like a sword studded with pearls of union; I make men living, not slaughtered, in the fighting. Blood does not shroud

84

the lustre of my blade; how should the errant wind sweep away my cloud? I am not a straw, I am a mountain of clemency and forbearing and justice; how should the fierce wind carry away the mountain? I am a mountain, and my being is His edifice; if I become as a straw, the wind transporting me is the remembrance of Him. My inclination is only stirred by His wind; my captain of cavalry is only the love of the One. Wrath is king over kings, but to me it is slave; even wrath I have bound under the bridle. The sword of my clemency has smitten the neck of my wrath; to me the wrath of God has come in the form of mercy. I am drowned in light, although my roof is ruined; I have become a garden, though men call me Father of Dust. Since the thought of other than God intervened, it behoved me to sheathe my sword, that my name may become He Loves For God's Sake, that my will may become He Hates For God's Sake, that my bounty may become He Gives For God's Sake, that my being may become He Withholds For God's Sake. My miserliness is for God, my giving is for God alone; I am altogether God's, to none other I belong. What I do for God's Sake is no mere conformity, no fancy and surmise, but the true vision of God. I have been freed from personal effort and enquiry, I have attached my sleeve to the skirt of God. If I am flying, I behold whither I must soar; if I am spinning, I behold the axis on which I turn. If I am dragging a load, I know whither I must bear it; I am the moon, and the Sun goes before me as my guide. I am free of self-interest: hear the witness of a freeman, for the witness of slaves is not worth two barley-corns. Since I am free, how should rage fetter me? Nothing is here but the attributes of God, so enter in! Enter in, for the grace of God has made you free, in that His mercy had precedence over His wrath. Enter in now, for you have escaped from the peril; you were a common pebble, God's alchemy has made you a precious stone. You have escaped from unbelief and its tangle of thorns; blossom now like a rose in the cypress-arbour of God. You are I, I am you, my much honoured friend; you were Ali—how then should I slay Ali? You committed a sin better than any piety; you have traversed all Heaven in a single instant. Enter in: I have opened the door to you. You spat upon me, and behold, I bestow upon you a present. Such things I give to the worker of wickedness; see how I offer my head to the foot of the transgressor. What then do I bestow upon the doer of righteousness? Know for sure, I bestow treasures and kingdoms everlasting. Such a man I am, that the honey of my gentleness did not turn into a sting in wrath even against my murderer. The Prophet whispered into the ear of my servant that one day he would strike off this head of mine from its neck; inspired by the Friend, the Prophet announced that my destruction in the end would be encompassed by my servant's hand. My servant said, "Slay me first, that this monstrous sin may not be wrought by me." I said, "Since my death is to come about through you, how can I seek to outwit my fate?" He fell before me crying, "O generous master, for the sake of God cleave me in twain so that this evil end may not come upon me and so that my soul may not burn for destroying its own life." I said, "Begone: the ink of the Pen of Fate is dry; by that Pen many a landmark is overthrown. No hatred is in my soul on account of you, for I do not recognize this deed as coming from you. You are the instrument of God; God's hand is the agent; how shall I reproach and resist the instrument of God?" '

'Why then,' asked the knight, 'is retaliation prescribed?'

'That too is of God,' said Ali. 'And it is a hidden mystery. If God objects to His own act, yet out of His objecting He makes fair gardens to grow. It is proper for God to object to His own act, seeing that in fury and gentleness He is One. Within this city of vicissitudes He is the Prince; He is the master of ordination in all kingdoms. If He breaks His own instrument, yet He amends that which has become broken. In the hour of battle,' the Prince of the Faithful continued, 'when you, good knight, spat in my face my spirit was stirred, my temper corrupted. Half of me fought for the sake of God, half out of passion, and partnership in God's business is not permissible. You were drawn by the hand of the Lord; you are God's handiwork, you were not of my making. Break God's image, but at God's command; shatter the Friend's glass, but with the Friend's stone.'

The infidel heard this, and a light appeared in his heart, so that he cut his Magian girdle.

86

'I was sowing the seed of wrongdoing,' he cried. 'I deemed you to be a man of a different kind. You were the balance of the One God's temper; nay more, you were the tongue of every true balance. You were my own tribe, my stock, my kin, you have been the light of the candle of my creed. I am the slave of that Lamp which seeks out every eye, from which your own lamp received its brightness. I am the slave of the billow of that Sea of Light which brings into view so fair a pearl. Offer to me the attestation of the true faith, for I perceive you to be the loftiest soul alive.'

Wellnigh fifty persons of his kindred and people turned their faces lovingly towards the true faith. He by the sword of clemency redeemed from the sword so many throats of so great a throng.

The sword of clemency is sharper than the sword of steel; nay, it wins more victories than a hundred hosts.

20

The fall of Adam, and the true friend

THE everlasting light dwells side by side with this mean world; the pure milk flows side by side with rivers of blood. Take two steps in this world without due precaution and your milk will turn to blood out of contamination.

Adam took one step in carnal pleasure; banishment from the heights of Paradise clutched his soul like a collar. The angels fled from him as from a devil; how many tears he shed, all on account of one loaf! Though the sin he had committed was slender as a hair, yet that hair had sprouted in his two eyes. Adam was the eye of the eternal light; a hair in the eye proved a mighty mountain. If Adam had taken counsel concerning that matter, he would never have uttered excuses in penitence, for when one intellect is paired with another intellect it becomes an inhibitor of evil action and evil speech; but when the carnal soul associates with another carnal soul, the partial intellect becomes futile and useless.

When out of loneliness you fall into despair, under the shadow of a true friend you become radiant as the sun. Go, swiftly seek the friend of God; when so you do, God Himself is your friend.

He who has fastened his gaze upon seclusion after all learned to do so also from the friend. One must seek seclusion from strangers, not from the friend; the fur coat is for winter, not for the spring. Let intellect be paired with another intellect and the light will be augmented, the road become plain. You who are at the chase, the friend is your eye; see that you keep it clean of chips and straws. Beware, do not make a dust with the broom of your tongue; do not make a traveller's present of chips to your eye.

Seeing that the believer is a mirror for his fellow-believer, his face is secure from every defilement. The friend is a mirror for the soul in time of sorrow; O soul, do not breathe on the face of the mirror; lest it cover up its face because of your breath, you must be swallowing down your breath every moment.

Are you less than earth? When a parcel of earth finds a friend in a spring shower, it discovers a myriad blossoms. The tree that is conjoined with a friend, even the sweet air, flowers forthwith from head to foot; but in autumn when it sees a contrary companion, it withdraws its face and head under the blanket, saying, 'An evil companion is a stirrer up of trouble; since he has arrived, my best course is to sleep.'

Sleep is true wakefulness when accompanied by wisdom; alas for the man awake who sits with the ignorant! When the crows pitch their tent in the month of January, the nightingales hide themselves and keep silence, for without the rose-garden the nightingale is hushed; the absence of the sun slays its wakefulness.

The sense of the body eats the food of darkness; the sense of the soul pastures on the Sun.

21

Omar and the man who thought he saw the new moon

OMAR was caliph; the month of the fast had come round. A crowd of people ran to the top of a hill to draw a good omen from the sight of the crescent moon.

'See, Omar!' cried one. 'The new moon!'

Omar did not see any moon in the sky.

'This moon,' he remarked to the man, 'has risen from your imagination. Otherwise, how is it that I do not see the pure crescent, seeing that I am a better scanner of the skies than you? Wet your hand,' he went on, 'and rub it on your eyebrow, then take another look at the new moon.'

The man wetted his eyebrow, and no more saw the moon.

'The moon is no more, King!' he cried. 'It has vanished.'

'Yes,' commented Omar. 'The hair of your eyebrow became a bow and shot at you an arrow of surmise.'

One hair through becoming crooked had waylaid him completely, so that he falsely claimed boastfully to have seen the moon.

If one crooked hair can veil the whole sky, how will it be if all your parts are crooked?

22

The man who stole a snake,
on the answer to prayer

A THIEF once stole a snake from a snake-catcher, and in his folly accounted it a rich prize. The snake-catcher escaped from the bite of the snake; the man who had stolen his snake was killed by it most miserably. The snake-catcher saw him, and recognized him.

'Well, well,' he remarked. 'My snake has robbed him of life. My soul was begging and beseeching God that I might find the thief and take my snake back from him. Thanks be to God that my prayer was rejected. I supposed it to be a loss, and it turned out a gain.'

Many a prayer there is that involves loss and destruction, which the Holy God in his great goodness does not hear.

23

Jesus and the dead bones, the fool's prayer answered

A FOOL who was bearing Jesus company espied lying in a deep ditch some bones.

'Fellow-traveller,' he said, 'teach me that Exalted Name whereby you make the dead to live, so that I may perform a good deed and endow these bones with life.'

'Hold your peace!' said Jesus. 'That is not your work; it is not appropriate to your breath and speech, for it requires a breath purer than rain, more penetrating in effect than the angels. Many lives were needed for the breath to be purified and to become the trustee of the heavenly treasury. Just suppose you have taken this rod firmly in your hand, whence will your hand acquire the craft of Moses?'

'If I am not the man to chant mystic spells,' said the fool, 'do you yourself recite the Name over the bones.'

'Lord,' cried Jesus, 'what are Thy mystic purposes? What is this fool's hankering after such unrewarding work? How is it that this sick soul has no care for himself? How is it that this dead hulk has no care for his life? He has dismissed his own dead soul and seeks to repair the dead bones of a stranger!'

God said, 'The backslider seeks after backsliding. The thorn that has sprouted in him is the harvest of his sowing.'

Jesus thereupon recited the Name of God over the bones in response to the young fool's importunity, and for the sake of that raw fellow the decree of God brought to life the dead form of the bones. Up sprang a black lion, struck once with its paw and utterly destroyed the fool's figure; it rent his skull so that all his brains poured out—the brains of a nut forsooth, for brains were not in that skull. If he had had a brain, his breaking to pieces would have inflicted no injury save upon his body.

'How was it that you mauled him so quickly?' said Jesus to the lion.

'Because he badgered you so much,' the lion replied.

'How was it that you did not drink the man's blood?' asked Jesus.

'Because it was not my destined allotment to drink it,' answered the lion. 'My killing this prey,' the beast explained, 'O Messiah, was simply that others might take warning therefrom. If there had still been provision for me to receive in this world, what business would I have had to be already with the departed?'

24

The Sufi and his unfaithful servant, on the peril of associating with evil companions

A CERTAIN Sufi who was wandering round the world spent one night as a guest in a hospice. He tethered his beast in the stable, then took his place at the high table with his colleagues. Later he engaged with his friends in meditation; to dwell in the presence of a true friend is like studying a volume. The book of the Sufi indeed is not made up of ink and words, it is nothing but a heart white as snow. The scholar's provision is the marks scratched by a pen; the Sufi's provision is the footmarks of the saint.

When the circle of the Sufis seeking spiritual profit closed in ecstasy and mystic joy they laid dishes of food before their guest, who then remembered his beast.

'Go to the stable,' he said to the servitor. 'See to some straw and barley for my beast.'

'Heavens above!' exclaimed the servitor. 'Why such detailed orders? This has been my job for a long, long time.'

'First moisten his barley,' the Sufi went on. 'He is an old ass, and his teeth are not strong.'

'Heavens above!' the other repeated. 'Why do you tell me this, master? I teach others to make these arrangements.'

'Mind you take off his saddle before anything else, then spread some ointment on his sore back.'

'Heavens above! Old wiseacre, I have had a hundred thousand guests just like you, and every one of them has gone away satisfied. We value our guests as highly as our kin and our own lives.'

'Give him some water, but make sure it is milk-warm.'

'Heavens above! Really, I am quite ashamed of you.'

'Put only a little straw in his barley.'

'Heavens above! Please cut your speech short.'

'Sweep his stall thoroughly of pebbles and dung, and if it is wet sprinkle dry earth on it.'

'Heavens above! Call the heavens above to stop your mouth! A few words are sufficient to a messenger who knows his job.'

'Take the comb and curry the ass's back.'

'Heavens above! Father, do have some shame.'

So saying, the servitor briskly girded up his loins.

'Off I go,' he cried. 'First I will fetch the straw and barley.'

He took his departure, and promptly forgot all about the stable, giving the Sufi to suppose he was vigilant as a hare. Off went the servitor to join a merry rabble, holding to high ridicule the Sufi's counsel.

The Sufi, wearied by the journey, stretched himself out and closed his eyes. Presently he dreamed that his ass was held fast in the clutch of a wolf which was tearing strips off his back and thighs.

'Heavens above!' he exclaimed. 'What sort of madness is this? Good gracious, where is that attentive servitor?'

He dreamed again that his ass while on the road was falling now into a well, now into a ditch; all kinds of disagreeable scenes he kept seeing, and he recited over and over *The Opening* and *The Clatterer*.

'What is the best thing to do?' he asked himself. 'My friends have all deserted me. Clean away they have gone, and shut every door in my face. That miserable servitor—now I wonder; did he not take bread and salt with us? I showed him nothing but civility and gentleness; why does he on the contrary treat me so spitefully? There must be some solid basis for every enmity; otherwise, common fellowship should dictate faithfulness. Take Adam now,' he went on. 'He was a kind and generous fellow; when had he done any injury to the Devil? What did man ever do to snake and scorpion that they should always be desiring his hurt and his death? It is in the nature of the wolf to rend and tear; the selfsame envy, after all, is visible in mankind. No, no,' he would proceed. 'To think evil is a sin; why do I entertain such dark thoughts about my brother? Yet on the other hand, dark thoughts are common prudence; how can a man who never thinks evil remain unharmed?'

While the Sufi was torn by such anxieties, his donkey was in such a plight that one could only wish for one's enemies. There the poor ass was, with only earth and stones for company, his saddle awry, his halter in ribbons, killed by the long haul, all night long without any fodder, now at the last gasp, now about to expire.

'Dear God,' the ass intoned all night, 'I forgo the barley, but is one handful of straw too much? Good elders, have some pity,' he mutely entreated. 'That impudent stripling has utterly destroyed me.'

Such pain and torment that poor ass suffered as a land-bird suffers when the torrent strikes; all through the night till morning he rolled on his side, wracked by consuming hunger.

With the morn along came the servitor, hurriedly looked for the saddle and laid it on the ass's back, then like an ass-dealer stuck him twice or thrice with the goad, treating the wretched ass like the cur that he was. The sharpness of the prick set the donkey jumping; what tongue has the ass to express his feelings? The Sufi mounted and set off; at once the ass fell on his face, and so went on all the time. Each time the people picked him up, all thinking he was ill. One would give his ear a good tweak, another looked for the ulcer under his bit, another searched for a stone in his shoe, another poked at the pus in his eye.

'Good shaikh, what is the cause of this?' they were saying. 'Did you not say yesterday, "Thank God, this ass is strong"?'

'The ass had nothing to eat but good heavens all night,' said the Sufi. 'Naturally this is the only way he can go along. Since good heavens was his food last night, last night he glorified good heavens, today he thanks heaven on his knees.'

Be on your guard, and heed not the blandishments of an evil friend; see the snare, do not stride securely upon the earth. Look at the hundred thousand devils all crying 'Good heaven!' Adam, see in the serpent the Devil himself! The attention of base men is like the servitor in the story; better to have nobody for friend than the fawning of nobodies.

25

The king and his falcon, on penitence

A FALCON once flew away from his royal master to an old woman who was sifting flour, to bake pasties for her children. Her eyes lighted upon the fine, high-born falcon and at once she tied its feet and clipped its wings, cut its talons and gave it straw to eat.

'Unworthy persons have not treated you properly,' she said. 'Your wings have grown beyond measure, your talons are too long. The hand of the unworthy is sure to make you ill; come to your mother, she will look after you.'

The king hunted all day for his bird, and finally came to the old woman's tent where he suddenly sighted the falcon all amongst the smoke and dust. The king wept bitterly over the bird and made lament.

'Though this is the just reward for what you did, seeing you did not keep true faith with me, yet how could you flee to Hell from Paradise? Did you not heed God's words, ''Not equal are the inhabitants of the Fire and the inhabitants of Paradise''?'

The falcon was all the while rubbing its wings against the king's hand as if to say, 'I have sinned.'

'King, I have sinned,' the falcon said. 'Now I am penitent. I am converted. I am a Moslem anew.'

26

The saint and the halwa, an example of true charity

A CERTAIN shaikh was perpetually in debt by reason of the openhandedness for which he was famous. He borrowed countless sums from the affluent which he expended upon the world's poor; he had also built a hospice on debt, and had devoted his wealth, his hospice and his very life to God. God, who made flour out of sand for Abraham's sake, was for ever paying his debts out of every quarter.

The Prophet said that in every bazaar two angels ever stand, offering up this prayer: 'O God, accord to the prodigal a good return, and O God, accord to the miserly ruin.' Especially does this apply to the man who has been prodigal with his life, offering his own throat as a sacrifice to the Creator; he has offered his throat to the knife like Ishmael, but the knife proves ineffectual against his throat. For this reason the martyrs live in felicity: regard not like an infidel the body only, for God has accorded them in return life everlasting, life secure from all sorrow and suffering and misery.

The debtor shaikh had done business like this for many years, taking with one hand and giving with the other just like an almoner, sowing seeds till the day of his death that on the day of his death he might be a prince most glorious. Now the shaikh's life had come to its end; he saw in his body the signs of death, while his creditors were gathered seated around him, the shaikh melting gaily away like a cendle. The creditors for their part had turned desperate and bitter, the anguish of their lungs matching the anguish of their hearts.

'Just look at these evil-minded men!' said the shaikh. 'Does God not possess four hundred gold dinars?'

Outside a boy was shouting 'Halwa!', vaunting of his sweet-meat in hope of a few pence. The shaikh nodded to the servitor, bidding him to go out and purchase the whole of the halwa, 'For,' thought he to himself, 'when my creditors eat the sweetmeat, for a little while they will not look sourly at me.' The servitor at once went out and bought with gold the whole of the halwa.

'How much is your halwa by the lump?' he asked.

'Half a dinar and a bit,' answered the boy.

'No,' said the servitor. 'Do not ask too much from Sufis. I will give you half a dinar. No more words.'

The boy deposited his tray before the shaikh. Now mark the mysterious inward thoughts of the shaikh: he motioned to the creditors as if to say, 'Look, here is a present for you. Eat and enjoy it, it is lawful food.'

The tray was soon empty. Thereupon the boy took it saying, 'Give me the dinar, wise old man!'

'The dinar?' cried the shaikh. 'Where would I get even a dirhem? I am in debt, and on my way to dissolution.'

The boy hurled the tray on the ground in mortification, sobbing his heart out at being swindled.

'Oh! oh!' he cried. 'I wish my legs had been broken. I wish I had mucked around the bath-stove and never passed by the door of this hospice! Grovelling, greedy Sufis, washing their faces like cats but hounds at heart!'

All the neighbourhood, roused by the boy's uproar, gathered round him.

'Hard-hearted shaikh!' he cried, running to his bedside. 'Know for sure, my master will kill me. I tell you he will kill me if I go back to him with nothing in my hands. Will you let him do that to me?'

The creditors too turned on the shaikh, incredulous and indignant.

'What sort of game is this?' they demanded. 'You gobbled up our money, and now you are taking your sins off to the next world. What is the idea of this culminating iniquity?'

The boy went on weeping till the time of afternoon prayers. The shaikh closed his eyes and disregarded him; indifferent to abuse and remonstration, he had withdrawn his moon-bright face under the blanket, happy with eternity,

99

happy to be dying, serenely indifferent to the reproachful words of high and low.

He is whose face the Beloved smiles sweetly—how can he be hurt by the sour looks of men? The king drinks wine on the verge of the stream till dawn; listening to the minstrels, he is unaware of the frogs' croaking.

When the time for afternoon prayer came, a servant entered with a platter on his palm, as if from Hatim the bountiful. A man of wealth and substance, having knowledge of the shaikh, had sent him a present—four hundred dinars, and in the corner of the tray another half-dinar in a screw of paper. The servant advanced, did obeisance to the shaikh, and placed the platter before the incomparable master. When the shaikh uncovered the dish the people present witnessed the miracle he had wrought. Sighs and lamentations went up at once on all sides.

'Shaikh of shaikhs and king of kings, what wonder is this? What secret, what sovereign power, lord of the lords of mystery? We did not know. Forgive us. Very reckless were the words that we uttered. We who brandish sticks blindly, inevitably we shatter lamps.'

'I absolve all your idle words,' said the shaikh. 'It was natural that you should speak so. The secret of this happening is that I asked God for guidance, and consequently He showed me the right way, saying, "Though that dinar is a little matter, its payment depends upon the outcry of the boy. Until that boy selling halwa weeps, the sea of My mercy does not surge".'

27

The Sufis and the dervish's ass, on the mortal peril of greed

A DERVISH on his wanderings arrived at a certain hospice. He led his beast along into the stable, where with his own hand he gave it a little water and some fodder—a very different dervish from the one we spoke of before. This man took due precaution against neglect and muddle-headedness; but what profits precaution against the inexorable march of destiny?

The Sufis dwelling in that hospice were poor and destitute: poverty, goes the saying, wellnigh encompasses soul-destroying disbelief.

Rich man with your full belly, beware, do not laugh at the crookedness of the suffering poor.

Because of their destitution that flock of Sufis resolved unanimously upon selling the ass.

'In time of necessity,' they said, 'carrion is lawful meat. Many a corrupt act has become, through necessity, a righteous deed.'

In that very instant they sold the poor little ass, fetched fine pastries and lit candles; the hospice rang with great merriment.

'Pastries to eat tonight, music and dancing, plenty to eat! How much longer must we go begging with our wallets? How long endure hardship and three-day fasting together? We too are God's creatures,' they cried. 'We too have souls. Luck is with us tonight: we have a guest.'

After this manner they were sowing the seed of falsehood, deeming to be the soul that which was not the soul. The traveller for his part, worn out by the long journey, took what he saw as a fine reception and the fondest welcome, for the Sufis made a great fuss of him one after another, playing well the backgammon of flattering attention.

Seeing them so affectionate towards him, the dervish exclaimed, 'If tonight I do not make merry, pray, when shall I do so?'

They ate the pastries, and began the music and dancing; the hospice was filled to the rafters with smoke and dust— smoke from the kitchen, dust from the stamping of feet, every soul in a commotion of yearning and ecstasy. Now, fluttering their hands, they would stamp their feet; anon in deep prostration they swept the floor with their brows.

When the spiritual concert had run its full course, the minstrel struck up a deep and solemn air.

'The ass is gone, the ass is gone'; so commenced his song, stirring up all present to an equal share in the ditty. To this same rhythm they continued stamping their feet till dawn, clapping their hands and shouting, 'The ass is gone, the ass is gone!'

The dervish, imitating the others, also began to chant impassionately, 'The ass is gone!'

At last the joyous excitement passed. The music ceased. It was dawn. All cried, 'Farewell!' The hospice was deserted. The dervish found himself alone.

The traveller set to work to shake the dust off his baggage; he humped the baggage out of his cell to tie it on his ass. Not wishful to journey alone, he was hurrying to rejoin his fellow-travellers. He entered the stable, but did not find his ass.

'That servitor has taken it to water,' he said. 'It drank very little water last night.'

The servitor came along then, and the dervish asked him where his ass was.

'Look at your beard, you silly old man!'

The servant's answer set off a fine quarrel.

'But I entrusted my donkey to you. I put my ass in your charge. Come, straight to the point,' cried the dervish. 'No arguing. Hand back to me what I entrusted to you. I am simply asking for what I gave you. Return immediately what I sent you. The Prophet said, "Whatever your hand has taken must in the end be given back." If that does not satisfy you, with your impudence, come, let us go together and call on the Cadi.'

'I was overpowered,' the servitor replied. 'The Sufis all rushed on me, and I was afraid for my life. Do you fling liver and lights at a pack of cats and then expect to find any trace of it? One loaf of bread among a hundred hungry mouths? One mangy cat before a hundred dogs?'

'I take it they seized the ass from you by force intending to spill my blood, poor wretch that I am. So,' the dervish concluded, 'you did not dare to come and tell me they were carrying off my donkey. If you had, I could have bought it back from whoever had it, or they might have made a round robin for my benefit. There were a hundred ways of making good the damage when they were here; now every one of them has gone off in a different direction. Whom can I set hands on and hale before the Cadi? It is you yourself who have brought this judgment upon me. Why did you not come to me and tell me, "Stranger, such a terrible wrong has been committed"?'

'By Allah, I came many times to inform you of what had occurred,' said the servitor. 'But you kept on saying "The ass is gone" with greater gusto than any of them. Consequently I returned again, thinking, "He knows all about it; he is content with this judgment; he knows the mind of God".'

'They were all chanting the words so merrily,' said the dervish, 'that I too found enjoyment in chanting them. Blind imitation of them has destroyed me entirely: two hundred curses on that blind imitation!'

If you want purity of vision, mind and hearing, tear to shreds the curtains of greed; because greed inspired that dervish to imitate the others, his mind was blinded to light and illumination. Greed for the pastries and eagerness to share in the excitement and the concert impeded his mind from knowing what was happening.

28

The scoundrelly bankrupt and
the Kurd, on the same

THERE was once a bankrupt without hearth or home who had long dwelt in prison and unremitting bondage. He gobbled up the morsels of all the prisoners, his greed making him a Mount Qaf pressing down on the hearts of the inmates. None of the others had the gall to swallow so much as one mouthful of bread, for that gluttonous gobbler pounced on it immediately. He had trodden all virtue underfoot; his snatching for bread had converted the prison into a veritable hell.

At last the other prisoners came to complain to the Cadi's agent, a discerning man.

'Convey our respects to the Cadi,' they said, 'and relate to him what we are suffering at the hands of this vile man. He has taken up permanent lodging in this prison, the idle waster, the base groveller, the squalid nuisance. He turns up impudently like a fly at every meal, uninvited and without so much as a good day to you. The rations for sixty people is simply nothing to him; if you tell him, "Enough, now" he makes out he is deaf. Not a morsel reaches any of us other prisoners, or if by a hundred tricks one of us comes upon a bite up he comes immediately, with his throat like the throat of Hell, citing in justification God's commandment, "Children of Adam, eat!" Justice! Give us justice against such a three-years' famine, and may the shadow of our master continue for ever! Either let this buffalo go out of prison, or make him a regular allotment of food out of some charitable trust.'

The gracious agent went straight to the Cadi and reported the complaints to him in every detail. The Cadi summoned the bankrupt to appear before him, then he made enquiry about him of all his officers. The complaints levelled by the gaol-flock were all proved to his satisfaction.

'Get up and leave this prison,' the Cadi ordered the bankrupt. 'Go on back to your own miserable hovel.'

'The only hearth and home I have is your beneficence,' he answered. 'Like the infidel in the saying, your prison is my Paradise. If you refuse me and drive me out of prison I shall surely die of destitution and in torment.'

'Prove to me you are penniless,' the Cadi commanded.

'Here are my witnesses,' he replied. 'The inmates of this prison.'

'They are suspect witnesses,' the Cadi answered. 'They are running away from you, shedding tears of blood. Moreover, they are demanding to be delivered from you, and the testimony they offer, being interested parties, is void.'

'We testify,' cried all the people of the tribunal, 'both as to his insolvency and his depravity.'

'Wash your hands of this bankrupt, my lord,' advised everyone the Cadi consulted.

'Parade him all round the town for everyone to see,' ordered the Cadi. 'Let everyone know him for the bankrupt rogue he is. Proclaim him from street to street; beat the drum of his bankruptcy everywhere in public view. Let no man sell to him on credit, let no man lend him a single sou. Whoever may charge him with fraud here again, I refuse to put him in prison any more. In my opinion his bankruptcy is proven, he possesses nothing, whether in cash or kind.'

The excitement started. They brought along the camel belonging to a Kurd who sold firewood. The wretched Kurd protested loudly; he also rejoiced the officer in charge with a sixpenny bribe; but all the same they commandeered his camel from breakfast-time till nightfall—his lamentation was of no avail. On the camel squatted that heavy famine of a bankrupt, while the owner of the camel ran in the camel's wake. From quarter to quarter, from street to street they lumbered till the whole city knew him by sight; in front of every public bath and every market-place all the people stood and stared at his features. Ten loud-voiced criers proclaimed— there were Turks, Kurds, Greeks and Arabs—'This man is bankrupt. He owns nothing. Let no man lend him so much as one farthing. He possesses not one grain, openly or in secret. He is a bankrupt, a fraud, a cheat, a bladder of lard.

Be on your guard! Have nothing to do with him: if he sells you an ox, be sure you knot it securely! Take note that if you bring this rapscallion to judgment, I will not commit a dead bag of bones to gaol. Sweet of speech he is, and his throat is pretty wide; his shirt may be new, but his coat is in tatters. If he puts on that garment in order to deceive, even it is borrowed to gull the common people.'

When the bankrupt dismounted from the camel at nightfall the Kurd said to him, 'My home is a long, long way off. You have squatted on my camel ever since dawn; I let you off the barley, but at least give me the price of the straw.'

'Why, what do you think we have been going round the town for?' the bankrupt countered. 'Where is your sense? Is nobody at home? The drum drumming me a bankrupt has echoed to the seventh heaven, yet apparently you have not heard the bad news! Simple greed must have filled your ears; so it is true, my lad, that greed makes people deaf—and blind!'

The seal of God rests upon the hearing and sight. There are many shapes and sounds within the Veil, and God transmits to the eye such beauty, perfection, charm as He wills, transmits to the ear what He wills of music, glad tidings, joyous shouts. The world is full of remedies, but you have none for your ill until such time as God opens a window for you.

29

The ruined house, on false happiness

DO not say to yourself, 'So-and-so found a treasure suddenly.
I wish I could too, and be done with work and workshop!'
Such things are a matter of luck, and very rare too; one must
earn one's living so long as the body is capable. In any case,
does earning a living prevent you finding a treasure? Do not
give up work; treasure follows in the wake of work.

Mind you never become a prisoner of the little word 'if'
saying, 'If I had only done this or the other.' The understanding Prophet forbade us to say 'if' and declared, 'If is a
bit of hypocrisy.'

A stranger was once hunting for a house in a hurry. A
friend took him to a dilapidated building.

'If it only had a roof,' he said, 'it would make you a fine
home, and right next door to me. Your family too would
be very snug in it if only it had another room.'

'Quite so,' answered the stranger. 'It is fine to live next
door to friends. But dear soul, one cannot live in "if"!'

The whole world is seeking for happiness; it is because of
false happiness that they are all afire. Old and young, all are
prospectors for gold, but the ordinary eye cannot tell alloy
from gold.

Learn to recognize the false dawn from the true; distinguish
the colour of the wine from the colour of the cup. Then it
may be that patience and time may produce, out of the
spectrum-viewing sight, true vision, and you will behold
colours other than these mortal hues, you will see pearls
instead of stones. Pearls, did I say? Nay more, you will
become a sea, you will become a sun travelling the sky.

30

The man who killed his mother,
on mortification of the flesh

A CERTAIN man in anger killed his mother, stabbing her with a dagger and beating her with his fist.

'Your rotten nature,' observed a bystander, 'made you forget what is due to a mother. Listen, tell me why you killed your mother. Tell me, you scoundrel, whatever had she done?'

'Something that was a shame and a disgrace to her,' he answered. 'I killed her so that the earth should cover up her shame.'

'Kill the one who sinned with her, my dear sir,' said the other.

'In that case,' said the man, 'I should be killing a man every day. I killed her, and so escaped from shedding the blood of many. Better to cut her windpipe than the throats of a multitude.'

That depraved mother is your carnal soul, pervading every part of you with its corruption. Then mortify it, because for the sake of that vile thing every moment you are attacking a being most precious. It is your carnal soul that makes this fair world distressful to you; on its account you are at war with God and men. Mortify the flesh, and you will have done with lame excuses; you will no longer have a single enemy in the wide world.

31

The king and the two slaves,
on true discrimination

A CERTAIN king bought two slaves cheap. He had conversation with one of the pair and found him both quick-
witted and sweet of response; without a moment's reflection
he would speak in such a manner as others only after five
hundred reflections. You would have said that within him
was an ocean, the whole of that ocean pearls of eloquence,
the light that glittered from every pearl a sure criterion
between truth and falsehood.

Having observed that this slave had a penetrating mind,
the king beckoned to the other slave to come forward. When
the second one stood before him the king observed that his
teeth were black and that his mouth stank. Though the king
found his conversation disagreeable, nevertheless he persisted
to search out his secret thoughts.

'With a face like this and a stinking mouth sit at a distance,'
the king ordered him. 'But not too far. You would be good
at writing letters and documents, but hardly an agreeable
friend and companion. However, let us see if we can cure
that mouth of yours. You shall be the beloved patient, I the
skilful physician. Burn a new blanket because of one flea?
Never; it would not be right for me to shut my eyes on you
entirely. For all your faults, sit down and tell me two or
three tales so that I may see properly the shape of your mind.'

Then the king sent the sharp-witted one off on a job.

'Off to the baths with you and give yourself a scrub,' he
said.

'Splendid!' he said to the other one. 'You are a clever
fellow—a hundred slaves rolled up in one, to tell the truth.
You are not in the least as your fellow-servant indicated.
Envious wretch, he wanted to turn me cold towards you. He

said you were a thief, a crook, a twister, a sodomite, a pansy, and all the rest.'

'He has always been one to speak the truth,' said the slave. 'I have never seen anyone so truthful as he is. Telling the truth is inborn in his very nature; whatever he says, I would never say it is baseless. I do not consider him crooked; he thinks good thoughts; it is myself that I hold suspect. It may well be, your majesty, that he sees faults in me I do not see in myself.'

'Well now,' the king said, 'speak about his faults, just as he spoke of yours. Then I shall know whether you are devoted to my interest, a good steward of my property and my affairs.'

'King, I will tell you his faults, though I find him a very agreeable fellow-servant,' the slave answered. 'His faults are affection, loyalty, manliness, sincerity, sagacity, good companionship. His least fault is chivalry and generosity—a chivalry that is ready even to give up life. I will tell you another of his faults: he is not conceited, in fact he is always looking for faults in himself. He has always been one to find fault with himself and look for his own faults—kindness itself to everyone, very hard on himself.'

'Do not be so eager in praising your friend,' said the king. 'Do not sing your own praises under cover of praising him. I am going to put him to the test, and the consequence will be that you will be put to shame.'

'No, by Allah,' protested the slave. 'By Allah the Most High, Lord of the Kingdom, Merciful, Compassionate! By the God who sent forth the prophets, not out of need of them but in grace and majesty! By the Lord God who created out of humble earth majestic paladins, cleansing them of contamination with terrestrial beings and causing them to outrun the celestials! By Him who took of the Fire and fashioned into pure Light, so that it outpaced all other lights, that lightning-shaft which shone over the spirits, so that Adam discovered of that Light godly knowledge! That which grew from Adam the hand of Seth gathered, and Adam, seeing it, made him his vicegerent. Noah, having enjoyment of that selfsame Substance, showered pearls in the air of the ocean of Spirit. The soul of Abraham, possessing that massive radiance, went without fear into the flaming fire. Ishmael, falling into the river of that Light, laid his head before Abraham's lustrous knife. David's spirit was heated by its rays, so that the iron became pliant in his hand-loom. Solomon being suckled upon the milk of union with that Light, the demons became obedient slaves to his command. When Jacob bowed his head before the decree Divine, scenting his son long lost, his eyes were brightened by that Light. Moon-faced Joseph, beholding that Sun, became wakeful indeed in the interpretation of dreams. When the rod imbibed that Light from the hand of Moses it made one mouthful of all Pharaoh's kingdom. When Jesus, Mary's son, found the ladder to it, he swiftly scaled the heights of the fourth heaven. When Muhammad attained that kingdom and bliss, in a moment he split in two halves the disk of the moon. Abu Bakr, becoming a sign of Divine favour, was Companion to such a King, and men called him the Trusty. Omar, distraught with love for that Beloved, became a criterion, like the heart, between truth and falsehood. When Othman became the fountain of that vision, he was light overflowing, and was called Lord of the Two Lights. Beholding its countenance, Ali scattered pearls of wisdom and became the Lion of God in the pasture of the spirit. Junaid, being reinforced by its battalions, advanced along spiritual stages past all number. Bayazid saw the way into its superabundance and heard God naming him Pole of the Gnostics. Karkhi, posted as guard over its citadel, became the vicar of Love, inspired by the breath Divine. The son of Adham joyfully galloped his steed thither and became the Sultan of Sultans of equity. Shaqiq, by cleaving that glorious Way, became a sun of judgment, sharp of vision. Multitudinous emperors, hidden to mortal eye, hold their heads high beyond this transitory world; their names remain secret because of God's jealousy, and are not pronounced by the tongue of every beggar. By the truth of that Light, by the truth of those enlightened ones who are as fishes swimming in that Sea—whether I call it the Soul of the Sea or the Sea of the Soul, it fits it not; I am seeking a new name for it—by the truth of that That from which spring this and that, all kernels being as mere husks in relation to it, I swear that the qualities of my fellow-servant and friend

III

exceed a hundredfold all that I have said. What I know of the attributes of that boon-companion would never be credited by you; what then shall I say, noble king?'

'Now speak of what concerns yourself,' the king ordered. 'How long will you speak of what concerns this one and that? What do you possess? What have you acquired? What pearls have you fetched from the bottom of the Sea? On the day of death these senses of yours will become void; have you that inner light to companion your heart? When in the tomb dust fills these eyes, do you have that which will light up the grave? In the time when your hands and feet are torn to pieces, do you have plumes and wings for your soul to soar? In the time when this animal soul remains no more, you must set in its place the eternal spirit. When God said, "Whoso brings a good deed," the condition was not the doing but the bringing of the good deed into the presence of God. You possess a substance, be it of man or be it bestial; how shall you bring these mere accidents that have passed away? These accidents of prayer and fasting—since that which endures not for two moments together is annihilated, it is impossible to transport the accidents, but they may free the substance of its ailments so that the substance becomes changed by such accident, as when an ailment is removed by continence. By effort continence, the accident, becomes the substance; through continence the acid mouth becomes as sweet as honey. By sowing fields of earth are turned into fields of corn, by treating the hair the hair is made into curly tresses. Intercourse is the accident; it passes away, and the substance, the child, is produced of us. Mating horse or camel is the accident; the object is the birth of colt, the substance. The planting of the garden is likewise the accident; the substance is the garden's produce, which was the object. Know too the practice of alchemy for the accident: if any substance results from that alchemy, then produce it! To burnish a mirror is the accident, good sir; from this accident is born the substance, translucency. Therefore do not say, "I have done this and that"; show me the yield of those accidents, do not burke the issue. Mere description of qualities is an accident. Hold your tongue; do not slay the goat's shadow as a sacrifice!'

'King,' said the slave, 'the mind must needs despair, if you say that accidents cannot be transported. Your majesty, there is nothing left for a man but to despair if the accident, once departed, shall never return. Were there no transporting and resurrection of accidents, all acts would be meaningless, all words but babble. These accidents are transported, but in another guise; the resurrection of everything transient is another kind of existence. Everything is transported after the fashion that becomes it; what befits the herd is the driver of the herd. When the Resurrection comes, every accident shall have its form, and the form of every accident shall have its turn. Consider well yourself: were you not an accident, the motion of copulation, a copulation with a purpose? Consider houses and cottages: they were as tales in the architect's mind. Such a house for instance, which appeared to us beautiful, harmoniously designed its estrade, roof and door—it was the accident, the thoughts of the architect that produced the tools and beams from the various crafts. What is the origin and source of every handicraft but fantasy, accident, a thought in the craftsman's mind? Consider without prejudice all the parts of this world: they are the product of nothing but accident. The beginning, thought, comes to an end in action; know that such was the construction of the world in eternity. The fruits exist first in the thought of the heart, and only in the end do they manifest in fact. When you have done the work and planted the tree, finally you recite what you inscribed at the beginning. Though bough, leaf and root come first, all these are despatched for the sake of the fruit. So the secret Thought which lay at the core of yonder heavens finally materialized in him for whom the world was made. Our discussion and debate is itself a transporting of accidents; the lion and the jackal are a transporting of accidents. All created beings indeed were once accidents, so that it was with this meaning that God said, "Has there come on man a while of time when he was a thing unremembered?" Whence are these accidents born? From ideas. And whence are these ideas born? From thoughts. This universe is a single thought proceeding from the Universal Mind: the Mind is like a king, the ideas are his messengers. The first world is the world of probation; the second world is the recompense for this and that conduct. When your servant, O king, commits a crime that accident proceeds to become—chains and prison. When your servant performs seemly service, does not that accident become a robe of honour in the battle? Accident and substance are like the egg and the bird; this comes from that and that from this successively.'

'Let us concede this to be the meaning,' said the emperor. 'How is it then, that these accidents of yours have not produced one substance?'

'Divine Wisdom has kept it hidden,' said the slave, 'so that this world of good and evil may be a mystery. For if the forms of thought were to become visible, infidel and believer would speak of nothing but God's praise. Moreover, were this clearly seen and not hidden, O king, if the inscription of faith and unbelief were to be readable on the forehead, how would there be idols and idolaters in this world? How would any man have the gall to mock at the holy? This world of ours would be the Resurrection indeed, and who sins and commits wrong at the Resurrection?'

'God,' said the king, 'has veiled the recompense of evil, but only from the common herd, not from His elect. If I ensnare one prince, I keep it hidden from the other princes, but not from the vizier. God has shown to me the recompense of work and countless multitudes of the forms of actions. Give me a token, for I know all; the cloud does not veil the moon from me.'

'What then is the purpose of my speaking,' asked the slave, 'since you know the nature of that which has been?'

'God's wisdom in manifesting the world,' said the king, 'is that that which was known should come forth visibly. Until He made visible that which He knew, He did not impose upon the world the pains and throes of delivery. Not for a single moment can you sit inactive, without some evil or goodness issuing from you. These cravings for action were committed to you so that your secret heart might become visible. How should the reel, the body, ever be at rest seeing that the end of the thread, the mind, is always tugging it? The token of that tugging is your restlessness; to be inactive is for you like the agony of death. This world and the world beyond are forever giving birth; every cause is a mother, whereof the effect is the child. As soon as the effect is born it becomes a cause, so that other marvellous effects may be born of it. These causes mount back generation on generation, but it requires a very illumined eye to see the links.'

The king had reached this point in his discussion with the slave—either he observed in him a token, or observed it not; if that diligently searching king saw such, it were no marvel, but we have not authority to mention the fact—when the other slave arrived back from the hot bath. The exalted king called him to him.

'I wish you health and lasting happiness!' he cried. 'Now you look very fine and handsome and elegant. What a pity! If only there were not those things in you which So-and-so declares, everyone seeing your face would feel happy; the very sight of you would be worth the kingdom of the world.'

'Give me a hint, king,' said the second slave, 'of what that bane of the faith has said about me.'

'In the first place,' answered the king, 'he described you as double-faced. He said that to outward appearances you were a remedy, but secretly a sickness.'

Hearing from the king how malicious his colleague had been, the sea of his anger surged mightily. He foamed and turned scarlet, so that the billows of his abuse passed all bounds.

'From the very first moment of our association,' he cried, 'he has been a great eater of dung, like a dog in a famine.'

He went on abusing him at regular intervals like a bell tolling, till the king put his hand on his lips.

'That is quite enough. From what you have said I now know you and him apart. You have a foul spirit; your colleague has only a foul mouth. So sit at a distance,' the king ordered, 'you foul of soul! He shall give the orders and you will obey them.'

Know then that a fine and handsome exterior when paired with a bad character is not worth a sou; whereas if the exterior is unpleasing and contemptible but the disposition is good, you may gladly die at such a person's feet. Know that the external form passes away, whereas the world of inner truth abides eternally.

115

32

The falcon and the owls,
a parable of the soul

A FALCON lost its way and fell into the wilderness; in the wilderness it fell among owls. Forthwith a great tumult broke out amongst the owls.

'The falcon has come to grab our home,' they hooted, like scavenger dogs of the street falling upon a stranger's coat.

'How does it beseem me to consort with owls?' cried the falcon. 'I would gladly surrender a hundred such wildernesses to the owls. I do not wish to dwell here. I am going. I will return to the king of kings. Do not kill yourselves with alarm, owls. I am not settling here, I am going to my homeland. In your eyes this ruin is a thriving abode; my place of delight is the forearm of the king.'

'The falcon is scheming,' cried one of the owls, 'scheming to root you out of hearth and home. He will grab our houses by his cunning. He will tear us out of our nests by his subterfuge. This adorer of cunning makes out to be satisfied, but by Allah! he is worse than all the greedy ones put together. In his greed he devours clay as though it were date-syrup: friends, trust not the sheep's tail to the bear! He brags of the king and the king's hand only to lead us simpletons astray. How should a common bird be the king's congener? If you have even a little sense, do not listen to him! Is he the king's congener, or even the vizier's congener? Is garlic a suitable ingredient of walnut-cake? As for his cunning and tricky saying, "The king is searching for me with his courtiers," there is a monstrous mad notion for you! What a stupid brag, what a snare for catching fools! It would be sheer idiocy for anyone to believe that; how should a scarecrow of a bird hobnob with royalty? If the least of us owls should peck at his brains, where is he likely to get help from the king?'

'If a single feather of mine is broken,' said the falcon, 'the king of kings will root out the entire owlery. An owl? Why, if a falcon should vex my heart and mistreat me, in every lowland and highland the king will heap up hundreds of thousands of stacks of falcons' heads! His loving kindnesses keep watch over me; wherever I go, the king follows after me. My image is dwelling in the Sultan's heart; without my image, the Sultan's heart would be sick. When the king sends me winging upon his way, I fly up to the heart's zenith like a sunbeam to the sun; I fly like the moon and the sun, I rend the curtains of the skies. The light of all intellects is drawn from my thought, the rending of heaven is of my nature. I am a falcon, yet the phoenix himself is lost in amazement at me; what is an owl, that it should know my secret? For my sake the king was mindful of the prison and set at liberty a hundred thousand in bonds. For one moment he made me to consort with the owls, and through my words converted the owls into falcons; happy is the owl that by good fortune comprehended my mystery in my soaring. Cling to me, that you may be joyous birds, and that, though you are owls, you may be royal falcons! He who is beloved of such a king, why should he be a stranger wherever he may alight? He for whose pain the king himself is the cure, though he wail like reed, he is not without riches. I am the possessor of the kingdom, I am no groveller; the king is beating for me the falcon-drum in the beyond, drumming the message "Return!" God is my witness, despite the adversary. True, I am not the king of king's congener; far be it from him; but he has revealed himself, and I have light from him. Congenerity is not in respect of shape and essence. Water becomes the congener of earth in the plant; air becomes the congener of fire in consistency; wine in the end becomes the congener of the body's constitution. Since my genus is not the genus of my king, my ego has passed away for the sake of his ego. Since my ego has passed away, he remains alone; I roll like dust before his horse's feet. The soul has become dust, and the only signs of it are the mark of his feet on its dust; become dust before his feet for the sake of this sign, that you may be the crown on the head of the tall and proud. Let not my shape deceive you: before I am transported, enjoy the transport of my sweets!

33

The man who tore down a wall, an analogy
of the believer at prayer

A HIGH wall stood by the brink of a stream, and on the top of that wall was perched a thirsty man in great anguish, for the wall prevented him from reaching the water and he was in sore straits for the water, like a fish on dry land.

All of a sudden he threw a brick into the water, and the plash of the water came to his ears like words spoken, like the words of a sweet and delightful friend. The sound of the water intoxicated him like wine, and from the pure pleasure of hearing the water plash that sorely tried man began to tear bricks off the wall and to fling them into the stream.

'Hey, you!' the water seemed to cry. 'What advantage do you gain from pelting me with bricks?'

'Twofold advantage, O water,' the thirsty man replied. 'I will by no means withhold my hand from this work. The first advantage is just to hear the sound of the water, which to the thirsty makes music as sweet as the rebeck; the sound of it is like the trumpet of Israfil putting life anew into one that was dead. Or it is like the sound of thunder in the days of spring, hearing which the garden adorns itself in such fine array; or it is like the days of almsgiving to the poor man, or the message of release to the prisoner. It is like the breath of the All-merciful coming out of Yemen, unbreathed by any mouth, unto Muhammad, or like the breath of the glorious Apostle himself coming to the sinner in intercession, or like the breath of Joseph, the lovely, the charming, beating upon the soul of Jacob wasted with grief. The second advantage is that with every brick I tear off I draw nearer to the "running water" of God, for as the bricks get fewer, each time one is torn off the high wall becomes lower. The lower the wall, the nearer I get to the water; break it away entirely—that is the prescription for attaining the water.'

Tearing down the firm-clinging bricks—that is prostration, a cause of drawing nigh to God. God says, 'And bow thyself and draw nigh.' So long as the wall of arrogance lifts its neck high, it is an obstacle to bowing the head; I cannot prostrate myself upon the Water of Life until I find deliverance out of this earthly body.

34

The man who let his thornbush grow, on the evil of procrastination

A CERTAIN hard-hearted but soft-spoken man planted a thornbush in the middle of the road. Those who passed along that way reproached him, begging him to root it up; but he did not do so. All the while the thornbush was growing bigger; the people's feet were bleeding from its pricks. The people's clothes were torn by the thorns; the feet of the poor were sorely wounded.

'Root it up!' the governor ordered him peremptorily.

'Very well, one day I will root it up,' the man replied.

So for a long while he promised 'tomorrow' and 'tomorrow'; meanwhile his thornbush became strong and thrived.

'Crooked promiser,' said the governor to him one day, 'get on with my job. Do not bum your way back.'

'There is plenty of time still, uncle,' the man answered.

'Hurry up at once,' cried the governor. 'No postponing settlement.'

You with your talk of 'tomorrow', know that with every day that passes the evil tree grows more vigorous, while the digger-up is getting old and doddery.

Blessed is he who profits of the days of his youth to settle his debts, in the days when he has the power, when he has health and strength of heart and vigour; when that season of youth, like a fresh green garden, brings forth produce and fruit unstintingly; when the springs of vigour and lust are flowing, so that the soil of the body is made verdant; when he is like a well-built house whose roof is very high, its walls symmetrical, unbuttressed and unclamped; ere the days of old age arrive and bind your neck with 'a rope of palm-fibre'. For then the soil grows sour, crumbling and weak—

121

never did plants thrive in brackish soil—the water of strength and lust is cut off; a man has no profit either of himself or of others. The eyebrows are drawn down like a crupper-strap, the eyes are grown moist and dim, the face is wrinkled like a lizard's back; speech, taste and teeth have all gone out of use. The day has grown late, the bag of bones is lame, the way is long; the shop is ruined, the business is all in disorder. Then the roots of bad habits are firmly established, and the power to pull them up is sadly diminished.

35

The baptism of God

THE 'baptism of God' is the dyeing-vat of Divinity wherein all parti-coloured things become of one hue. When the mystic falls into that vat, and you say to him, 'Arise!' in rapture he answers, 'I am the vat: do not reproach me.'

His saying 'I am the vat' is the same as saying 'I am the Truth': though he is of iron, he has the colour of fire. The hue of the iron is obliterated in the hue of the fire; though a silentiary, the iron vaunts of its fieriness. When it turns crimson as gold in the mine, then tonguelessly it boasts, 'I am the Fire'; exalted by the hue and the nature of the fire, 'I am the Fire,' it cries, 'I am the Fire.'

'I am the Fire,' it repeats. 'If you have any doubt or hesitation make experiment, thrust your hand into me. I am the Fire; if what I say seems doubtful to you, lay your face on my face just for one moment.'

When Man receives light from God he is worshipped by the angels, being the chosen of God; likewise he is worshipped by him whose spirit, like the angel, has been liberated from insolence and doubt.

36

Dhu 'l-Nun in the madhouse, a story of true friendship

IT so fell out that a new fervour and fury possessed Dhu 'l-Nun the Egyptian; his fervour waxed so great that the salt of it was felt by every lacerated heart even to above the sky. The people could not endure his fury; the fire of it was ravaging their beards! When that fire fell upon the beards of the uninitiated they bound him hand and foot and thrust him into prison.

Friends went to the prison to enquire after the story of what had happened to Dhu 'l-Nun, and expressed certain views concerning it.

'Perhaps he does this on purpose, or there is some hidden wisdom in it,' they said. 'He is a model, a shining example of our religion. Far be it from his understanding deep as the sea that madness should inspire him to folly. God forbid, considering the perfection of his station, that the cloud of sickness should obscure his moon. He has gone into the house to flee from the mischief of the common people; he has become mad because of the infamy of the sane—gone of conscious purpose and become mad because of the disgrace of the dull, body-pampering intellect. "Bind me fast," he cried, "and with the tail of the cow smite me on head and back, and dispute not thereon, that from the blow of that member I may discover life even as the man who was slain came to life through Moses' cow, my trusty ones!" '

'Who are you? Take care!' cried Dhu 'l-Nun when those persons approached him.

'We are friends of yours,' they answered respectfully. 'We have come here in all reverence to enquire after you. How are you, ocean of manifold intelligence? What calumny against your intelligence is this reported madness? How should the smoke of the bath-stove reach to obscure the sun? How should the fabulous simurgh be discomfited by the raven? Hold not back the truth from us; explain this report. We are your lovers; do not treat us so. It is not right to drive lovers away, or to delude them by masquerade and imposture. Lay bare your secret in our midst, O king; hide not your countenance in the cloud, O moon! We are very loving, and true, and heart-sore; we have bound our hearts upon you in this world and the next.'

Thereupon he began to curse and swear abominably, mumbling and mouthing like a gibbering madman. He sprang up and let fly with stones and staves, and the whole company fled for fear of being struck. Then he laughed aloud, and wagged his head.

'Look at the wind in the beards of these self-styled friends!' he cried. 'Just look at my friends! Where is the sign of their friendship? To true friends, suffering is as dear as life itself.'

How should a friend run away from the pain inflicted by his friend? Pain is the kernel; friendship is only as the husk to it. The sign of true friendship is joy in affliction, calamity and suffering. A friend is as gold, and affliction is like the fire: pure gold rejoices in the heart of the fire.

37

Luqman's answer, on the nature of slavery

LUQMAN, the devoted slave, was nimble night and day in the service of his master, who preferred him above all others in his employment, deeming him better even than his own sons. For though Luqman was born a slave, in truth he was a master-man, being free of sensual desire.

(A certain king said to a dervish in the course of conversation, 'Ask me to bestow some gift upon you.' The dervish answered, 'O king, are you not ashamed to say such a thing to me? Come and see! I have two slaves, contemptible creatures, yet those two are governors and princes over you.' The king said, 'What two? Surely you are mistaken.' The dervish replied, 'One is anger, the other is lust.')

Luqman's master was like a master outwardly, but in reality his master was Luqman's slave. He was well aware of this state of affairs, for he had seen the sure token in Luqman; that royal traveller knew the secret perfectly, but kept on driving the ass for the sake of the good he had in mind. He would have set Luqman free from the first, but desired only what should be pleasing to him; for Luqman's wish was to remain a slave, so that none should know the secret of that lion-hearted youth.

Whenever food was brought to the master, he would at once send a messenger to Luqman for him to reach out his hand to it first, purposing that he, the master, should eat his slave's leavings. He would eat the remnants with utmost rapture, and would throw away any food that Luqman had not touched, or if he ate of it, it was without heart and appetite—surely a sign of unlimited conjunction.

One day he was brought a melon as a present.

'Go, call my son Luqman,' the master cried.

He cut the melon and gave Luqman a slice; Luqman

swallowed it down as if it were sugar and honey. Seeing with what pleasure he ate it, the master gave him a second slice, and so continued till he had reached the seventeenth piece and only one slice remained.

'I will eat this one myself,' said the master. 'Then I can see what a sweet melon it is. The pleasure he shows in eating is enough to whet anyone's appetite.'

The master ate the slice, and its sourness was like a flaming fire blistering his tongue and burning his throat. For a while he was quite out of himself because of the bitterness, but presently he addressed Luqman.

'O my soul and my whole world,' he said, 'how did you convert so much poison into an antidote? How did you reckon this oppression a kindness? What fortitude is this? Why this forbearance? Or perhaps you consider your life your deadliest foe? Why did you not artfully advance some plea, saying, "I have a good excuse; let me be for a little"?'

'I have eaten so much from your munificent hand,' answered Luqman, 'that I am doubled up with shame. Master of wisdom, I was ashamed not to eat one bitter thing from your hand. The melon had had the pleasure of being touched by your sugar-bestowing hand; how then could any bitterness be left in it?'

Love makes bitter things sweet; love converts base copper to gold. By love dregs become clear; by love pains become healing. By love the dead is brought to life; by love a king is made a slave.

38

The unbelieving philosopher, on repentance

A CANTOR was reciting the verse from the Koran: 'What think you? If in the morning your water should have vanished into the earth, then who would bring you running water?' 'If I stop the water from the spring, if I conceal the water in the depths and make the springs dry and a land of drought, who shall bring water into the spring again apart from Me, the incomparable, the Lord of grace and glory?'

A certain philosopher, a contemptible logician, happened to be passing by the school at that time. When he heard the verse he remained in great disapproval, 'We will bring the water back with the shovel; with a few strokes of the spade and the sharp axe we will bring the water up from the depths!'

That night when he fell asleep he dreamed that a lion-hearted man struck him on the face and blinded both his eyes.

'Miserable wretch,' the man cried, 'if you speak the truth, bring up some light with your axe from these two springs of vision!'

Rising with the dawn, he found himself blind in both eyes; from both his eyes the light abundant had vanished.

If he had made lament and asked God's forgiveness, the vanished light would have appeared again by God's grace. But we have not of ourselves the power even to ask God's forgiveness; the sweet savour of repentance not every drunkard tastes. The monstrousness of his deeds and the hideousness of his blasphemy had barred the way of repentance against his heart.

Repentance requires an inward glow and the water of tears; lightning and clouds are the sole condition of repentance. For the fruit to mature fire and water are needed; clouds and lightning are necessary for this display. Without there be lightning in the heart, clouds in the eyes, how shall the fire of God's menace and wrath be allayed? How shall grow the herbage of the joy of Divine union? How shall the fountains of limpid water gush forth? How shall the rose-bed tell its secrets to the meadow? How shall the violet make covenant with the jasmine? How shall the plane-tree open its hands in prayer? Or how shall any tree toss its head in the air? How shall the blossoms in the days of spring ever shake from their sleeves their bounty of petals? How shall the anemone's cheeks flame like blood? How shall the rose bring forth gold out of its purse?

These beauties are all the token of a witness; they are the footprints of a man devoted to God.

39

The coming of Wisdom

WISDOM, said the Prophet, is like a stray camel: like a broker, it guides to the presence of kings.

You see in a dream a person of handsome mien who gives you a promise and a sign that your desire will come true. This is the sign (he says): tomorrow So-and-so will encounter you. Here is another sign: he will be on horseback. Another sign: he will clasp you to his breast. Another sign: he will smile before you. Another sign: he will fold his hands before you. Another sign: when tomorrow comes, you will not tell this dream to a soul, much as you would like to do so.

It was in connexion with the last sign that God said to the father of John the Baptist, 'Thou shalt not utter any word for three days. For three nights keep silence as to all that passes with thee, good and ill: this shall be the sign that John will be born to thee. For three whole days breathe not a single word, for this silence is the sign that thy desire shall be fulfilled. Beware that thou speak not of this sign, but keep this speech hidden within thy heart.'

Such are the signs that the phantom will sweetly tell the dreamer. Yet what signs are these? There are a hundred others.

This is the sign that you will gain from God the kingdom and glory you are seeking—that you weep all through the long nights, and burn at your supplication in the hour of dawn; that without the object of your quest, your day is darkened, your neck shrunk to the thinness of a spindle; that you have given in alms all that you possess, your goods given in charity like the alms of those who gamble all; that you have sacrificed all your goods, your sleep, your health, your life, so that you have become thin as a hair; so often you have sat in the fire like aloes-wood, so often you have sallied to meet the sword, like a helmet. A hundred thousand such acts of helplessness past all reckoning are the habit of the lovers of God.

When you have dreamed this dream by night, the day dawns, and in the hope of its realization your day is a day of triumph. You turn your eyes to left and right: where is that sign, where are those tokens? You are a-tremble like a leaf: what if the day passes, and the sign is not fulfilled? You run through the streets and the bazaars and from house to house like one who has lost a calf.

'Good news, master? Why are you running hither and thither? Who is it belonging to you that you have lost here?'

'Good news,' you answer. 'But no one must know my good news except me. If I tell it, my sign will elude me, and when the sign is missed, the hour of death is come.'

You peer into the face of every man on horseback. 'Do not stare at me like a madman,' he tells you. You answer him, 'I have lost a friend; I am searching for him. Good luck be yours for ever, rider! Have mercy on lovers; pray forgive them!'

When you have searched earnestly and attentively, earnest seeking cannot fail: so said the Prophet. Suddenly there comes a blessed horseman, then he clasps you tightly to his breast.

40

Moses and the shepherd, on the
indulgence of God

ONE day Moses encountered a shepherd on the way, and
heard him saying: 'O God who electest whomsoever Thou
wilt, where art Thou, that I may become Thy servant and
stitch Thy shoes and comb Thy head, wash Thy clothes and
kill Thy lice and bring Thee milk, O most worshipful! Kiss
Thy little hand and rub Thy little foot, sweep Thy little
room when bedtime comes, O Thou to whom may all my
goats be a sacrifice, O Thou in remembrance of whom I cry
ah and ah!'

The shepherd was talking nonsense after this fashion.
Moses said to him, 'Whom are you addressing?'

'Him who created us,' the shepherd answered. 'Him by
whom this earth and heaven were brought to sight.'

'Ah, you have become indeed a backslider!' Moses said.
'You have ceased to be a Muslim, you have become an
unbeliever. What is this babble, this unbelief and gibberish?
Stuff some cotton-wool into your mouth! The whole world
stinks with the stench of your blasphemy; your blasphemy
has turned to rags the silk robe of religion. Shoes and socks—
such things are suitable for you, but how are they fit for the
Sun Divine? If you do not stop up your throat from saying
such words, a fire will come and burn up all the people.'

'Moses, you have stitched up my mouth and burned my
soul with repentance,' the shepherd said. Heaving a sigh, he
rent his garment and hastily set forth into the desert.

Thereupon a revelation came to Moses from God: 'You
have put asunder My servant from Me. Did you come in
order to unite, or to tear apart? Take no step to separate,
so far as you are able; the most hateful of all things to Me
is divorce. I have ordained for every man a manner of conduct;

I have given to every man his own way of expression. In regard to him it is praiseworthy, in regard to you it is blameworthy; in regard to him it is honey, in regard to you it is poison. I am independent of all purity and uncleanness; I am far above all sloth and alacrity. I made not any commandment that I might make profit, but that I might be bountiful to My servants. To Indians the usage of Hind is praiseworthy, to Sindians the usage of Sind is praiseworthy; I am not sanctified by their magnificats, it is they who are sanctified so that they scatter pearls. I do not regard the tongue and the speech; I regard the inward soul and the spirit's state. I look into the heart, whether it be humble even though the words spoken be far from humble. For the heart is the substance; speech is only the accident; therefore the accident is adventitious, the substance is the true object. How many more of these phrases, these concepts, these metaphors? What I want is burning, burning; attune yourself to burning! Kindle a fire of love in your soul, burn utterly all thought and expression!'

Thereafter God hid in Moses' secret heart such mysteries as cannot be spoken.

When Moses heard this rebuke from God he ran into the desert in quest of the shepherd, driving on over the footprints of that man distraught, scattering dust from the skirt of the desert.

Finally Moses overtook and sighted the shepherd. He gave him the good tidings.

'Licence has come from God. Search not after any particular rules or order of worship; whatever your distressed heart desires, declare it. What I called your blasphemy is in fact true religion, and your religion is the light of the spirit. You are saved, and through you a whole world is in salvation. "God does whatsoever He wills": these words have set you free; go, loose your tongue in whatever manner you please.'

'Moses, I have gone beyond that,' said the shepherd. 'Now I am weltering in my heart's blood. I have transcended the "Lote-tree of the Boundary"; I have gone a hundred thousand years' journey beyond. You applied the whip; my horse shied, bounded, and passed beyond the sky. May the Divinity be intimate with my humanity: blessings be upon your hand

and upon your arm! My state now is beyond all telling; this that I am telling is not my true state.'

Beware and beware! Whether you praise God or give thanks to Him, know that your lauds are as the foolish words of that shepherd. Though your praise is superior in comparison with his, yet in relation to God it too is halting and maimed. God's accepting your commemoration is of His abounding mercy.

41

The prince and the man who swallowed a snake, on true compassion

A WISE man was riding along on his horse when he saw a snake entering the mouth of a sleeping man. He sought with haste to drive the snake away but found no opportunity of doing so. Being well endowed with intelligence, however, he struck the sleeper several hearty blows with his mace, which sent him running headlong to shelter under a tree. Now many rotten apples had fallen from that tree; the prince stuffed so many of the apples in the man's mouth that they were falling out again.

'Eat of these, my poor fellow in your agony!' he urged.

'Why, prince, did you set on me so?' cried the man. 'What have I ever done to you? If you have a fundamental quarrel with my being alive, please strike me once with your sword and shed my blood forthwith. It was a luckless hour when your eyes lighted on me; thrice happy is the man who never saw your face. Guiltless, without sin whether great or small—why, even atheists would not deem such injustice justified. Even as I speak the blood gushes from my mouth. God, I beseech Thee, visit him with due retribution!'

Every moment he hurled a fresh curse at the prince. The prince kept on beating him and saying, 'Run! Run in the wilderness!'

Down came the mace; the horseman was swift as the wind. The man went on running, every now and then falling on his face. Stuffed full he was and sleepy, utterly worn out; his feet and face were covered with a thousand wounds. The prince drove him to and fro all the while till nightfall, till his bile overcame him and he vomited. Up came everything he had eaten, bad and good alike, and along with the rest of his vomit out shot the snake.

When he saw he had got rid of the snake, he fell on his knees before his benefactor; the moment he sighted the horror of that huge, black, ugly snake all his sorrows departed from him.

'You are a very Gabriel of compassion, or God Himself,' he cried. 'You are the very Lord of Bounty. Blessed was the hour when your eyes lighted on me. I was a dead man: you have given me new life. Thrice happy is the man who sees your face, or who suddenly alights in your street. O lauded of the pure Spirit, how many idle and foolish words I spoke to you! Lord, emperor, prince, it was not I that spoke, but my folly: take me not to task for it. If I had had the slightest notion of the facts, how could I ever have spoken such foolish words? I would have uttered much praises of you, man of qualities so fair, if you had only given me one hint of the true state of affairs. But you kept silence, seeming much disturbed; without a word you went on pummelling my head till my head became dizzy and my wits flew away—more especially seeing that my head has but little brain. Pardon me, man handsome alike in looks and deeds! Overlook the things I spoke out of insanity.'

'If I had spoken even a hint of it,' the prince replied, 'your gall would immediately have turned to water. If I had told you the qualities of the snake, sheer terror would have brought you to give up the ghost. You would not have had the power to eat; neither would you have had the means or the will to vomit. I listened to your maledictions and quietly went on with the work, repeating under my breath, "Lord grant an easy issue!" I had not licence to tell you the cause, neither was it within my power to abandon you. All the while in my heart's anguish I repeated the Prophet's prayer, "Guide my people; verily they know not".'

The man, delivered out of woe, kept falling on his knees.

'My happiness, my good fortune, my treasure! Noble sir, you will find your reward from God; weak as I am, I have not the power to thank you. God Himself will say thanks to you, my leader; I have not the lips, the chin or the voice so to do.'

Such is the 'enmity' of the wise: their poison rejoices the soul. But the friendship of the fool is misery and perdition.

42

The blind beggar, on the power of compassion

THERE was once a blind man who all the time cried, 'Have pity! I am doubly blind, people of this passing time. Attend therefore, and show me double compassion, for I have two blindnesses, and exist between them.'

'We see your one blindness well enough,' remarked someone. 'What may the other blindness be? Pray explain.'

'I have an ugly voice and an unpleasing tone,' he replied. 'An ugly voice, and blindness—there you have the double. My ugly cry makes people annoyed, so that their affection is diminished by my cry. Wherever my ugly voice betakes itself, it becomes the source of anger, annoyance and hatred. Have double compassion upon my double blindness, make room in your hearts for one who is denied all room.'

The ugliness of his voice was lessened by this lament, so that the people with one heart took compassion upon him. By telling his secret, his voice was made beautiful by the sweet accents of the voice of his heart. But the man whose heart's voice is also evil, that triple blindness dooms him to everlasting exile.

Yet it may be that the bountiful ones who give without cause will lay a hand upon his hideous head. Since the beggar's voice became sweet and plaintive, the hearts of the stony-hearted became soft as wax.

43

The man and the bear, a parable
of misplaced trust

A DRAGON was pulling a bear into its jaws; a lion-hearted man, observing the bear's plight, went to its rescue. Resourcefulness and courage supporting one another, by this strength the man slew the dragon.

The bear, having escaped from the dragon and having been treated so nobly by that courageous man, like the dog of the Men of the Cave attended at his heels constantly. The good man, having borne the brunt, laid down his head in weariness, while the bear, utterly devoted, stood guard over him.

'What ever is happening, brother?' asked a passer-by. 'What is the relationship between this bear and you?'

The man told his tale and the incident of the dragon.

'Fool!' cried the passer-by. 'Do not set your heart on a bear. The friendship of a fool is worse than his enmity. Drive the bear away by whatever means you can.'

'He said this out of envy, by Allah,' said the man to himself. Then he added aloud, 'Why do you regard its bearishness? Just look how affectionate it is!'

'The affection of fools beguiles the heart,' said the other. 'My "envy" is better than its affection. Come along with me now. Drive the bear away. Do not choose the bear as your companion; dismiss not your fellow-man.'

'Go away, you envious fellow, mind your own business!'

'This was my business, but you were fated not to trust me. I am not less than a bear, noble sir. Abandon it, and let me be your comrade. My heart trembles with anxiety for you. Do not go with such a bear into the jungle. Never to no purpose has my heart trembled: this is the light of God, no false pretence or bragging. I am a believer, and so see by the light of God. Beware, beware! Flee from this fire-temple!'

All this the other said, but it did not penetrate the man's ear: dark thoughts are a mighty barrier to a man. The other seized him by the hand, but he drew his hand away.

'I am off,' he cried. 'You are no friend and guide. Off with you. Do not trouble yourself on my account. Not so much wisdom-mongering, you interfering busybody!'

'I am not your enemy,' the other assured him. 'It would be a kindness for you to come after me.'

'Leave me alone! I am sleepy,' the man shouted. 'Now go!'

'Now do submit to your friend,' the other pleaded. 'Then you will sleep in the shelter of a wise man, in the protection of a true friend who has a heart.'

The other's earnestness put quite a fanciful idea in his mind. He became furious and quickly turned his face away.

'Maybe he is after my blood, a murderer!' he thought. 'Or he has some other ulterior motive—he is a beggar and a vagabond. Or perhaps he has made a bet with his friends that he will scare me against my companion.'

Not a single good thought entered his mind, so wrong-headed was he. All his good opinions were reserved for the bear; you might well think he was the bear's soul-mate! Cur that he was, he suspected a wise man and deemed a bear affectionate and just.

The good Muslim thereupon quitted the fool and hurried home, muttering under his breath, 'Now only God can help him!' He said, 'The only result of my earnest advice and disputation is that more fanciful notions still are born in his mind. The road of advice and good counsel is therefore closed. I can only obey God's command, "Turn thou away from them".'

The man fell fast asleep. The bear kept driving the flies away, but despite its efforts they were soon back again. When this had happened several times that bear got furious with the flies and went off to the mountain, where he picked up a huge great stone. Returning with the stone, he saw that the flies were once more cosily settled on the face of the sleeper. He seized that millstone and flung it at the flies to scare them away. The stone made mincemeat of the face of the sleeper, proclaiming this proverb to the world at large:

'A fool's love is for sure the love of a bear: when he hates he loves, and when he loves he hates.'

44

Galen and the madman

GALEN said to his companions, 'One of you administer to me such-and-such a drug.'

'Learned professor,' one of them replied, 'the drug you name is prescribed in cases of lunacy. Far be this from your powerful mind! Do not speak of it again!'

'A lunatic,' Galen explained, 'turned his face to me, looked into my face agreeably for a while, winked at me, and pulled me by the sleeve. If I had not been to some extent his congener, how would that ugly creature have turned his face towards me? How would he have approached me, had he not seen in me one of his own kind? How would he have flung himself upon one of another kind?'

When two people rub shoulders together, without a doubt there is something common between them. Does a bird fly save with its own kind?

The company of the uncongenial is the grave and the tomb.

45

A story of Moses, on consorting with the saints

GOD spake unto Moses reproachfully, saying, 'O thou who hast seen the moon rise out of thy bosom, whom I have illumined with the Light Divine, I who am God fell sick; why camest thou not to visit Me?'

'O Thou who art all-glorious and all-perfect,' Moses cried, 'what mystery is this? Explain it to me, O Lord.'

God spake again unto Moses, saying, 'When I was sick, why didst thou not kindly enquire after Me?'

Moses answered, 'Lord, there is no imperfection in Thee: I have lost my reason: uncover these words to me.'

God said, 'Verily a chosen and well-loved servant of Mine fell ill. I am he: mark it well: his exemption is My exemption, his sickness is My sickness.'

Whosoever would sit with God, let him sit in the company of the saints. If you are severed from the company of the saints you are in destruction, being a part without the whole.

46

The Sufi, the Fakih and the Sharif, and
how their solidarity was destroyed

A GARDENER one day saw in his orchard three men,
seemingly come to rob it—a Fakih, a Sharif and a Sufi, each
one an insolent and perfidious rogue.

'I have a hundred proofs of their rascality,' he murmured.
'But they are united, and in union is strength. I cannot
single-handed overcome the three of them; so first I must
divide them one from the other. I will isolate each one of
them from the others, then, when he is alone, I can pluck
out his beard.'

By a trick he got the Sufi away from the other two, intending to set his colleagues against him.

'Go into the house,' he said to him. 'Fetch a rug for your
comrades.'

The Sufi went. Then the gardener said to his two companions, 'You are a Fakih, and you are an eminent Sharif. It
is in accordance with your legal judgment'—this to the Fakih—
'that we eat bread; it is by the wings of your wisdom that
we fly. And the other of you, he is our prince and sovereign;
he is a Sayyid of the family of the Prophet. Who, pray, is
this gluttonous, ignoble Sufi, that he should sit with kings
like yourselves? When he returns, you two shake him off and
have the freedom of my orchard and villa for a week. What
is an orchard after all? My life is at your disposal. You have
always been as dear to me as my right eye.'

His devilish whispers duped them completely. They drove
the Sufi off, and when he was gone the gardener, their common foe, followed after him with a thick stick.

'You dog!' he cried. 'Is it part of your Sufism that you
hop into my orchard in my despite? Did Junaid and Bayazid

show you this way? From which Shaikh and Pir did you get this instruction?'

Having got the Sufi by himself he gave him such a beating that he cracked his head and half killed him.

'My troubles are over!' exclaimed the Sufi. 'But now you, my comrades, look out for yourselves! You considered me an outsider; but beware! I am no more of an outsider than this cuckold. What I have tasted you will also have to taste; such a draught as this is the recompense of every rotter.'

The gardener, having finished with the Sufi, hit upon the same kind of pretext as before.

'O Sharif,' he called, 'pray go to the house. I have baked some delicious wafers for breakfast. Shout to Qaimaz from the door to fetch the wafers—and the goose as well.'

Having got him out of the way, the gardener said to the Fakih, 'Far-sighted sir, it is clear and sure that you are a Fakih. But he—a Sharif? What a ridiculous claim he makes! Who knows who made his mother? Many a fool has attached himself to Ali and the Prophet!'

The Fakih fell under his spell. Off at once the rascal went in the wake of the Sharif.

'You ass!' he cried. 'Who invited you into this orchard? Is thievery all that you have inherited from the Prophet? The lion-cub takes after the lion, but tell me, in what respect do you take after the Prophet?'

That mightily resourceful man then dealt with the Sharif as a Khariji rebel would deal with the family of Muhammad. The Sharif was devastated by the scoundrel's blows.

'One dip is enough for me!' he cried to the Fakih. 'You paddle there alone if you like, all on your own. Give him your belly to beat like a drum! If I am no Sharif and unworthy, unfit to be your comrade, at least I am no worse for you than such a scoundrel.'

The gardener, having finished with the Sharif, addressed himself to the Fakih.

'What sort of a Fakih do you call yourself? You put to shame every fool alive. Is this your legal judgment, you amputated thief, that you may enter my garden without so much as a by your leave? Did you read such a licence in the *Intermediate*? Is this problem so resolved in the *Comprehensive*?'

'You are perfectly right,' said the Fakih. 'Beat me: I am in your power. This is the due recompense for one who breaks with his friends.'

Whoever the Devil cuts off from the men of nobility, finding him isolated, he proceeds to devour him. To quit the congregation of the saints for so much as a moment—that is the chance for Satan's cunning. Know this well.

47

Bayazid and the man who claimed to be the Kaaba, on the spiritual preceptor

THAT shaikh of the Muslim community Bayazid was speeding towards Mecca to perform the greater and lesser pilgrimages. In every city through which he passed his first care was to search out the mighty men of God.

'Who is there in this city,' he would ask as he went around, 'who leans upon the pillars of spiritual insight?'

One day he espied an old man bent as the crescent moon; he saw in him the dignity and the address of true men of God. Though blind of eye, his heart was radiant as the sun— he was as an elephant dreaming of his native India. Bayazid sat down before him and enquired after his estate; he found him to be a dervish and also a family man.

'Where are you making for, Bayazid?' the old man asked. 'Where are you dragging your baggage, traveller in a strange country?'

'At dawn I start for the Kaaba,' Bayazid replied.

'Well, and what provisions for the road do you have with you?'

'Two hundred silver dirhems. See, they are tied tightly in the corner of my cloak.'

'Go round about me seven times,' said the old man. 'Count that as better than the circuit of the pilgrimage. And set those dirhems before me, generous man. Know that you have made the greater pilgrimage and your desire has been attained. The lesser pilgrimage also you have made, and gained the life everlasting; you have sped over Mount Safa, and are now safe and pure. I swear by the truth of the God whom your soul has seen that God has preferred me above His Holy House. Though the Kaaba is His house of pious service, my body likewise is the house of His inmost secret. Since He

made the Kaaba He has never gone into it; into this house
that is I none but the Living God has gone. In seeing me you
have seen God; you have circled about the Kaaba of truthfulness. To serve me is to obey and give praise to God; let
you not think that God is apart from me. Open well your
eyes and look upon me, that you may see the Light of God
in human flesh.'

Bayazid heeded those subtle sayings, and held them in his
ear like a golden ring.

Make haste every moment to seek the shadow of the kings,
that in that shadow you may outshine the sun.

48

The man who married a harlot,
on living dangerously

THE prince of Tirmidh said one night to his court-jester Dalqak, 'You have taken to wife a harlot in your haste. You should have mentioned the matter to me, then we might have married you to a respectable woman.'

'I have already married nine respectable and virtuous women,' said the jester. 'They all became harlots, and I wasted away with grief. Now I have taken this harlot not knowing her previously so as to see how this one would turn out in the end. I have tried good sense often enough already; henceforward I intend to cultivate madness!'

Let safety go, and live dangerously; forsake good repute, be notorious and a scandal. I have made trial of provident good sense; hereafter I am going to make myself mad.

49

The saint who feigned to be mad
in order to be free to serve God

A CERTAIN man announced, 'I wish to find someone of good intelligence, to consult him about a difficult problem that confronts me.'

'There is no one of good intelligence in our city,' a bystander told him, 'with the exception of that man over there who appears to be mad. Look, see him mounted on a cane, riding it like a hobby-horse all among the children. He is a man of sound judgment, bright as a spark of fire, exalted as heaven, lofty as the stars. His royal splendour is the soul of the Cherubim; he conceals his glory in this madness.'

'You riding on the cane there,' the enquirer shouted. 'Drive your horse this way just a moment.'

'Say what you have to say as quickly as you can,' said the saint, riding towards him. 'This horse of mine is pretty wild and hot-tempered. Hurry up or he will kick you. State clearly what you want to know.'

Seeing that he had no chance of telling him the secret of his heart, the man evaded the issue and bantered with the saint.

'I would like to marry a woman from this street,' he said. 'Who would be suitable for a man like me?'

'There are three kinds of women in the world,' the saint answered. 'Two are a pain in the neck, and one is the soul's treasure. One when you marry her is yours entirely; one is half yours and half another's; the third, let me tell you, is not yours at all. So now you know. Stand away with you. I am just off: away, or my horse will let fly a kick at you so that you will fall down and never get up again.'

The saint rode off among the children. The man called to him once more.

'Come here and explain what you said. You said women are of three sorts. Pick them out one by one.'

'Choose a virgin,' said the saint, riding towards him, 'and she will be yours entirely, and you will escape from all sorrow. The one who is half yours is a childless widow. The one who is not yours at all is a married woman with a child; having had her child by her first husband, her affection and all her thoughts will be directed to it. Now stand away, or my horse may aim a kick, the hoof of my wild horse may land on you.'

With a whoop of joy the saint rode back and called the children to him again. The man called to him yet a third time.

'Here! There is just one question left, your majesty.'

'Say what you have to say as quickly as you can,' the saint said, riding back. 'That child over there has stolen my heart away.'

'Your majesty,' said the man, 'with such intelligence and learning, what is the meaning of this feigning act? It is marvellous! You transcend in exposition the Universal Mind itself. You are a shining sun; how is it you are veiled in madness?'

'These scoundrels,' the saint explained, 'have it in mind to make me Cadi of their city. I objected, but they said, "No, there is no one as learned and accomplished as you. With you here, it would be wicked and unlawful for someone inferior to you to hold office as Cadi. The sacred law gives no licence for us to make anyone less than you our ruler and leader." Under this compulsion I turned crazy and mad, but inwardly I am the same as I always was. My intelligence is the treasure, I am the ruin concealing it; if I were to reveal the treasure I would be mad indeed. My knowledge is of substance, not of accident; this precious gift is not to be wasted on mere worldly interest. My purchaser is God: He is drawing me aloft. "God has bought from the believers their selves".'

When the student of heavenly science uses his knowledge not for the sake of enlightenment but as a bait for popular applause, he is no whit better than the student of base worldly wisdom; for he is seeking knowledge to impress all and sundry, not in order that he may find release out of this world.

50

The policeman and the drunkard,
on spiritual intoxication

A POLICEMAN on his beat at midnight saw a man lying asleep at the base of a wall.

'Hi, you are drunk,' he called to him. 'Tell me, what have you been drinking?'

'The contents of the bottle,' the man replied.

'Well, what may the contents of the bottle be?' the policeman asked.

'Some of what I have drunk,' said the man.

'Ah, but that is out of sight,' said the policeman. 'Come on, what have you been drinking?'

'What is out of sight in the bottle.'

The questions and answers went round and round. The policeman remained like a donkey stuck in the mud.

'Say ah now,' the policeman ordered.

'Hu, hu,' the drunkard stammered.

'I said, Say ah, and you are saying hu,' the policeman said.

'That is because I am happy, while you are bent double with grief,' the drunkard replied. 'People say ah when they are in pain or sorrow or when they have been wronged. Winebibbers shout hu hu out of happiness.'

'I know nothing about that,' said the policeman. 'Get up, get up. Enough chiselling high notions. Stop this wrangling!'

'Go away!' the man retorted. 'What business have you with me?'

'You are drunk,' the policeman said. 'Up with you now. Come along to the lock-up.'

'Officer, leave me alone,' said the drunkard. 'Go away.

How can you carry off a pledge from a naked man? If I had had the power to walk I would have gone to my own home, and then how would all this have happened? If I had been in my right reason and human contingency I would still be sitting on the bench, holding forth like the shaikhs.'

51

A vision of the Last Day

AT the resurrection the believers will say to the Angel, 'Is
it not true that Hell was the common road along which
believer and infidel alike must pass? Yet on this road we
have seen neither smoke nor fire. Behold, here is Paradise,
and the Palace of Security; where then was that vile place
of passage?'

Then the Angel will say, 'That green garden you saw in
a certain place as you passed, that was Hell and the dread
place of chastisement. For you it became a garden, full of
herbs and trees. Since you strove hard against this carnal
soul of hellish temper, this fiery miscreant craving after
rebellion, and it became full of purity, and you put out the
flame of it for the sake of God; since the flaming fire of lust
has become the verdure of piety and the light of guidance;
since the fire of wrath in you has turned to forbearance, and
the darkness of ignorance in you has turned to knowledge;
since the fire of cupidity in you has turned to unselfishness,
and thorn-like envy has turned to roses; inasmuch as long
ago you put out all these fires in you for the sake of God,
making the fiery carnal soul like a garden in which you cast
the seed of fidelity, and the nightingales of the remembrance
and glorification of God sang sweetly in that garden beside
the river; inasmuch as you answered the call of God's
Messenger and brought water into the flaming hell of your
carnal soul; on account of this our Hell in respect to you
became green herbage and a rose-bower, and riches abounding.'

52

The two thieves, a parable of the greater and the lesser good

A CERTAIN man saw a thief in his house, and at once gave chase to him. He chased him over two or three squares until exhaustion brought him out in a sweat. His impetus had carried him close to the thief and he was just about to leap on him and seize him when a second thief shouted out to him.

'Come and see the havoc he has wreaked. Come back quickly, man of action, and see the terrible state of affairs here.'

'Perhaps there is a thief over there,' the man said to himself. 'If I do not return quickly, it will all be up with me; he will lay hands on my wife and child. What would I gain then from trussing up this thief here? The good Muslim is calling me out of pure kindness; if I do not return quickly evil will come upon me.'

Relying on the sympathy of that supposed well-wisher, the householder gave up chasing the thief and took another way.

'What is happening, my good friend?' he called. 'Whose fell hands have caused your lamentation and outcry?'

'See, here are the thief's footprints!' the other shouted. 'That pimp of a thief has gone this way. Look at the cuckold's footprints! After him! Follow this clue!'

'Fool, what are you telling me?' the householder cried. 'Why, I had as good as caught him, but when you shouted I let the thief go. I took you for a sensible man, you ass! What nonsense and gibberish is this, fellow? I had found the real thing; what use is the clue?'

'But I am giving you the clue to the real thing,' the other replied. 'This is the clue. I know all about the real thing.'

'You are either a knave or a fool,' said the householder.

'No, you are a thief. You know all about the affair. I was just on the point of haling my foe along when you let him escape, with your shout of clues.'

Devotion in the vulgar is sin in the elect; union in the vulgar is exclusion in the elect.

53

The Devil's debate with Moawiya,
on the same

IT is related that the caliph Moawiya was once asleep in a corner of his palace; the door of the palace was fastened from the inside, for he was worn out with people always calling on him. All of a sudden a man awakened him; when he opened his eyes the man had vanished.

'No one had admission to the palace,' Moawiya said to himself. 'Who had the boldness and impudence to do this?'

He went round the palace, searching for a sign of the vanished man. Behind the door he saw an unfortunate wretch who was hiding his face between the door and the curtain.

'Hey, who are you? What is your name?' he demanded.

'In plain language,' said the other, 'my name is Iblis the Damned.'

'Why were you so anxious to wake me up?' asked Moawiya. 'Tell me the truth. Do not speak at cross purposes.'

'The time for prayer is almost over,' said Iblis. 'You must run quickly to the mosque. "Hasten your devotions before the time is past": so spake the Prophet, threading a pearl of truth.'

'No, no,' Moawiya replied. 'It would never be your object to be my guide to any good. If a thief enters my dwelling in secret and then tells me, "I am keeping watch," how can I believe that thief? How should a thief know the reward of good works?'

'At first I was an angel,' Iblis replied. 'I trod the path of obedience to God with all my soul. I was the confidant of all who follow the Way; I was the confederate of those who dwell near the Throne. How should a man forget his first vocation? How should one's first love depart out of the heart? If on your travels you see Rum or Khotan, how should the love of your homeland vanish from your heart? I too have been one of those intoxicated by this wine; I too have loved His court. From the cutting of my navel I was predestined to love Him; the seed of love for Him was sown in my heart. I have seen good days from Fortune; I have drunk the water of Mercy in the springtime. Was it not the hand of His grace that sowed me? Was it not He that lifted me out of non-existence? Many are the loving kindnesses that He has shown me; many a time I have walked in the garden of His good pleasure. He would lay the hand of compassion on my head, He would open the fountains of grace within me. Who found milk for me in the season of my infancy? Who rocked my cradle? It was He. From whom did I drink milk other than His milk? Who nurtured me but His providence? The habit that has entered into men's being with their mother's milk, how can it ever be expelled from them? If the Sea of Bounty has rebuked me once, yet how have the doors of Bounty been shut? The root substance of His coin is giving and grace and goodness; wrath is only a dust-speck of alloy on that coin. Out of pure goodness He made the world; His sun cherished the motes dancing in its beams. If separation from Him is pregnant of His wrath, yet it is that one may know the worth of union with Him, that separation from Him may chastise the soul and that the soul may know the worth of the days of union. The Prophet said that God declared, "My purpose in creating was to do good. I created that My creatures might have profit of Me, that they might smear their hands with my honey; not in order that I might Myself profit, wresting a coat from a creature naked." During these few days since He drove me from His presence, my eyes have continued fixed upon His beauteous face: "Such wrath from such a beauteous face? Amazing!" Every one being preoccupied with the secondary cause, I do not regard the cause, which is temporal, for the temporal only occasions something temporal. I regard the grace preceding, and tear in twain all that is temporal. Granting it was out of envy that I would not bow down to Adam, yet that envy sprang from love, not from rebellion. It is sure that all envy arises from love, lest any other should consort with the beloved. Smouldering jealousy is the condition of love, just as "God

158

bless you'' follows upon sneezing. Since no other play was possible on His board, and He said, ''Play!'' what more can I do? I played the only move that was open to me—I cast myself into calamity. Even in calamity I taste His delights: mated by Him am I, mated by Him am I, mated by Him! Good sir, how can anyone within these six dimensions deliver himself out of the square of six? How shall the part of the six escape from the whole of the six, especially when the Matchless match-player sets all awry? Whoever is trapped in the six is already in Hell; only the Creator of the six can set him free. Whether he be doomed to faith or to unbelief, he is the hand-spun of the Most High and His creature.'

'All this is true,' replied the caliph. 'But your share in these things is lacking. You have waylaid countless multitudes like me; you have drilled a hole and entered the treasury. You are fire: shall I not be burnt by you? Inevitably. Who is there whose raiment is not torn to shreds by your hand? Fire, since it is your nature to set things burning, inevitably you must be setting something burning. That is God's curse on you, that He has made you a burner, that He has made you the master of all thieves. You have conversed face to face with God; how should I be a match for your cunning, O enemy? Your store of knowledge is like the fowler's whistle: it is the whistle of the birds, but it catches birds. That whistle has waylaid countless multitudes of birds; the bird is deluded, thinking a friend has come; hearing the sound of the whistle while on the wing, it swoops down out of the air and is trapped here, a captive. Through your craft the people of Noah know lamentation, their hearts consumed with fire, their breasts torn to shreds. You gave over the people of Ad to the wind of destruction, adding to their sorrows anguish and torment. Through you the people of Lot were rained with stones, through you they were drowned in the black waters. Through you Nimrod's brain crumbled away, you who have aroused countless turmoils. Through you the mind of Pharaoh, that shrewd philosopher, became blind so that he found no understanding. Through you Bu Lahab also became unworthy; through you Bu'l-Hakam too became a Bu Jahl. On this chessboard, to testify to your skill, you have checkmated hundreds of thousands of masters; you have

159

burned many hearts by your inextricable gambits, and your own heart has thereby been blackened. You are the sea of cunning, and all creatures are but a drop; you are as a mountain, and we simpletons but a mote. Who shall escape from your cunning, adversary? We are drowned in the Flood, save him whom God defends. Many a lucky star by you has been consumed; many a marshalled army by you has been scattered.'

'Undo this knot,' said Iblis. 'I am the touchstone for the spurious and the true coin. God has made me the test of lion and cur, God has made me the test of true coin and spurious. When have I ever blackened the face of the counter- feit coin? I am only a money-changer; I assess its worth. To the righteous I act as a guide: I tear off the withered branches. To what end do I proffer this fodder? To reveal what kind of animal it is. When a wolf bears young to a deer and there is doubt whether the young is wolfish or deerlike, scatter before it grass and bones and watch in which direction it makes haste. If it runs to the bones, then it is canine; if it desires the grass, surely its stock is deer. Wrath and gentleness were wedded together, and of the twain was born a world of good and evil. Offer grass and bones, offer the food of the flesh and the food of the soul: if he seeks the food of the flesh, he is of no worth; if he desires the food of the spirit, he is a leader. If he serves the body, he is an ass; if he enters the sea of the soul, he will discover pearls. Although the twain, good and evil, are different yet both the twain are engaged in one work. The prophets of God proffer devotions, the enemies of God proffer lusts. How should I make a good man bad? I am not God; I am only the tempter, I am not their creator. How should I make the beautiful ugly? I am not the Lord; I am a mirror for the beautiful and ugly—God made me a tale-bearer and a truth-teller to tell where the ugly one is and where the beautiful. I am a witness: is prison the right place for a witness? I do not deserve prison, as God is my witness. Whenever I see a fruitful sapling I nurture it tenderly as a nurse; wherever I see a sour and dry tree I chop it down, so that the musk may be separated from the dung. The dry tree says to the gardener, ''Young fellow, why do you chop off my head without any fault of mine?" The gardener answers, "Silence, ugly-tempered tree! Is not your dryness a sufficient crime in you?" The dry tree says, "I am straight, I am not crooked; why are you hacking at my heels without any sin of mine?" The gardener answers, "If you had been born under a lucky star, would you had only been crooked, if only you were sappy. You would have drawn up the Water of Life; you would have been steeped in the Water of Life. Your seed was bad, and your root was bad; you were not joined to a good tree. If a sour branch is joined to a sweet one, that sweetness pene-trates into its nature".'

'Highwayman!' the caliph cried. 'Stop your arguing. You cannot get under my guard, so do not look for a way. You are a highwayman, I am a stranger and a merchant; do you think I will buy any old rags you bring? Do not sniff round my goods, infidel that you are; you are not one to buy goods from anyone. A highwayman never buys from anyone, and if he makes out he is a buyer, it is only trickery and fraud. What has this envious one, I wonder, in his gourd? Help us, O God, against this adversary. If he breathes one more enchantment over me this highwayman will surely rob me of my coat! All this talk of his is like smoke: take my hand, O God! Succour me, or my coat will be blackened. I cannot match Iblis in argument: he is the tempter of noble and ignoble alike. Adam himself, the great one whom God taught the names, all of them, was helpless before the lightning rush of this cur; he flung him out of Paradise upon the face of the earth, so that he fell from Pisces like a fish into his net lamenting, "We have wronged ourselves." Truly there is no limit to Satan's guile and deceit. There is wickedness in every word he utters; spells innumerable are stored up in his mind. In an instant he strangles the manhood in a man; he kindles the fire of lust in woman and man. Iblis, you destroyer of men, ever seeking to tempt them to destruction, to what end did you waken me? Declare the truth!'

'The man who harbours evil thoughts,' Iblis replied, 'will not listen to the truth, though a hundred signs point to it. The mind that is used to meditating fanciful notions—produce your proof, and its fancies only increase. Let sound words enter such a mind and at once they are sick: the sword of the champion of the faith becomes a tool for a thief. So the best answer for him is a tranquil silence: it is madness to bandy words with a fool. Why do you complain to God of me, you simpleton? Complain of the wickedness of your own base carnal soul. You eat sweets and you come out in boils; fever seizes you, your temperament is disturbed. You curse Iblis, though he is innocent; why do you not see that the delusion comes from yourself? It is no fault of Iblis, it is your own fault, misguided creature, that you are running after the sheep's tail like a fox. When you see a sheep's tail in the grass, it is a snare; why do you not know this? You do not know it because your longing for the tail has driven you far from knowledge, blinded your eye and reason. The Prophet said, "Your love of things renders you blind and deaf"; no more quarrelling, it was your black soul that sinned. Do not put the guilt on me, do not see things crooked; I loathe evil and cupidity and hatred. I did an evil thing, and I am still repenting, waiting for my night to turn to day. I have become an object of suspicion among men; every man and woman attribute their evil actions to me. The impotent wolf, though hungry, is suspected of living in luxury; when he can scarcely crawl along because of feebleness people say it is indigestion, through eating too rich food.'

  'Nothing but the truth will save you now,' said the caliph. 'Justice is calling you to speak the truth. Tell the truth, so that you may escape from my clutches; cunning will never lay the dust of my warfare.'

  'How do you know the difference between lies and the truth,' asked Iblis, 'you with your idle fancies, full of strange ideas about me?'

  'The Prophet,' said the caliph, 'has given an indication; he has laid down the touchstone distinguishing counterfeit from good coin. "Lies," he declared, "is a disquiet in men's hearts; truthfulness is a joyous tranquillity." The heart is not tranquillized by lying words; water mixed with oil kindles no flame. Only in truthful talk does the heart become tran-quil; truths are the bait that ensnares the heart. Sick surely and of evil mouth is the heart that knows not the taste of truth from lies; when the heart is healed of sickness and disorder, then it knows very well the flavour of falsehood

162

and truth. When Adam's greed for the forbidden fruit waxed great, it robbed his heart of health; then he gave ear to your lies and blandishments, he became deluded and drank the fatal poison. Men are intoxicated with desire and passion, therefore they are ready to fall for your fraud. Whosoever has rid his nature of idle passion has made his eye familiar with the inner secret. Once upon a time they appointed a cadi, and he wept. His deputy said, "Cadi, why are you weeping? This is not the time for you to weep and lament, it is the time for you to rejoice and to receive congratulations." "Ah," the cadi replied, "how shall an unenlightened, ignorant man pronounce judgment between two who have knowledge? These two adversaries are apprised of their own dispute; what does the wretched cadi know of the two tangles? He is ignorant and quite unaware of the true state of affairs with them, how then can he proceed in the matter of their lives and belongings?" "True, the contestants know their case, yet they are unqualified to judge it," answered the deputy. "You are ignorant of the matter, yet you are the light of the community since you are not impeded by prejudice. That impartiality is in truth a light to the eyes; whereas the two litigants, though knowing the facts, are blinded by self-interest and prejudice has buried their knowledge. Lack of prejudice makes ignorance wise, but prejudice makes knowledge crooked and unjust. So long as you accept no bribe, you see straight; act out of appetite, and you are blind and a slave." I have cleansed my nature of all idle passion; I have not devoured appetizing morsels. My heart, the taster, has become bright as a mirror and distinguishes truly between truth and lies. Why did you awaken me? Cheat, you are the enemy of wakefulness; you are like poppy-seed, putting everyone to sleep, you are like wine robbing men of reason and knowledge. Ha, I have nailed you down: come on now, speak the truth. I know the truth; do not look for evasions. I only expect of anyone what is in his nature and constitution; I do not look for sugariness in vinegar, I do not take a sodomite for a soldier. I do not do as the heathens do, seeking of an idol to be God or even a sign from God. I do not look for the odour of musk in dung; I do not look for dry bricks in river-water. I do not expect ol Satan, whose nature is quite other, that he should awaken me with good intentions.'

Though Iblis spoke many words of trickery and treachery the caliph did not heed him; he continued tenaciously to wrestle with him. At last Iblis declared most reluctantly, 'Fellow, you may as well know that the reason I awakened you was that you might join the congregation in prayer, following the Prophet of lofty estate. If the time of prayer had passed with you still sleeping, the world would have become dark for you and without radiance. Out of vexation and grief tears would have poured from your eyes like water from a water-bag; for every man tastes joy in an act of devotion, and therefore cannot endure to miss it even for a moment. That vexation and grief would have been the equivalent of a hundred prayers; what is ritual prayer compared with the glow of such supplication? Noble prince, I must expose my trickery before you. If at that time you had missed the prayer, many sighs and laments you would have uttered out of your aching heart, and that regret and lamenting and supplication would have surpassed two hundred recollections and ritual prayers. I awakened you fearing that such a sigh would burn the veil; so that such a sigh should not be yours, and that you should have no way to uttering it. I am envious, and out of envy I acted thus; I am the enemy, and my work is trickery and hatred.'

'Now you have spoken the honest truth at last,' said the caliph. 'Trickery comes natural to you; you are well qualified to cheat. You are a spider, and flies are your prey; dog, I am not a fly, so spare yourself the trouble. I am a white falcon, I am the prey of the King; how should a spider weave his web about me? Off with you! Go on catching flies as much as you can; invite the flies to taste your whey; or if you call them to honey, that too will be lies, and sour milk for sure. You awakened me, but that awakening was slumber; you showed me a ship, but that ship was a whirlpool. You were calling me to good, but your purpose in calling me was to drive me away from the better good.'

54

The Mosque of Opposition, an example of perversity

YOU should listen to another parable of perversity as it is related in the Koran. The Hypocrites played just such a crooked game of odds and evens with the Prophet himself.

'Let us build a mosque for the glory of the Muhammadan faith.'

So they spoke; but their intention was apostasy. Just such a crooked game they were playing; they built a mosque other than the Prophet's mosque. Well they fashioned its floor and roof and dome, but they desired to disunite the community.

Then they came to the Prophet in supplication, kneeling before him like a camel.

'Messenger of God,' they cried, 'as a pure kindness will you give yourself the trouble of walking to yon mosque, that it may be made blessed by your advent—may your days be green till the resurrection! It is a mosque for days of mud and days of cloud, a mosque for days of distress in time of poverty, that a stranger may find there charity and shelter and that this house of service may be much frequented. So the rites of the faith shall abound and be multiplied; a bitter task is sweetened when shared with friends. Honour that place with your presence a little while; sanctify us by your blessing, praise us before men. Cherish the mosque and those who founded it. You are the moon, we are the night; suffer with us a moment so that by your beauty our night may become as day—that beauty which is a sun lighting up the night.'

Ah, would that their words had come from the heart, so that their desire might have been accomplished!

They recited their spells over God's Messenger; they galloped the steed of guile and cunning. That loving and compassionate Messenger vouchsafed them no answer save a smile of content. He expressed his thanks to that company, gladdening the envoys with his acceptance. Their trickery indeed was apparent to him in every detail, like a hair floating in milk; but the courteous Prophet feigned not to see the hair and with utmost politeness pronounced the milk excellent.

When the Prophet had resolved to go forth to their mosque the Divine jealousy cried to him, 'Hearken not to the tempter! These evil men have contrived much craft and cunning; all that they have advanced is the opposite of the truth. Their whole intention was to blacken the face of the faith; when have Christians and Jews sought the welfare of the true religion? They have built a mosque upon the bridge of Hell; they have played the backgammon of treachery with God. Their aim is to disunite the Messenger's companions; how should any graceless busybody comprehend the grace of God? They have built their mosque to import a Jew from Syria who by his preaching has made the Jews delirious.'

'Yes, I consent,' said the Prophet to those Hypocrites. 'But at the moment we are about to march, to set out on a campaign. The moment I return from this expedition I will immediately proceed to your mosque.'

So he put them off, and hastened to the battle, playing with those tricksters a hand of trickery. When he returned from the campaign, they came back again demanding the fulfilment of his former promise.

God said to the Prophet, 'Prophet, declare their treachery and, if it be war, then let war be!'

'Posturing people,' the Prophet cried, 'be silent! Not a breath, lest I speak your secret thoughts.'

When he had given a few indications exposing their inner thoughts they were much discomfited. The deputation turned back from him exclaiming, 'God forbid! God forbid!' Every Hypocrite came fraudulently, Koran under his arm, to the Prophet to swear oaths—'Oaths as a covering'—for the taking of oaths is a custom of the crooked.

'Am I to take your oath as true, or God's oath?' said the Prophet.

Again the people swore another oath, the Koran in their hands and on their lips the seal of fasting.

'By the truth of this holy, true word,' they swore, 'the

mosque we have builded is for the sake of God. Therein is no strategem to deceive; therein is only the remembrance of God, sincerity and calling on the Lord.'

The Prophet answered, 'God's voice is coming into my ears like an echo. God has set a seal upon your ears so that they race not to hear His voice. Behold, the voice of God is coming to me distinctly, filtered for me clear, like pure wine dredged of the dregs.'

So it was as when Moses heard the voice of God proceeding from the bush, saying, 'O fortunate one!' He heard proceeding from the bush, 'I am God'; and with the words appeared also lights.

Inasmuch as the Hypocrites were deserted by the light of inspiration, they began once more to recite oaths anew.

'You have lied!' cried the Prophet bluntly, giving them the lie direct.

Now one of the companions of the Prophet disapproved of that revocation.

'This Prophet is putting to shame so many venerable greybeards,' he remarked. 'What of generosity? What of the cloaking of sins? What of shame? The prophets cloak a great multitude of faults.'

Then again in haste he asked forgiveness of God lest he be put to shame by his opposing the Prophet. So the villainy of succouring the Hypocrites made that true believer wicked and disloyal as they.

'O Thou who knowest the secret heart,' he implored again, 'leave me not persistent in unbelief. My heart is not in my control as is my sight, otherwise this very moment I would burn my heart in wrath.'

As he was so meditating, slumber seized him. It seemed to him in a dream that their mosque was full of dung, a place corrupted, its stones stinking with ordure, black smoke belching up from the stones. The smoke penetrated his throat and made it smart; terrified by the acrid smoke, he sprang out of sleep, fell forthwith upon his face and wept.

'These things, O God, are the sign of their unbelief,' he cried. 'It is better to be wrathful against them, O God, than forbearing as I was, with a forbearance that separated me from the light of the faith.'

167

55

The stray camel, a parable of Divine wisdom

YOU have lost a camel and searched for it energetically; when you find it, how should you not know that it is yours?

What is that that is astray? A lost she-camel, fled from your hand into a hidden place. The caravaneers have begun to load, but your camel has vanished from the train. Lips parched, you are running this way and that; the caravan is gone far away, and the night is nigh. Your baggage is dumped on the ground, upon the way of fear, while you are running around hunting for your camel.

'Muslims,' you cry, 'who has seen a camel that slipped away this morning out of a stable? Whoever gives me a clue where my camel is gone, I will reward him with so many dirhems.'

You go about asking everyone for a clue; every low scoundrel is making fun of you.

'We saw a camel going in this direction—a russet camel, making for yonder pasturage.'

'It was crop-eared,' says one.

'Its saddle-cloth was embroidered,' says another.

'It only had one eye,' says a third.

'It had lost its hair through the mange,' says a fourth.

Every vile rascal offers at random a hundred clues for the sake of the reward.

Even so, regarding the knowledge of God, every man describes differently the great Unseen. The philosopher propounds his own explanation; the theologian invalidates his statement. A third authority gibes at both of them; a fourth wears himself to a shadow with his fraudulent erudition. Each of them gives these indications of the Way so that it may be thought they belong to that village.

168

Know this for the truth, that all of these are not in the right, neither is the herd wholly astray. Nothing false appears without the True. Unless there be truth, how should there be falsehood? Falsehood acquires its lustre from the truth.

56

The old man and the doctor,
on inveterate wickedness

AN old man said to a doctor, 'My brain is giving me hell.'

The doctor said, 'That infirmity of brain comes from old age.'

The old man said, 'I see dark spots in front of my eyes.'

The doctor said, 'That comes of old age, ancient one.'

The old man said, 'I get terrible backaches.'

The doctor said, 'That comes of old age, skinny old fellow.'

The old man said, 'Everything I eat repeats on me.'

The doctor said, 'A weak stomach comes from old age.'

The old man said, 'It hurts me when I breathe.'

The doctor said, 'Yes, it is probably asthma. Old age brings on two hundred ailments.'

The old man said, 'You fool, your needle has stuck; that is all you have learned of medicine. Addle-pate, your intellect has not taught you that God has appointed a cure for every pain. Idiot of a donkey, it is sheer incapacity that keeps you stuck in the mud; you have not the feet to pick yourself up.'

The doctor said, 'Sexagenarian, your bad temper and rage are also of old age. Since all the functions and parts of your body are attenuated, your self-control and patience have also become feeble.'

An old man cannot endure two words together, he cries out at once; he cannot keep down a single gulp, he vomits it straightaway—except of course the Elder intoxicated with God, whose inward being God endows with 'a goodly life'. Outwardly he is old, but inwardly he is youthful.

57

Goha and the orphan, on the unregenerate soul

A CHILD was weeping bitterly and beating his head beside his father's coffin.

'Father, where are they taking you,' he was saying, 'to press you under a parcel of earth? They are taking you to a narrow and stinking house without carpets and without a couch, no lamp at night and no bread in the day, no smell of food nor even a sign of it there, no well-built door, no way to the roof, not a solitary neighbour to give you shelter. Your body, which people delighted to kiss—how now should it enter a house dark and gloomy, a house unsheltering and a narrow place, where neither face nor complexion remains.'

After such a fashion he was enumerating the properties of the house, while from his eyes he wrung tears of blood.

Goha said to his father, 'Honourable sir, by Allah! they are taking this corpse to our house.'

'Do not be a fool!' said Goha's father.

'But listen to details, Papa,' Goha replied. 'Everyone of the details that the boy mentioned belongs to our house, without hesitation or doubt. No bed, no lamp, no food, no well-built door, no court, no roof.'

Even so sinful men have a hundred marks upon them, but how should they see them? The house, the heart, that remains unillumined by the rays of the sun of the Divine majesty—that house is narrow and dark as a Jewish soul, destitute of the savour of the loving King; neither has the glow of the Sun shone into that heart, neither has it an open door and a spacious court. Better for you is the tomb than such a heart: come, rise up now out of the tomb of your heart!

171

58

The Bedouin and the philosopher, on the uselessness of mundane science

A BEDOUIN had once loaded his camel with two huge sacks, one full of grain, and was seated on the top of the sacks, when he was questioned by a word-spinning philosopher who asked him about his homeland, and in the course of his inquisition let fall some penetrating remarks.

'And what are those two sacks stuffed with?' he finally asked. 'Come, tell me the truth.'

'There is wheat in one of my sacks,' answered the Bedouin. 'In the other is sand, no food for men.'

'Why did you load this sand?' asked the philosopher.

'So that the other sack should not remain alone,' said the Bedouin.

'For goodness' sense,' said the philosopher, 'pour half the wheat from that bag into the other. Then both sacks will be lighter, and the camel too.'

'Admirable, worthy and noble philosopher!' cried the Bedouin. 'Such subtle thought and excellent judgment! And you naked like this, and on foot, and so fatigued!'

The Bedouin took compassion on the philosopher and, good man that he was, decided to sit him on his camel.

'Eloquent philosopher,' he addressed him again, 'give me some slight account of your circumstances too. With such a brain and such competence you must be a vizier or a king. Come, tell me the truth.'

'Neither, I am just an ordinary commoner. Look at my condition. Look at my clothes.'

'How many camels have you got? How many cows?'

'None of either. Do not cross-question me.'

'Well then, what goods do you have in your shop?

'Where do I have a shop or a place of my own?'

'Then let me ask you about money. How much have you? You certainly go it alone, and your advice is highly prized. You possess the alchemy that turns all the world's copper into gold. Such a brain, such knowledge is studded with precious pearls.'

'By Allah, chief of the Arabs,' cried the philosopher, 'in all that I own there is not the price of food for the night. I run around naked and barefoot, going wherever anyone will give me a loaf. All that I get out of this philosophy and learning and science is—fancy ideas and a good headache!'

'Then please go a long way away from me!' the Bedouin said. 'Please do not let your bad luck rain down on my head! Take your luckless philosophy a long way away from me; your discourse brings bad luck to everyone alive. Either you go that way, and I will run this, or if your road is ahead, I will go back. Better for me is one sack of wheat and another of sand than all your brilliant machinations. My foolishness is a very blessed foolishness, for my heart is well provisioned and my soul is godfearing.'

The wisdom of this world increases surmise and doubt; the wisdom of true religion soars beyond the sky.

59

The miracle of the needles

THE true king is he who is a king in himself, not made king by treasuries and armies, so that his kingship remains everlastingly, even as the kingdom of the Muhammadan faith.

So it is related of Ibrahim ibn Adham that, being on a journey, he sat down by the margin of the sea. He was stitching his patched cloak, when a prince walking along the shore suddenly came to that place. Now the prince was a servant of the saint; recognizing him, he at once prostrated himself. He was amazed at the saint and his dervish cloak, so greatly his nature and his outward form had changed. He marvelled that he should have abandoned so mighty a kingdom and preferred poverty so exceeding slender, that he should have given up the sovereignty of the seven climes and beggar-like was plying the needle on his dervish cloak.

The saint became aware of his thoughts; for a saint is as a lion, and men's hearts are his thicket—he enters into their hearts, like hope and fear, and the secrets of all the world are patent to him.

The saint quickly threw the needle into the sea, then with a loud voice he called for the needle. Countless multitudes of Divine fishes, in the mouth of each fish a needle of gold, lifted their heads out of God's sea, saying, 'Receive, O shaikh, the needles of God!'

The saint turned to the prince and said, 'Prince, which is better—the kingdom of the heart, or so mean a dominion?'

When the prince perceived how the saint's command took effect in the coming of the fishes, he was overcome with ecstasy.

'Ah, the fishes know the Elder,' he cried. 'Fie upon him who is excommunicated from the court Divine! The fishes know the Elder, and we are far from him; we are doomed to lose this felicity, they are lucky to enjoy it!'

So saying, he prostrated himself and departed, weeping and desolate.

60

The miracle of the wine

A CERTAIN man accused a shaikh, saying, 'He is wicked, he is not on the path of rectitude. He is a winebibber, a hypocrite and a profligate; what sort of help is he to his disciples?'

'Show a little respect,' said one of the disciples. 'It is no small matter to harbour such thoughts about the great. Far is it from him, and far from his saintly qualities, for his clear spirit to be darkened by any torrent. Lay not such slander upon the people of God! This is pure imagination on your part. Turn a new page. What you say is quite untrue; and even if it were true, land-bird that you are, what has the Red Sea to fear from one corpse? The shaikh is not less in magnitude than two jugfuls, or a small cistern, so how can just one drop of impurity defile him?'

The evil-minded wretch still went on spouting rubbish about the shaikh: a squint-eyed man always has a twisted mind.

'I saw him at a party,' he babbled. 'He is naked and bereft of all piety. If you do not believe it, get up and go out tonight and you will see your shaikh's dissoluteness with your own eyes.

That night he took the disciple to a window.

'Look at the debauchery and making merry!' he cried. 'Look at the hypocrisy by day and the debauchery by night! By day a Muhammad, by night a Bu Lahab; by day called God's servant, by night—God preserve us! And a wine-cup in his hand!'

The disciple saw a full beaker in the Elder's hand.

'Master, is there a tumour even in you?' he exclaimed. 'Did you not always say that in a cup of wine the Devil micturates hurriedly and deliberately?'

'They have made my cup so full,' said the shaikh, 'that there is not room in it for so much as one grain of rue. Look, is there room here for a single mote? Some misguided fellow has got the matter all wrong. This is not a cup,' he went on, 'and this is not wine. Come down, unbeliever, and look at it for yourself!'

He came, and saw it was purest honey. That wretched enemy of God was covered with confusion.

Thereupon the Elder said to his disciple, 'Go and fetch me some wine, good sir. I am in pain; I am constrained; I am past starvation because of the pain. In time of constraint any carcase is ritually clean—a curse be on the head of the unbeliever!'

The disciple went round the wine-cellar, tasting of every jar for the sake of the shaikh; but in all the wine-cellars he found no wine at all; the jars of wine had become full of honey.

'Drinkers!' he cried. 'What is this state of affairs? What has happened? I cannot find wine in any jar.'

All the drinkers came to the shaikh, weeping and beating their heads with their hands.

'Most noble shaikh,' they cried, 'you entered the tavern and because of your advent all the wines have turned to honey. You have changed the wine and cleansed it of defilement; change our souls also, and purify them of nastiness!'

61

The mouse and the camel, a warning against spiritual pride

A LITTLE mouse once caught in its paws a camel's head-rope and in a spirit of emulation went off with it. Because of the nimbleness with which the camel set off along with him the mouse was duped into thinking himself a champion. The flash of his thought struck the camel.

'Go on, enjoy yourself,' he grunted. 'I will show you!'

Presently the mouse came to the margin of a great river, such as would have cast down any lion or wolf. There the mouse halted, struck all of a heap.

'Comrade over mountain and plain,' said the camel, 'why this standing still? Why are you dismayed? Step on like a man! Into the river with you! You are my guide and leader; do not halt half-way, paralysed!'

'But this a vast and deep river,' said the mouse. 'I am afraid of being drowned, comrade.'

'Let me see how deep the water is,' said the camel, and quickly set foot in it.

'The water only comes up to my knee,' he went on. 'Blind mouse, why were you dismayed? Why did you lose your head?'

'To you it is an ant, but to me it is a dragon,' said the mouse. 'There are great differences between one knee and another. If it only reaches your knee, clever camel, it passes a hundred cubits over my head.'

'Be not so arrogant another time,' said the camel, 'lest you are consumed body and soul by the sparks of my wrath. Emulate mice like yourself; a mouse has no business to hobnob with camels.'

'I repent,' said the mouse. 'For God's sake get me across this deadly water!'

'Listen,' said the camel, taking compassion on the mouse. 'Jump up and sit on my hump. This passage has been entrusted to me; I would take across hundreds of thousands like you.'

Since you are not the ruler, be a simple subject; since you are not the captain, do not steer the ship.

62

The miracle of the pearls

A DERVISH was once voyaging in a ship; he had taken for his bolster the goods of virtue. While he was asleep a purse of gold was reported missing and everyone on board was searched. He too was pointed out.

'Let us search this sleeping fakir also,' they cried.

The anxious owner of the money awakened him.

'A handbag is missing on board,' he explained. 'We have searched everybody; you cannot escape. Take off your dervish robe, come, strip yourself so that you may be cleared of people's suspicions.'

'Lord,' cried the dervish, 'these vile creatures have accused Thy servant. Accomplish Thy decree.'

Since the heart of the dervish was pained by that suspicion, forthwith countless multitudes of fishes on every side put forth their heads from the depths of the ocean, in the mouth of each a marvellous pearl—multitudes of fishes out of the swarming ocean, in the mouth of each a pearl, and what pearls! Every single pearl the revenue of a kingdom.

'These are from God. They are shared by none else.'

He cast down a number of pearls upon the ship, then sprang aloft, making the air his throne. There he sat cross-legged in comfort, like a king on his throne, he high in the zenith and the ship before him.

'Go!' he cried. 'Have your ship, and I will have God. Then you will not be plagued with a beggarly thief. We will see who is the loser by this separation. I am happy to be paired with God and at odds with men. He does not accuse me of theft; He does not give me over to the mercy of an informer.'

'Noble chief,' the people of the ship cried aloud, 'why has such a high station been vouchsafed to you?'

'For casting suspicion on fakirs and vexing God for the sake of a mean trifle! God forbid!' he replied. 'Rather it was for reverencing kings, in that I entertained no dark thoughts against fakirs—those gracious fakirs sweet of breath in magnification of whom God revealed the Sura *He frowned*.'

63

The Indian tree, on the multiplicity of names

A LEARNED man once told the following legend: 'In India there is a certain tree such that whoever plucks and eats of its fruit, he grows not old nor ever dies.'

A king, hearing this tale from a truthful reporter, fell in love with the tree and its fruit and sent a learned envoy, one of his secretaries, to India in search of the tree. For many years his envoy travelled about India upon the quest, wandering from city to city in search of it; he left no island, no mountain, no plain unvisited. Everyone he questioned held him up to ridicule.

'Who would search for such a thing, except a madman in chains?'

Many poked him playfully; many said, 'Prosperous fellow, how should the enquiry of so clever and brilliant a man as you prove fruitless or in vain?'

The respect show by the latter was like another slap in the face to him, harder to bear than the physical slap.

'Great man,' they mockingly extolled him, 'in such and such a place there is an enormous tree. In such and such a forest there grows a green tree, very tall, very broad, every branch of it huge.'

The king's envoy, his loins girt for the quest, kept hearing a different sort of report from everyone he asked. Much he travelled over many years, and all the while the king kept sending him money. He suffered much weariness in that foreign land, till at last he became incapable of searching farther. Not a trace was visible of the thing he sought, nothing but the report appeared of the object of his quest, so that the thread of his hope was snapped and his search in the end was abandoned. He resolved to return again to the king; shedding many tears, he trudged along the way.

Coming to a halting-place in utter despair, the king's intimate there fell in with a wise shaikh, a noble 'Pole'.

'Hopeless as I am, I will go to him,' he said to himself. 'From his threshold I will set out on the road, that haply his blessing may go along with me, since I am desperate of gaining my heart's desire.'

His eyes brimming with tears, he went before the shaikh; the tears poured like rain from a cloud.

'Shaikh,' he cried, 'now is the time for compassion and pity. I am in despair; now is the hour for loving kindness.'

'Declare the reason for your despair,' said the shaikh. 'What is the object of your quest? What do you seek?'

'The emperor,' said the envoy, 'chose me out to search for a certain well-branched tree. For there is a tree, unique in all the world, whose fruit is the substance of the Water of Life. Many years I have searched, but I have seen no sign of it, save the banter and ridicule of those merry-makers.'

'Simpleton,' the shaikh laughed, 'this tree is the tree of knowledge in the learned man, very high, very huge, very wide-spreading—Water of Life from the Ocean Divine. You have gone after the form only, and have gone astray; you have abandoned the reality, and therefore cannot find it. Sometimes it is named "tree" and sometimes "sun"; sometimes it is named "sea" and sometimes "cloud". It is that one Thing from which effects multitudinous arise, and its least effects are life everlasting. Though it is single, it has a thousand effects; names innumerable are proper to that one. One person may be father to you, but son in regard to someone else, wrath and foe to another, to another loving kindness and good. Hundreds of thousands of names he has, yet he is one man; even he who possesses his every quality is blind to his quality. Whoever searches after the name only, though a man of trust, like you falls into despair and distraction. Why do you stick to this name "tree", so that you remain with bitterness in your mouth, utterly luckless? Pass on from the Names and contemplate the Attributes, that haply the Attributes may guide you to the Essence.'

Men's disagreements stem from names; when they proceed to the reality, peace ensues.

64

The men who ate the elephant, on the penalty of greed

HAVE you heard the tale of how a certain sage in India once espied a party of friends? Naked and destitute, without provender, ahungered, they were arriving from a far journey. His wisdom's love surged within him and he greeted them kindly, blossoming like a rose-bush.

'I know,' he said, 'what anguish has gathered upon you, hungry and empty, on this pilgrimage of pain. But by Allah I adjure you, illustrious folk, let not your food be the elephant's young! The elephant is in the direction where you are now going; give heed, and do not rend the elephant's child! Young elephants there are upon your way; to hunt them down would delight your hearts mightily. Very weak they are, and tender and very fat, but their mother lies in wait, searching for them; she would wander a hundred leagues seeking her offspring with many a moan and many a sigh. Fire and smoke issue from her trunk: beware that you harm not her fondly cherished little ones! The elephant takes a sniff at every mouth and twists her snout round the belly of every man, seeking where she may find the roast flesh of her offspring, that she may display her vengeance and her might.

'Listen to my advice,' the good counsellor went on, 'that your hearts and souls may not be sorely tried. Satisfy yourselves with grasses and leaves; go not in chase of the young elephants. Now I have discharged the debt of good counsel; what should the fruit of good counsel be but felicity? I came in order to deliver the Message, that I may rescue you out of repentance. Take heed, and let not greed waylay you, let not greed for the leaf tear you up from the roots!'

So saying, he wished them farewell and departed.

As they went on their way, their famine and hunger waxed

184

mighty. Suddenly they espied towards the highroad a fat young elephant, just newly born. Like ravening wolves they fell upon it, ate it clean up, and washed their hands.

One of the travellers however did not eat; he counselled his fellows, for he recalled what the dervish had said. The sage's words prohibited him from eating the roast flesh: old sense frequently bestows on you new fortune.

Then they all dropped to the ground and fell fast asleep; but the still hungry one watched like a shepherd amidst the flock. Presently he saw a terrible elephant approaching. First of all she came running towards him as he kept guard, and thrice sniffed his mouth, but no unwholesome odour came from it. Several times she circled him, and then departed; that huge queen-elephant harmed him not at all. Next she smelt the lips of every man that lay sleeping; the smell of her young one's flesh came to her from them each as they slumbered, for each had eaten of the roast-flesh of her offspring. The mother-elephant swiftly rent and slew them one by one, tossed each in the air at random so that he dashed upon the ground and split asunder.

On the Last Day the scent of pride, of greed, of concupiscence will become like the smell of onions when a man speaks. Though you swear an oath, saying, 'When have I eaten them? I have always abstained from onions and garlic,' yet the breath of your oath will inform against you and will smite the noses of those sitting with you. Many a prayer is rejected because of its smell; the crooked heart is revealed upon the tongue. The answer to such a prayer is 'Slink you into Hell'. The recompense of every fraud is the cudgel of rejection.

But if your words be crooked, yet if your meaning is true that crookedness of utterance shall be acceptable to God.

65

The prayer that was answered

A CERTAIN man one night was crying 'Allah!' till his lips were becoming sweet with the mention of his name.

'Why now, chatterbox,' said the Devil, 'where is the answer "Here am I" to all this "Allah" of yours? Not one answer is coming from the Throne: how long will you grimly go on crying "Allah"?'

The man became broken-hearted, and laid down his head to sleep. He saw in a dream mystic Khazir all in a green garden.

'Look now,' Khazir called, 'why have you desisted from the mention of God? How is it you repent of having called upon Him?'

'No answering "Here am I" is coming to me,' the man replied, 'and I therefore fear that I may be repulsed from His door.'

Khazir answered, 'Your cry of "Allah" (God says) is itself My "Here am I"; your pleading and agony and fervour is My messenger. All your twistings and turnings to come to Me were My drawing you that set free your feet. Your fear and love are the lasso to catch My grace. Under each "Allah" of yours whispers many a "Here am I".'

66

The countryman and the townsman, on the consequences of imprudence

ONCE upon a time, my brother, there was a townsman who was acquainted with a countryman. Whenever the countryman came to town he always pitched his tent in the street of that townsman; he would be his guest for two months or three, constantly in his shop and at his table. Whatever he needed during that time the townsman would furnish him with free of charge.

One day he turned to the townsman and said, 'Master, are you never coming to the village for a holiday? Bring all your children, for the sake of Allah. This is the very season of the rose-garden and spring. Or else come in the summer, the season of fruit, so that I may bind my loins to do you service. Bring your whole cavalcade, your children and people. Stay in our village for three months or four, for in the springtime the countryside is delightful with its sown fields turning green and charming anemones.'

The townsman was always putting him off with promises, till eight years had elapsed since the first promise.

'When do you mean to set out?' the countryman would ask each year. 'It is already December.'

'This year,' the townsman would always excuse himself, 'we have a guest who has come from such and such a place. Next year, if I am able to get away from pressing cares, I really will run down to your part of the world.'

'My family are longing to welcome your children, patron,' said the countryman.

Back he would come each year, like the stork, to take up residence in the townsman's pavilion. Each year the merchant would expend on him his gold and wealth, spreading wide his wings. For the final time that champion of chivalry laid the table for him night and morning, three months long, till in very shame the countryman protested.

'How long only promises? How long will you deceive me?'

'Body and soul, I am eager for the reunion,' said the merchant. 'But every removal depends upon the decree of God. Man is like a ship, a sail, he must await the Wind-driver to bring the wind.'

'Generous friend,' the countryman once more adjured him, 'take your children and come. See our country paradise.'

Thrice he took his hand in solemn covenant, saying, 'In Allah's name, come quickly, make the effort!'

After ten years—and every year the same entreaties, the same sugared promises—the children of the merchant themselves took up the tale.

'Father, even the moon, the clouds and the shadows have their journeys. You have laid many obligations upon him. You have taken infinite pains on his account. He wants to repay some part of that obligation when you become his guest. He has enjoined us often and often in secret: "Drag him to the village. Coax him to come".'

'All this is true, little apple,' said the townsman. 'But remember the adage, "Look out for evil from him you have done good to".'

The countryman employed every charm to wheedle the townsman, till he succeeded at last in fuddling the merchant's prudence. His children in approval happily chanted the words of Joseph's brethren, 'to frolic and play'. The prudent merchant brought forward all sorts of excuses and pretexts to counter the stubborn devil of a countryman.

'Just at present I have some important affairs to see to,' he pleaded. 'If I come to the country they will never be put in order. The king himself has charged me with a delicate business; he has not slept of a night waiting for me. I cannot abandon the king's command and come into the king's presence pale with shame. Every morning and every evening a high-ranking officer comes demanding of me the solution. Do you hold it right that I should come to the village, so that the sultan knits his brows in wrath against me? How should I cure his fury after that? I would surely be burying myself alive if I did this.'

A hundred pretexts of this sort he propounded, but his devices did not pair with the decree of God. When God's doom determined to try every strategem, the townsman was checkmated by the countryman. Despite countless prudent resolutions the merchant was checkmated; embarking on the journey, he soon found himself in trouble.

Gaily enough he made preparations for the journey; the bird of his resolve winged swiftly towards the village. His family and children also prepared for the excursion, heaping their baggage upon the buffalo of departure.

'We have tasted already the fruit of foreboding,' they cried as they hastened rejoicing on their way. 'Give good tidings of the village! The place we are making for is a delicious pasturage; our friend there is both generous and charming. He has invited us with thousands of fond wishes, he has planted for us the green sapling of generosity. We shall carry back from him to the town the entire store of the village to keep us through the long winter; indeed, he will place his whole orchard at our disposal, he will make a place for us in the midst of his soul!'

So the merchant and his children made ready an equipage and galloped upon their mules towards the village, chanting gaily as they drove through the open country the old saying, 'Travel bringeth gain'. By day they burned their faces in the sun, by night they learned the way from the stars. To them the hideous road appeared very fair; their excitement to see the village turned the way into Paradise. Fancying the gold was already pursed and knotted for them, the poor deluded creatures hurried on to the village. Whenever they encountered anyone coming from the village they rained on his cheeks kisses of joyfulness.

'You have seen the face of our friend,' they would cry. 'Therefore you are the soul of the Soul, and our very eyes.'

Presently a village came in sight, but it was not the one the townsman was seeking, so he chose another road. For wellnigh a month the party sped from village to village, not knowing well the way to their host's village. They suffered much anguish and agony on that road, like the torment of a land-bird fluttering through a torrent. They became quite sick of the village and the countryside, sick of the sugared utterances of so unskilful a spellbinder.

189

After a month they finally reached their destination, themselves out of provisions, their mules without fodder. Mark now how that countryman with the worst intentions piled new and greater calamities on the old. All day he kept his face hidden from them lest they should poke their snouts into his orchard. Having made enquiries, they discovered where he lived and hastened to his door as though they were his own kin. The people of his household barred the door in their faces.

The merchant became as one mad at this perversity, but it was not the time for rough measures; what is the use of fury when you have fallen into the pit?

For five days they remained at his door, by night in the cold, by day scorched by the sun. Not out of indifference or mulishness they remained there but of dire necessity and lack of a mule. From time to time the townsman caught sight of the countryman and saluted him.

'I am so-and-so,' he would say. 'Such and such is my name.'

'Very likely,' the countryman would answer. 'How should I know who you are, whether you are a filthy rascal or a fine gentleman?'

'This instant,' said the townsman, 'is like the resurrection when, as the Koran says, a man shall flee from his brother. I am the man,' he would then explain, 'at whose table you ate dainties in abundance. Do you not remember the day I bought you those goods? Every secret that goes beyond the two becomes public property. All the people heard the secret of our affection; benefits received generally engender some mark of respect.'

'Why do you blather so?' the countryman would reply. 'I know neither you, nor your name, nor where you live.'

On the fifth night such a storm of cloud and rain came on that the heavens themselves might well wonder at their deluge. This was the last straw. The merchant hammered at the door.

'Call your master!'

After a hundred importunities the countryman at last came to the door.

'Well, what is it now, good fellow?'

'I give up all those claims on your gratitude,' the townsman said. 'I renounce the repayment I was counting on. I have suffered five years of torture these five days, my wretched soul buffeted by all this fire and furnace. The sun of your affection is clearly towards setting. If you have shed my blood, I acquit you of guilt; but on this night of rain pray give us some nook to shelter in that at the resurrection your virtue may find its reward.'

'The gardener has a little nook,' said the countryman. 'He keeps watch there against the wolf, bow and arrow in hand to shoot if the mighty wolf should come. If you are willing to perform that service, the place is yours; if not, be so good as to look for another place.'

'I am ready to perform a hundred services,' said the townsman. 'Just give me the place, and put the bow and arrow in my hand. I will not go to sleep; I will keep guard over the vines; if the wolf should raise his head, be sure I will shoot him. For God's sake do not abandon me tonight, you double-faced hypocrite, with the rain-water overhead and the mud underfoot!'

A nook was duly cleared, and thither the townsman went with his family. The place was cramped, without room to turn round in; riding on one another like locusts, they huddled in fear of the torrent into the corner of the hollow.

'It serves us right, O God,' all night they chanted. 'It serves us right.'

All night, bow and arrow in hand, the townsman looked out for the wolf on this side and that. Every gnat, every flea in that tumbledown shack became as a wolf to them, biting them uninterruptedly; their dread of the ferocious wolf's onslaught left them no leisure so much as to drive away the gnats. For they feared that the wolf would wreak some havoc so that the countryman would tear out the townsman's beard. So they were gnashing their teeth till midnight, their souls mounting from their navels to their lips.

Suddenly from the top of a hillock appeared the likeness of a solitary wolf. The merchant loosed the arrow from the thumb-stall and shot at the animal, so that it fell to the ground. As it fell the animal farted. The countryman thereupon cried aloud and beat his hands.

'Ignoble wretch, that is my ass-colt!'

'No, it is that devil of a wolf. See, the features of a wolf show clearly in it. Its shape betrays its wolfishness.'

'Not so,' the countryman replied. 'I know that fart anywhere, just as I can tell water from wine. You have killed my ass-colt grazing in the meadow. May your soul never be delivered out of the clutch of Hell!'

'Make a better investigation,' the townsman pleaded. 'It is night, and at night the identities of things are obscured to the beholder. Night changes many things and shows them all wrong. Not everyone has the power of seeing straight by night. What with the night and the clouds and the torrential rain, this triple darkness is enough to create the most enormous error.'

'To me it is as clear as daylight,' the countryman declared. 'I recognize my ass-colt's fart. I know that fart amongst twenty farts, just as a traveller knows his own provender.'

Losing all patience, the merchant leaped up and seized the countryman by the collar.

'Fool, cutthroat, hypocrite!' he shouted. 'Why, you must have eaten opium and beng together! In a triple darkness you recognize the ass's fart; how then do you not know me, you blundering idiot? He who knows a colt at midnight, how should he not know his ten-years' companion?'

Prudence is this, that when wordly men invite you, you should not say, 'They are quite wild for my company.' Know their invitation to be as the whistle of the fowler, crouching hidden in his place of ambush. He puts forward a dead bird, making out that the plaintive song comes from it. The birds think it is one of their own kind and gather about it; the fowler rends their skins—all except forsooth the bird God has endowed with prudence, so that it may not be duped by that bait and blandishment.

67

The jackal that pretended to be a peacock

A JACKAL once got into a dyeing-vat and there tarried for a space. Then he got out again, and his skin was stained with the dye.

'See, I have become the Peacock of Heaven's Heights!' he cried.

Indeed, his dyed fur had acquired a delightful sheen, and when the sun shone upon those colours he beheld himself green and crimson, russet and gold. So he displayed himself to the other jackals.

'Little jackal,' they all exclaimed, 'what is the matter? Why is your head full of such perverse glee? You have gone apart from us in your exultation; what is the ground for your high disdain?'

'You there,' one of the jackals went up to him and cried, 'are you a pretender, or is your heart truly joyous? You have perpetrated a fraud so as to jump up on the pulpit and with your vainglory make all the people envious. You have laboured much but experienced no true ardour, so you have displayed a fraudulent piece of impudence.'

The multicoloured jackal slunk up quietly and whispered into the ear of the reprover.

'Why, just look at me! Look at my colours! No idolater possesses an idol like me. I have become lovely and many-hued as the garden. Do not turn your head from me: bow down before me! See my pomp and splendour, my sheen, my glitter, my colour! Call me the Pride of the World, the Pillar of the Faith! I have become the theatre of the grace Divine, I have become the tablet expounding the majesty of God. You jackals, beware! Do not call me a jackal; how should a jackal possess so much beauty?'

The jackals gathered about him like moths around a candle.

'Say, what shall we call you then, creature of pure substance?'

'A peacock,' he answered, 'proud as Jupiter.'

'Peacocks of the Spirit,' they then said to him, 'hold displays in the Garden of Roses. Do you make such a display?'

'No,' he replied. 'How should I tread the streets of Mina, never having gone into the desert?'

'Do you utter the peacocks' cry?'

'No,' he answered.

'Then you are not a peacock, father of lofty airs! The glory-robe of the peacock is the gift of heaven; how should you ever attain to it by means of dyes and false pretences?'

68

The birth of Moses

NOW whereas Pharaoh's endeavours lacked the blessing of God, all that he stitched together proved a ripping apart.

He had at his command a thousand astrologers, besides countless interpreters of dreams and magicians. He was shown in a dream the coming of Moses who should destroy Pharaoh and his kingdom.

'How,' he asked the interpreters and the astrologers, 'how may the ill-omened phantasm and dream be warded off?'

'We will devise a plan,' they all replied to him. 'We will waylay his birth, as brigands waylay the caravan.'

When the night arrived that Moses should be begotten Pharaoh's counsellors deemed it advisable early on that day to bring forth unto the maidan the royal throne and banquet.

'Welcome, all you Israelites! The king invites you to come, that he may show you his face unveiled and to do good unto you for the heavenly reward.'

For those captives might only stand afar; they were not permitted to look on Pharaoh, and if they encountered him upon the road the law required of them that they should lie flat on their faces. So the law prescribed, that no captive timely or untimely should behold the prince's countenance; whenever on the road he should hear the cry of the pursuivants, he must turn his face to the wall that he might not see. If he should nevertheless see his face, he would be deemed a criminal and the direst consequence would come upon his head. Those Israelites were covetous to see the forbidden countenance, since man is ever covetous for that which is forbidden.

'Captives, get you to the maidan, for there is hope that you may see Pharaoh and enjoy the imperial bounty.'

When the Israelites heard the good tidings they thirsted and yearned exceedingly to behold Pharaoh. Swallowing the bait, they hastened thither and prepared themselves for the promised display. Having by a trick brought them to the maidan, Pharaoh revealed to them his face fresh and fair, entertained them fondly and showered gifts upon them, bestowed on them indifferently both presents and promises.

Then Pharaoh said to them, 'As you value your lives, do you all sleep in the maidan this night.'

They answered him, saying, 'We will do you service; if it be your pleasure, we will dwell here a whole month.'

At nightfall the king returned to the city rejoicing.

'Tonight is the conception, and they are far from their wives.'

Imran his treasurer also attending him returned to the city, keeping Pharaoh company.

'Imran,' commanded Pharaoh, 'sleep at this door. See that you go not unto your wife or seek to lie with her.'

'I will sleep even at the door of your chamber,' said Imran. 'I will think of nothing except your pleasure.'

Now Imran was also one of the Israelites, but he was dear to Pharaoh as his own heart and soul. How then should Pharaoh have supposed that he would disobey him and do the very thing that Pharaoh's soul most feared?

The king departed, and Imran slept at his portal. At midnight his wife came to look for him. She fell upon him and kissed him on the lips, rousing him up from his night slumber. Awaking, he beheld his wife was very fair, raining kisses from her lips upon his lips.

'How was it that you came at this time?' Imran asked.

'Out of yearning,' she answered, 'and by the ordinance of God.'

The husband drew her lovingly into his embrace, no more contending with himself in that moment. He lay with her in union, then he said to her:

'Wife, this is no small matter. A steel has struck upon the stone and a flame has been born, a flame that shall take vengeance on the king and his kingdom. I am as the cloud, you are the earth, and Moses is the plant. God is the king on the chessboard and we are mated, mated. Know that checkmate and victory proceed from the king, my bride; do not suppose that to spring from us, do not jeer at us! The thing whereof

196

Pharaoh is afraid came into being this very moment when I lay with you. Make not public any of these things; do not breathe a word, lest a hundred sorrows come upon me and you. In the end the effects of this will become manifest, seeing that already, my darling, the tokens have appeared.'

At that moment cries from the people were coming from the direction of the maidan, and the air was full of noises. The king sprang forth from his chamber forthwith in terror, barefoot.

'What is all this clamour?' he cried. 'Hark, what is the noise and clamour coming from the maidan, scaring into flight even genie and demon?'

'Long live the king!' answered Imran. 'The people of Israel are rejoicing because of you. They are making merry because of the king's bounty; they are dancing and clapping their hands.'

'Perhaps it is so,' Pharaoh replied. 'But it has filled me with grave doubts and suspicions. This uproar has truly changed me, it has aged me with bitter grief and care.'

The king kept pacing to and fro; all night he was like a pregnant woman in the hour of childbirth.

'Imran,' he kept saying every moment, 'these cries have seriously discomposed me.'

Wretched Imran had not the courage to disclose how he had had intercourse with his wife, how his wife had crept into his arms so that the star of Moses came into sight.

Day broke.

'Go forth, Imran,' commanded Pharaoh. 'Apprise yourself of the meaning of that tumult and noise.'

Imran rode directly to the maidan.

'What was this tumult?' he demanded. 'The emperor has not slept.'

Every astrologer, with head bare and garment rent, kissed the earth like people in mourning; like people in mourning, their voices were choked with lamentation, their robes disarrayed. They had plucked out their beards and hair; they had torn their faces; they had scattered dust upon their heads; their eyes were bloodshot.

'Is all well?' Imran inquired. 'What is this fuss and confusion? Does this ill-omened year give you some evil sign?'

197

'O prince,' they apologized, 'the hand of Divine foreordaining has taken us captive. Tonight the star of that boy, to our great confusion, shone clearly on the brow of heaven; the star of that prophet shot up in the sky, and we were constrained to weep stars of tears.'

Imran, withal glad in heart, out of hypocrisy beat his hands against his head crying, 'Woe, all is lost!'

Making himself out to be wrathful and cross, he raged among them insensate, as though he were mad. He pretended to know nothing, and rushing forward addressed to the assembled company words exceeding rough.

'You have deceived my king,' he shouted angrily. 'You have not refrained from treachery and covetousness. You instigated the king to go to the maidan, you squandered the honour of our king. You smote your hands upon your breasts in guarantee that you would set the king free of all cares.'

The king also heard the astrologers' excuses.

'Traitors, I will string you up without any quarter,' he cried. 'I have made myself a laughing-stock. I spilled my treasure upon my enemies so that this night all the Israelites should remain far from encountering their wives. Now my wealth and honour are gone, and my labour is lost. Is this the friendship and action of noble men? For years you have carried off good stipends and robes of honour, you have devoured provinces at your own sweet will. Was this your famed judgment, your wisdom, your astrology? Grovelling tricksters all of you, birds of ill omen! I will tear you asunder, I will set you ablaze, I will pluck off your noses and ears and lips. I will make you faggots for the fire, I will make your past pleasure most unpleasant for you.'

'Khedive,' they made answer, prostrating themselves, 'if this once the Devil has outwitted us, yet for many years we have warded off afflictions; the imagination boggles at what we have done. Now it has got by us; the child is manifestly conceived; the semen is spilled, the foetus is in the womb. Yet we ask pardon for this; we will watch out for the day of birth, O king; we will observe by the stars the day of his nativity, so that this foreordinance may not elude us. If we do not keep watch for this then do you slay us: our thoughts, our minds are the slaves of your judgment.'

For nine months he was reckoning day by day, lest the arrow of the foe-transfixing doom should fly.

After nine months the king brought forth his throne to the maidan and made stringent proclamation.

'Women, go with your babes to the maidan! Go forth, all you children of Israel! In like manner as last year your men received robes of honour and bore away every one of them gold, this year, hearken you women, the good fortune is yours; each one of you shall obtain the thing that she desires. The king will give the women robes of honour and presents; he will set caps of gold too on the children's heads. Give ear! Every one of you who has given birth this month shall receive treasures from the puissant king.'

The women went forth with their babes; joyfully they came to the king's tabernacle. Every woman newly delivered went forth from the city unto the maidan, utterly unconscious of any guile or malice. When the women were all gathered about him his officers snatched from their mothers every male child and cut off its head.

'This is by way of precaution, to prevent the king's enemy growing up and that confusion may not increase.'

Imran's wife, who had taken Moses along with her, kept a safe distance from all that tumult and vapour.

Pharaoh, the sly one, sent the midwives into all the houses to spy. They informed on Imran's wife.

'Here is a child. His mother did not come to the maidan. She is under doubt and suspicion.' 'In this street there dwells a handsome woman. She has a child, but she is full of craft.'

Then came the officers. Bidden by God, she cast the infant into the oven. From the Omniscient revelation came to her that the child, being of the stock of Abraham, would be under the protection of Divine command, 'O fire, be coolness and safety!' According to the revelation the woman cast Moses into the sparks, and the fire had no effect upon his body.

Then the officers went away without accomplishing their purpose. Once again the informers, being apprised of the facts, raised a furore with the officers in Pharaoh's presence to gain a few pence.

'Officers, go back again to that quarter. Look very carefully in the upper chambers.'

199

Once more the revelation came to the mother of Moses.

'Cast him into the water. Be hopeful still. Tear not your hair. Cast him into the Nile, and put your trust in God. I will restore you to him, happy and serene.'

69

The snake-catcher and the frozen snake,
a cautionary tale

A CERTAIN snake-catcher went out to the mountains
to catch snakes by his magic spells. All around the mountains
in the days of snow he kept searching for a mammoth
snake. There he espied a mighty dragon, dead, and at the sight
of it his heart was filled with fear. Nevertheless he snatched up
the dragon and came to Baghdad, hoping to make a stir. For the
sake of earning a halfpenny he dragged along a dragon huge
as the pillar of a house.

'See, I have brought a dead dragon,' he cried. 'What I have
suffered in hunting it down!'

For he supposed that the dragon was dead; but it was alive,
only he did not see too well. It was frozen by the frosts and
snow and it was alive, but looked as though it were dead. He
set up a booth on the bank of the Tigris. The news ran like
wildfire through all Baghdad.

'A snake-catcher has brought a dragon. He has caught an
amazing rarity.'

Hundreds of thousands of boobies assembled, a prey, like
the man himself, to his own idiocy. They were expectant, and
he was waiting for the scattered population to assemble; for the
bigger the crowd, the better the begging and the larger the
collection. The idlers gathered in their hundreds of thousands
and formed a ring, sole rubbing sole.

The snake-catcher started to move the wrapping. The
assembled multitude stretched their necks. They saw that the
dragon, that had been frozen by the bitter cold, lay under a
hundred sorts of sackings and covers and bound with thick
ropes. The keeper had taken good precautions!

In the delay, while the people collected and waited, the
sun of Iraq shone full upon the snake. The sun of that hot

climate warmed it and the cold humours went out of its limbs. That which was dead now revived; to its astonishment the dragon began to uncoil itself.

The people's amazement was multiplied a myriad times on seeing the dead snake stir. They shrieked in astonishment and fled to a man. Meanwhile the snake was bursting its bonds, and what with the people shouting, every side went crack crack! The snake broke through its bonds and slid out from under them, a hideous dragon roaring like a lion. In the rout many people were killed; a hundred heaps were made of the fallen.

The snake-catcher was paralysed with fear on the spot.

'What,' he cried, 'have I brought from the mountains and the wilderness?'

The dragon is your carnal soul. How should it be dead? It is only frozen—by frustration and atrophy. Keep the dragon in the snows of segregation; beware, do not drag it into the sun of Iraq!

70

Moses and Pharaoh

'WHY, Moses,' said Pharaoh, 'did you slay the people and put fear into their hearts? The people have been put to rout by you; in the rout many folk slipped and were slain. Inevitably the people have taken you as their enemy; hatred of you has filled the breasts of men and women alike. You called the people to follow you, but the contrary has come to pass; the folk cannot escape from opposing you. I too, for all that I shrink back from your mischief, am cooking a pot to requite your evil. Put it out of your mind that you can hoodwink me, or that you will find any follower but your own shadow. Be not deceived by the thing that you have wrought; you have merely cast terror into the people's hearts. Produce a hundred such tricks, and you will still be exposed; you will become contemptible, a public laughing-stock. There have been many impostors like you, but in the end they have all been brought to shame in our Egypt.'

'I admit no partner with God in what He commands,' said Moses. 'If His command is that my blood be shed, I do not fear. I am well content; I am thankful indeed, my adversary; on this side I may be disgraced, but with God I am in high honour. Let me be contemptible in the eyes of the people, a miserable laughing-stock; in God's sight I am beloved, wooed, approved. So may men say of me; but tomorrow God shall blacken *your* face. Glory belongs to God and to His servants only; read in the Koran the token thereof, as shown in Adam and Iblis. The exposition of God, like God Himself, is infinite. Take heed; close your mouth, and turn the page!'

'The page is under my control!' answered Pharaoh. 'The scroll and register of authority is mine this moment. The people of all the world have singled out me; are you more intelligent than all, fine fellow? So, you have singled out yourself, Moses. Listen now: off with you! Have less conceit of yourself; let not yourself delude you. I will muster all the magicians of the world, that I may show your stupidity to the city. This will not happen in one day or two, however; give me respite till the forty days of Tammuz.'

'No licence for that is granted me,' said Moses. 'I am God's servant, and it is not commanded to accord you respite. If you are the master and I have no ally indeed, yet I am servant to God's command. With that I have nothing to do. As long as I am alive, I will contend with you earnestly. What matters it if I have no helper? I am the servant of God, I will fight until His decree comes to pass. It is He alone who parts adversary from adversary.'

'No, no! You must appoint a respite,' Pharaoh answered. 'A few less blandishments, beat not the wind so!'

Forthwith God Most High made revelation to Moses: 'Grant him an ample respite, be not afeared of that. Give him willingly the forty days' respite he asks for, that he may meditate plots of divers kinds. Let him labour! I am not asleep. Bid him be gone quickly, for I have forestalled him. I will confound all their knavish tricks, I will bring to little all that they build up. Let them fetch water, and I will make it fire; let them procure honey and sweetness, and I will make it bitter. Let them tie the bond of love, and I will destroy it; I will do that whereof they do not conceive. Have no fear, grant him a long respite; bid him gather his host and prepare a hundred tricks.'

'God's command has come,' said Moses to Pharaoh. 'Go, respite is granted you. I go to my own place; you are rid of me.'

He went his way, and at his heels went the dragon, wise and affectionate as a huntsman's dog, wagging its tail like a huntsman's dog, pounding stones to powder under its hoof. With its breath it sucked stones and iron into its jaws and visibly chewed the iron into little pieces. It disgorged foam from its gullet like a camel; whomsoever a drop struck, he was smitten with leprosy. The champing of its teeth would break the stoutest heart and reduce the soul of the black panther to a state of terror.

When God's chosen prophet reached his own people he

seized the corner of the dragon's mouth, and it turned again into a staff. Leaning upon it, he spoke.

'Amazing! Clear as the sun to me, but to my adversary dark as night! Amazing! How does this host not see a whole world filled with the sun at high morning? Eyes open, ears open, and this orb of day! I am astounded at how God blindfolds men. I am astounded at them, and they at me: born of the same springtide, but they are thorns and I am jasmine. Many a cup of purest wine I have laid before them, but its liquor turned to stone before this party. I bound a bunch of roses and brought it to them; every rose became as a thorn, the honey turned to a sting.'

So Moses returned home, and Pharaoh remained with his court. Forthwith he summoned his counsellors and advisers, who deemed it right that the king and ruler of Egypt should gather the magicians from all parts of the land. Thereupon he sent many men to all the provinces to gather the sorcerers.

Now there were two youths, celebrated magicians whose magic penetrated the very heart of the moon. Publicly and openly they drew milk from the moon; upon their journeys they rode upon a wine-jar. They made the moonlight to appear like a piece of linen which they measured out and sold with all speed, carrying off the money; the purchaser, becoming apprised of the deceit, would smite his hands on his cheeks out of grief. Hundreds of thousands of such wizardries they had invented, no mere imitations. In due course the king's message came to them.

'The king now desires your help, forasmuch as the two dervishes have come against the king, mounting an assault upon his palace. All that they have with them is a solitary rod, which turns into a dragon at Moses' bidding. The king and all his army are utterly helpless, all reduced to lamentation by these two persons. Some remedy must be devised in magic, that perchance you may save the lives of all from these two magicians.'

When the herald delivered this message to the two magicians, fear and love descended into the hearts of them both. The vein of congenerity with Moses began to throb in them; they laid their heads upon their knees in wonder.

'Mother, come, where is our father's grave?' they said presently. 'Do you show us the way.'

She took them and showed them the way to their father's grave. Then they kept a three days' fast for the sake of the king.

'Father,' they said after that, 'the king in great distress has sent us a message, that two certain men have brought him to sore straits and destroyed his reputation in the eyes of the army. These men have with them neither weapon nor soldiery, nothing but a rod, and in that rod much trouble and trial. You have departed into the world of the saints, though to mortal sight you are sleeping in earth. If it be magic those men are wielding, then inform us; if it be of God, spirit of our father, inform us likewise, that we may bow down before them and rub ourselves against their alchemy. We are in despair; yet a hope has dawned. We are in banishment; yet grace has drawn us.'

'Sons, life of my life,' came the answer, 'to declare this matter plainly is reserved to God. I have no licence to speak openly and freely, yet the secret is not far from my sight. Nevertheless I will show you a sign, that this hidden thing may become manifest to you. Light of my eyes, when you go thither become apprised of the place where Moses sleeps and in the time when that sage is asleep, make for the rod, putting fear aside. If you find you are able to steal it, he is a magician, and you have at your disposal the means of dealing with a magician; but if you cannot steal it, beware! He is of God, he is the messenger of the Lord of glory, divinely guided. Though Pharaoh should take the world, east and west, yet shall he be overthrown: to fight with God is foolishness. This sign I have given you, a true sign, soul of your father. Inscribe it upon your heart. Allah knows best the right course. Soul of your father, when a magician sleeps there is none to guide his magic and cunning. When the shepherd sleeps the wolf is secure; when the shepherd sleeps, his exertion is stilled; but the animal whose shepherd is God—how has the wolf hope or way to work it mischief? The sorcery that God works is true and right; it is an error to call that true thing sorcery. Soul of your father, this is the critical sign: even though the prophet die, yet God raises him up. Soul of your father, when a magician goes to sleep his work becomes lustreless and shines no more.'

The two youths kissed their father's grave and departed to Egypt, to engage in this dire struggle. Having come to Egypt for that great task, they straightway sought out Moses and his dwelling. It so chanced that on the day of their arrival Moses lay asleep under a palm-tree. The people gave them a clue where they might find him.

'Go, look yonder towards the palm-grove.'

When the two magicians saw Moses stretched out asleep they made ready to steal the rod, making for it quickly.

'We must get behind him and then snatch it,' they said.

As they prepared to approach a little nearer the rod began to tremble, quivering all over in such a manner that the two magicians were rooted to the spot, paralysed with fear. Then the rod turned into a dragon and charged at them; both took to flight; pale of face, they fell headlong in terror, tumbling over and over down every slope.

Then it became certain to them that Moses was from Heaven, for they were seeing the limitations of magic. Diarrhoea and fever overcame them; presently they found themselves at the last gasp, in the throes of death. Immediately they sent a man to Moses, asking his pardon.

'We put you to the test, and how would the idea of testing you have come to us if not for envy? We have sinned against the heavenly King; pray for us to be forgiven, most elect of the Court of God.'

Moses pardoned them, and forthwith they were healed. They struck their heads upon the ground before Moses.

'Nobles, I pardon you,' Moses said. 'Hell shall not have your bodies and souls. It is as though I never saw you; estrange yourselves to the making of excuses! Come as you are, outwardly strangers but in truth familiar, come to make battle in the cause of the King!'

The two men kissed the ground and departed. They were waiting for the time and the right occasion.

71

The elephant in the dark, on the reconciliation of contrarieties

SOME Hindus had brought an elephant for exhibition and placed it in a dark house. Crowds of people were going into that dark place to see the beast. Finding that ocular inspection was impossible, each visitor felt it with his palm in the darkness.

The palm of one fell on the trunk.

'This creature is like a water-spout,' he said.

The hand of another lighted on the elephant's ear. To him the beast was evidently like a fan.

Another rubbed against its leg.

'I found the elephant's shape is like a pillar,' he said.

Another laid his hand on its back.

'Certainly this elephant was like a throne,' he said.

The sensual eye is just like the palm of the hand. The palm. has not the means of covering the whole of the beast.

The eye of the Sea is one thing and the foam another. Let the foam go, and gaze with the eye of the Sea. Day and night foam-flecks are flung from the sea; oh amazing! You behold the foam but not the Sea. We are like boats dashing together; our eyes are darkened, yet we are in clear water.

72

Noah and Canaan

CANAAN was swimming in the waters, saying, 'I do not want the ark of Noah, my enemy.'

'Hey, come here!' cried Noah. 'Sit in your father's ark, miserable wretch, so that you may not be drowned in the Flood.'

'No,' answered Canaan. 'I have learned to swim. I have lighted a candle other than your candle.'

'Beware, do not do so! These are the billows of the Flood of calamity. Hands and feet and swimming today are nothing. It is the gale of wrath, the tribulation that puts out the candle. Only God's candle endures eternally. Hold your peace!'

'No,' Canaan replied. 'I will get me into that high mountain. That mountain will protect me from every hurt.'

'Beware, do not do so! The mountain this hour is but a straw. God will give security only to those He loves.'

'When have I harkened to your advice, that you should have hoped that I am of this household?' Canaan asked. 'Your words have never been agreeable to me. I am quit of you, in this world and the next.'

'Beware, do not do so, my dear one. This is no day for putting on airs. God has no kinship, He is without partner. Till now you have been disdainful; now the disdain is God's. Whose disdain cuts any ice in the Court of God? From eternity He is the unbegetting, the unbegotten; He has no father, no son, no uncle. How then will He suffer the disdain of sons? How will He listen to the disdain of fathers? "I am unbegotten," says God. "Old man, be not proud. I am unbegetting; young man, strut not so. I am not a husband, lust has no part of Me; lady, here put aside disdain." In this Presence naught but humility, servitude, surrender is of account.'

'You have been saying this for years, father,' said Canaan.

'Now you are saying it again. You are mad, demented. You have said plenty of such things to all and sundry, and you have received plenty of chilly answers! These chilly words of yours have not entered my ear, especially now that I have become wise and puissant.'

'What harm will it do, my dear one, if you listen once to your father's advice?'

Noah kept uttering gentle counsel of this kind, which Canaan likewise rejected rudely. The father wearied not of counselling Canaan; not one word penetrated the ear of that reprobate. While they were arguing, suddenly a fierce wave smote Canaan on the head, and he was dashed to pieces.

'Long-suffering King of Kings,' Noah cried, 'my donkey is dead, and Thy torrent has swept away the load. Thou didst promise me many times, saying, "Thy family shall find deliverance from the Flood." Simple as I am, I fixed my heart upon hope of Thee; why then has Thy torrent robbed me of my cloak?'

God said, 'He was not of thy family and kinsfolk. Saw you not that you are white, and he is blue?'

'I will have nothing,' said Noah, 'of aught other than Thy Essence. He who has become dead in Thee is not other than Thou. Thou knowest how I am to Thee: twenty times am I as the meadow is to the rain, of Thee living, through Thee rejoicing, a pauper fed without intermediary or intervention, neither united nor separated—O perfection!—without quality, without description, without causation. We are the fishes and Thou art the Sea of Life; by Thy grace we live, O Thou whose attributes are all good. Thou art not contained within the bosom of any thought; Thou art not conjoined with any effect as being a cause. Before this Flood and after it, to Thee I have addressed myself in every eventuality; with Thee I have been ever speaking, not with men, O Thou who givest speech both new and of old. Does not the lover night and day converse now with the ruins, now with the orts of the loved one's dwelling-place? To outward appearance he has turned his face towards the ruins; but to whom in reality is he uttering that anthem of praise? Thanks be, that Thou hast now let loose the Flood and removed the intermediary of the ruins, for they were vile and evil ruins, uttering neither a cry nor so much as an echo. I would address such ruins as answer back, like the mountain, with an echo, that I may hear Thy name redoubled, for I am in love with Thy soul-assuaging name. For that cause every prophet loves the mountains, that he may hear Thy name redoubled; the lowly mountain shallow as a heap of stones suits a mouse, not us, as a halting-place. For when I speak it befriends me not, and the breath of my speech remains without an echo. Better it is that Thou shouldst level it with the earth; it conspires not; trample it underfoot!'

God said, 'Noah, if thou so desirest I will muster them all together and raise them from the dust. I will not break thy heart on account of a Canaan, but I am apprising thee of their true estates.'

'Nay, nay,' cried Noah. 'I am well content that Thou shouldst drown me too, if that be necessary to Thee. Every moment be drowning me; happy am I. Thy decree is my very soul; I cherish it as my life. I look upon no man; or if so it be that I look he is only a pretext, Thou art the true object of my gaze. Whether in the hour of thanksgiving or of fortitude, I am in love with Thy handiwork; how should I be like an infidel in love with aught Thou hast made?'

All glorious is he who is in love with God's handiwork; an unbeliever is he who is in love with aught God has made.

73

The striker and the stricken, the dilemma of mystical bewilderment

A CERTAIN man struck Zaid on the neck. Zaid rushed at him to join issue with him.

'I have a question to ask you,' said the assailant. 'Answer me first, and then hit me back. I struck the nape of your neck; there was a sound of a slap. Now I have a question to ask you in all sincerity. That sound of a slap—was it caused by my hand or by the nape of your neck, highly honoured sir?'

Zaid replied, 'Because of the pain I have not the leisure to stand and reflect on this matter impartially. Since you have no pain, you do the pondering!'

74

The lover and the letter, on complete absorption

A LOVER, being admitted to sit beside his beloved, there-upon drew out a letter and read it to her. The letter, which was in verse, told over her praises together with much lament-ation, misery and supplication.

'If all this is for my sake,' said the beloved, 'to read this now you are with me is a sheer waste of time. Here I am beside you, and you read a letter! This is certainly not the sign of a true lover.'

'True, you are here with me,' the lover replied. 'All the same, I am not enjoying myself as well as I should. Though we are united now, I am not experiencing what I did last year on your account. I have drunk limpid water from this fountain, I have refreshed my eyes and my heart. I still see the fountain, but there is no water; perchance some footpad has cut off my water!'

'Then,' said his lady, 'I am not your beloved. I am in Tartary, while your desire is in Cathay. You are in love with me and with a certain emotion together, and the emotion eludes your grasp, young man. So I am not the entire object of your quest; at this moment I am only a part of your aim. I am the dwelling-place of the beloved, not the beloved her-self. True love is fixed on the gold and not on the coffer.'

75

David and the man who begged for food

THERE was a certain man living in the time of the prophet David who in the presence of every sage and before every fool used to utter the following prayer.

'O God, provide me with riches without any pain! Since Thou hast created me a slothful man, a punch-bag, a slacker, a lazybones, one really cannot put the load of horses and mules on the backs of galled, reluctant asses. Since Thou, who art all-sufficient, hast created me slothful, grant me my daily bread likewise by the way of slothfulness. I am slothful; I slumber in the shade of existence; I sleep in the shadow of all this munificence and bounty; surely Thou hast prescribed another manner of livelihood for such as are slothful and slumber in the shade. Every man with a foot to walk by seeks after some livelihood; be Thou very compassionate to those who have no feet. Send Thyself his daily portion to such an unfortunate; waft the rainclouds towards every land. Since the land has no foot, Thy munificence drives the rainclouds towards it in double measure; since the baby lacks the power to walk, its mother comes and pours its portion into its mouth. I would have a daily portion that comes suddenly, without fatigue, since the only effort I can make is the effort of begging.'

Such was his prayer for a long space of time, day unto night, all night unto morning. All the people laughed at his words, at his foolish hopes and fruitless labours.

'Amazing!' they said. 'What is this simpleton saying? Has somebody made him senseless with beng? Toil, pain and weariness is the way to get one's bread; God has given to every man a trade and a means to seek his living. Now the king and ruler and messenger of God is the prophet David, the all-accomplished; yet with all the pomp and pride that is in him, since the Friend has chosen him for His especial favours—

his miracles are innumerable and countless, the waves of his munificence surge incessantly; for what man since Adam even till today has possessed a voice like an organ, so that whenever he preaches he causes men to die, two hundred men annihilated by his sweet voice? In that hour the lion and the deer congregate together, heedless one of the other, to listen to his exhortation; the mountains and the birds chant in harmony with his voice, both are his confidants when he calls unto God. These and a hundred times as many miracles are his; the light of his countenance is both transcendent and immanent—yet with all this majesty, God must have made his daily bread to be bound up with seeking and searching, since without the weaving of coats of mail and no small labour his daily bread does not come to him, all-triumphant as he is. Yet so God-forsaken a malingerer, a stinking ruffian, an outcast from heaven, such a backslider wishes immediately, without trading, to fill his pockets with profit! Idiot that he is, he comes here boldly and says, "I will climb up to the sky without a ladder".'

This one would say to him mockingly, 'Go and get it! Your daily bread has arrived. Here comes the messenger of glad tidings!'

That one would laugh, 'Give us some of your present too, viceroy of the village!'

But for all the taunting and ridicule of the people he diminished in no wise his prayers and fawning, so that he became famous and renowned in the city as the man who looked for cheese in an empty bag. That beggar became proverbial for stupidity, yet he would never give up his solicitation.

Then one day suddenly at breakfast-time just as he was uttering this prayer, with sobbing and sighs, suddenly a cow ran into his house, butting with her horns and breaking the bolt and key. Boldly the cow rushed into the house; the man leaped forward and tied her legs, then straightway he cut the cow's throat without a moment's pause, without reflection, without mercy. Having cut her head off he went to the butcher so as to strip off her hide in right good haste.

'Hey,' shouted the owner of the cow, catching sight of him. 'You to whose unjustness my cow has fallen a victim, hey! Tell me, why did you kill my cow, you fool, you pickpocket! Play the game!'

'I was just asking God for my daily bread,' the man answered. 'I was dedicating all my thoughts to that entreaty. My prayer of old was answered by God. The cow was sent as my daily bread. So I killed her. There is my answer.'

The owner of the cow seized him angrily by the collar; unable to bear any more, he punched him several times in the face. Then he dragged him off to the prophet David.

'Come on, you crack-brained, crazy criminal!' he cried. 'Drop this stupid argument, you fraud; let your brain work, come to your senses! What was that you were saying? What do you say your prayer was? Do not mock my head and beard and your own, you wanton!'

'I have offered up many prayers to God,' said the other. 'I have sweated much blood at this supplication and now I am sure that my prayer has been answered. So go bang your head against a wall, you profaner!'

'Hey, gather round, Muslims!' shouted the owner of the cow. 'Just listen to the rubbish and gibberish this idiot is speaking! For God's sake, Muslims, how should a prayer make my property his? If such were the case, the whole world would carry off one another's belongings by force—by means of a single prayer! If such were the case, blind beggars would have become eminences and princes. Day and night they are praying and praising God, humbly entreating God and saying, "Give unto us, O God! Unless Thou givest, certainly no one will give us aught. Opener Thou to all who knock, open the bolt of Thy bounty!" It is by prayer and supplication that blind men earn their living, yet all they get in the way of a gift is a crust of bread.'

'This Muslim speaks the truth,' the people said. 'This prayer-monger is a seeker after injustice. How indeed should this prayer be a means to the acquisition of property? When did the religious law recognize this as a title? A thing becomes your property either by sale, or donation, or bequest, or gift, or something of this kind. In what tome is this new law to be found? Give him back his cow, you, or go to gaol!'

The beggar was turning his face to heaven.

'None but Thou knows the truth of my case! Thou Thyself didst put that prayer into my heart; Thou didst kindle in my heart a hundred hopes. Not at random was I uttering that prayer; like Joseph I had dreamed dreams. That cheat has called me blind for committing this crime. God, what a devilish inference he has made! When have I ever prayed after the fashion of the blind? When have I begged of anyone save the Creator? The blind man in his ignorance has hope of God's creatures; I have hope of Thee, for by Thee all difficulties are made easy. Blind blunderer himself—he numbered me among the blind; he has not seen my soul's supplication and my sincere devotion. This blindness of mine is the blindness of love; love, said the Prophet, makes a man blind and deaf. I am blind indeed—to all other than God, by whom I see: tell me, is not this what love demands? Thou, God, who art seeing, hold me not to be one of the blind; O Axis, I revolve about the hub of Thy grace. Just as to Joseph the veracious Thou didst show a dream and it became a support to him, even so Thy grace has shown me a dream; that unending prayer of mine was no idle play. Thy creatures know not my secret thoughts, and so they deem my words to be drivel, and they have good right so to do; for who knows the secret of the Unseen, save the Knower of all secrets, the Veiler of all faults?'

'Turn your face to me and tell me the truth!' said his ad-versary. 'Why have you turned your face to heaven, nuncle? You are a practised fraud, an accomplished liar; you brag of love and of being near to God. Since you are dead in your inward heart, with what sort of cheek have you turned your face towards the heavens?'

Thereat a great clamour arose in the city. The good Muslim laid his face upon the ground.

'O God, put not Thy servant to shame,' he cried. 'If I am evil, yet do not disclose my secret. Thou knowest the truth, aye, and the long nights know it through which I was calling to Thee with a hundred supplications. What though my supplications are of no account in the sight of men, in Thy sight they are even as a shining lamp.'

'Hey!' cried the prophet David, appearing on the scene. 'What is going on here? What is it all about?'

'Justice, prophet of God!' called the plaintiff. 'My cow happened to stray into his house, and he killed it. Ask him why he killed my cow. Demand an explanation of the matter.'

'Speak, father of nobility!' David said to the beggar. 'How did you come to destroy the property of this gentleman? Be careful, do not speak at random! Produce your plea, so that this claim and cause may be settled once and for all.'

'David,' said the beggar, 'for seven long years I prayed and petitioned night and day. This is what I was seeking from God: "O God, I desire daily bread that shall be lawful, and without labour." Men and women are apprised of my lament; the children can well describe the matter exactly. Ask anyone you like for information about this; there is no need for torture or duress, anyone will tell you. Question the people both in public and secretly what this poor beggar with the ragged gown used to say. After all this praying and making lamentation, suddenly I saw a cow in my very house. My eyes were darkened, not on account of the fine banquet but for joy that my long entreaty had been accepted. I killed the cow, that I might give alms in thankfulness because the Knower of all things unseen had heard my prayer.'

'Expunge those words,' said David. 'Enter a legal plea in this action. Do you think it proper that without a regular plea I should establish an invalid precedent in the city? Who gave you the cow? Did you buy it? Did you inherit it? On what grounds do you take the crop? Are you the farmer? Know, good man, that the acquiring of property is like agriculture— unless you sow the land, the produce does not belong to you. What you sow, that you reap; that belongs to you. Otherwise this charge of injustice is proved against you. Go, give the good Muslim his money; do not twist your words. Go, look for a loan and pay him his due; do not seek to do wrong.'

'King, you are saying to me exactly what the oppressors say.'

So the beggar answered; then he prostrated himself.

'O Thou,' he prayed, 'who knowest the inward fire, kindle that flame in the heart of David. Plant in his heart that which Thou didst secretly cast into my heart, O my Benefactor!'

So saying, he began to weep piteously so that David's heart was moved within him.

'Plaintiff,' he said to the man demanding redress for his cow, 'grant me today a respite. Do not press your complaint. Give me the time to go into solitude to pray, that I may ask the Knower of all mysteries about these matters. It is my habit in prayer so to turn to God according to the Prophet's saying, "My delight is in the appointed prayers." Then the window of my soul is opened, and the Book of God comes to me out of the realm of purity, without intermediary. The Book, the Rain, the Light fall through my window, out of my origin, into the house of my heart. Like the sun, I am then utterly plunged in Light; I cannot differentiate between myself and the Light. My going to prayer and to that solitude is that I may teach the people the Way.'

David continued speaking after this fashion; the understanding of the people was about to be burned up. Then some one pulled his collar from behind.

'I have no doubt for my part as to the Unity of God.'

Hearing these words, he came to himself and cut short his discourse, closed his lips and set forth for the place where he would be alone. He shut the door and hastened to the prayer-niche, to the prayer that is answered by God. God made revelation to him wholly and completely; he became apprised of who merited the punishment.

On the following day all the disputants came and formed ranks before David the prophet. The matters at issue came up once again; the plaintiff plunged immediately into violent vituperation.

'Silence!' cried David. 'Go, give up your claim, acquit this good Muslim of malfeasance touching your cow. Since God has covered your sin, young man, go, say no more, acknowledge your due to God who veils men's sins.'

'Ah, woe is me!' cried the plaintiff. 'What judgment, what justice is this? Do you propose to establish a new law on my account? The fame of your equity has gone so far abroad that earth and heaven too are fragrant with the fame of it. Even blind dogs have never suffered such injustice. Rock and mountain are suddenly riven asunder by this inequity.'

After this manner he reviled David before all the people: 'Oyez! Oyez! Now is the time of injustice!'

'Refractory wretch!' David then said. 'Give all your wealth to him immediately, otherwise your position will become very precarious. I have spoken to you thus, so that your wrong-doing may not be made manifest through him.'

The plaintiff scattered dust on his head and rent his clothes.
'Every moment you pile one wrong upon another,' he
shouted.

He continued this sort of abuse for another while. Then
David summoned him to his presence again.

'Blind of fortune, since it was not your fortune to get off
lightly,' said David, 'little by little your wrongdoing has
come to light. You drop your ordure, then sit yourself down
on the seat of honour. Shavings and straw would be too good
for a donkey like you. Depart! Your children and your wife
have become his slaves. Say no more!'

The plaintiff dashed stones against his breast with both his
hands and ran up and down dale in his witlessness. The people
also started to reproach David, being unaware of the hidden
motives of the plaintiff's action.

'Prophet elect, so loving towards us,' that party cried,
turning their faces to David, 'this is unworthy of you. This is a
patent injustice, visiting your wrath on an innocent man for
nothing.'

'Friends,' said David, 'the time has come for his hidden
secret to be revealed. Arise all of you and let us go forth, that
we may become apprised of that hidden secret. In such and
such a plain there stands a great tree, its branches numerous
and dense and intertwining. Very firm are its tabernacle and
its tent-pegs, and the stench of blood is coming to me from
its roots. Blood has been spilled at the base of that fair tree;
this misbegotten wretch has killed his master. God's clemency
has hidden the crime till now; at last, thanks to the ingratitude
of that pimp, it has come to light. Never for a single day has he
looked upon his master's family, not even on New Year's Day
nor at the other festive seasons. He never sought to relieve the
destitute children with so much as a morsel, neither did he
remember his obligations of aforetime. And now, for the sake
of one cow, the accursed wretch is striking to the ground his
master's child. He himself has lifted the veil from his crime;
otherwise God would have concealed his guilt.'

When they went out towards the tree David commanded
them to tie the man's hands behind him.

'Now I will disclose the crime he committed, that I may
plant the banner of justice in the field. Dog,' he turned to the

prisoner, 'you killed this man's grandfather. You, a slave, in this manner became a master. You killed your master, and plundered his wealth. God has made manifest what transpired with him. That wife of yours was his handmaid; she acted unjustly towards the selfsame master. Whatever children she bore to him, whether female or male, all of them, from first to last, are the property of his heir. You are a slave; your earnings and goods are his property. You demanded the Law: take the Law! Now go. It is well. You slew your master by violence and miserably; it was on this very spot that your master begged for mercy. You hurriedly hid the knife under the soil on account of the terrible phantom you beheld. See, here is his head together with the knife, under the soil. Dig away the soil, like this! The name of this dog is even written on the knife; how hurtfully and treacherously he treated his master!'

They did accordingly. When they cleft the soil they found in the earth the knife and the head. A great howl thereupon went up from the people; every man cut the zone of unbelief away from his waist.

'Come, you claimant of justice!' David then cried. 'Take your justice, with your blackened face!'

He ordered retaliation—that he should be slain with the selfsame knife. How should his cunning deliver him from the knowledge of God? Though the clemency of God performs many favours, yet when the sinner transgresses all bounds God exposes him.

When the mystery of that murderer's affairs had been unveiled, the miracles wrought by David became doubly evident. All the people came bare of head and bowed their heads to the ground in prostration.

'We have all been as blind from birth,' they exclaimed. 'Yet we have seen you work a hundred kinds of marvels. Now this miracle is more potent than all before it. Truly you bestow life that endures eternally.'

This is indeed the soul of all miracles, that it bestows eternal life upon the dead soul. The wrongdoer was killed, and the whole world became alive; every one became anew a true servant of God.

76

The schoolboys who made their teacher think he was ill

SOME boys in a certain school, having suffered much weari-ness and exertion at the hands of their master, took counsel together how they might hinder the work and compel the teacher to let them free.

'What can we do?' they debated. 'He is never overtaken by any illness that would make him absent himself for a few days, so that we might escape out of this prison, these res-trictions and all this work. Why, he is as immovable as a granite rock!'

The cleverest of the boys hit upon a plan. He would say, 'Teacher, how is it you are so pale? I hope nothing is wrong with you. Your colour is not at all normal; it must be the effect of the foetid air, or of fever.'

The boy explained his plan further. 'He will begin to ima-gine things a bit when I say that. You, brother, help me by saying the same sort of thing. As soon as you enter the door of the school, say, "I hope you are feeling well, teacher." That will set his imagination working a little more; imagination soon drives even the most reasonable man insane. After us, let a third, fourth and fifth boy express his sorrow and sym-pathy in like manner. When thirty boys in succession have unanimously told the same story, it will get fixed in his mind.'

'Congratulations, you clever chap!' all the boys exclaimed. 'May your luck always rest on the special favour of God!'

They engaged together in a firm covenant that not one of the gang should vary the formula. Then the ringleader made them all take an oath, so that no telltale should split on what was towards.

Next day the boys left home for school with this one thought in mind. They all stood outside, waiting for the ringleader to go in first, since he was the originator of the idea. He entered and saluted the master.

'Good day, sir! I hope all is well with you. Your face is quite pale.'

'There is nothing wrong with me,' the teacher answered. 'Go and sit down at once. Do not talk rubbish.'

Though he denied it, the dust of evil fancy suddenly struck into his heart a little. Another boy entered and spoke likewise; that fancy grew a little greater. The others went on in the same vein, till his fancy gained strength and he found himself wondering a good deal about his state of health. He became quite unnerved by fancy and fear; he jumped up from his seat and dragged his cloak after him, furious with his wife.

'Her love for me must be very feeble, with me in this state, and not so much as a "How are you feeling?" from her. She did not even tell me about my colour. Clearly her purpose is to escape from the shame of being married to me! Drunk with her own beauty and fine feathers, she has not noticed how shattered I am, like a bowl that has fallen from a roof.'

Returning home, he opened the door brusquely, the boys meanwhile following in his wake.

'Is everything all right?' asked his wife. 'How is it you have come home so soon? I trust no evil may befall your goodly self.'

'Are you blind?' he shouted. 'Look at my colour and condition. Even strangers are sympathizing with my distress, while you in my own home out of hatred and hypocrisy do not see how I am all on fire.'

'My good man, there is nothing wrong with you,' his wife retorted. 'It is simply your baseless fancy and nonsensical idea.'

'Do you still persist in wrangling, you whore?' he screamed. 'Do you not see this change, this trembling that has come over me? If you have become blind and deaf, is that any fault of mine? And me so ill, and in such misery and distress.'

'My good man, I will fetch a mirror,' she said. 'Then you will realize that I am guilty of no crime.'

'To the devil with you and your mirror!' he shouted. 'You have always been hateful, malicious, vicious. Spread my bed at once, so that I may repose. My head is heavy.'

223

Still the wife hesitated. The husband yelled at her.

'Hurry up, hateful woman! That is just like you.'

The old woman brought the bedclothes and spread them out on the floor. She could not speak, though her heart was burning. She said to herself, 'If I speak, he will suspect me, and if I say nothing, things will get really serious. If I tell him the truth, he will at once imagine, "My wife is contriving to get the place to herself. She is driving me out of the house. She is plotting and deceiving for some wicked purpose".'

She made his bed, and the master fell down upon it, sighing and groaning all the time.

The boys meanwhile sat there, inwardly reciting their lesson with a hundred sorrows.

'We did all this, and still we are prisoners,' they thought. 'It was a rotten building, and we are rotten builders.'

'Admirable chaps,' said the clever boy presently, 'recite your lesson at the top of your voice.'

They started to recite.

'Lads,' he said, 'the noise we are making will really do the master mischief. His headache will be made worse by our noise. Is it worth while that he should suffer for the sake of a few pennies?'

'What he is saying is perfectly true,' said the master. 'Off with you! My headache is worse. Clear out!'

'Noble sir,' they said with a bow, 'may suffering and danger be far from you!'

With that they skipped off to their homes, like birds hungry for grain. Their mothers became very angry.

'What, today a schoolday, and you do nothing but play?'

'Stop, mother,' each of them said in self-defence. 'The sin is not ours. It is not our fault. By the decree of Heaven our master has fallen sick and ill and is suffering.'

'It is a trick and a lie,' the mothers said. 'You produce a hundred lies, all out of greed for wheys. In the morning we will go and see the master, so as to get at the bottom of your trick.'

'In Allah's name, go!' the boys replied. 'Find out for yourselves whether we are lying or telling the truth.'

Next morning the mothers came and found the master in bed, like someone seriously ill. He was sweating under a pile

224

of blankets; his head was wrapped, his face was buried under the quilt; he was sighing in a whisper.

'Only God can help him now!' they all began to mutter. Then to him—'We hope all will be well, master. Your poor headache—by your life, we had no idea it was so bad.'

'I had no idea of it, either,' the master replied. 'It was those sons of whores that made me aware. I did not notice it, being so wrapped up in my teaching. All the time such a heavy sickness was in me.'

When a man is busy in earnest he is entirely blind to his own pain. The body is like a garment; go, seek the wearer of the garment, do not lick the garment. You are made in such wise that without the body you possess another body; so do not dread the departure of the soul out of the body.

77

The prescient goldsmith

A CERTAIN man came to a goldsmith.

'Give me the scales,' he said. 'I want to weigh some gold.'

'Go away,' said the goldsmith. 'I do not have a sieve.'

'Give me the scales,' repeated the man. 'Have done with such jokes.'

'I do not have a broom in the shop,' said the goldsmith.

'Enough, enough!' said the man. 'No more of these jests. Give me the scales I am asking for. Do not make out you are deaf. Do not hop about in all directions.'

'I heard what you said,' said the goldsmith. 'I am not deaf. Do not get the idea that I am doddering. I heard all right. But you are a trembling old man. Your hand shakes, your body is not upright. That gold of yours moreover consists of the tiniest filings. Your hand shakes, and so the fragments of gold will spill. Then you will say, "Master, bring me a broom, so that I may hunt for my gold in the dust." When you sweep up you will gather dust along with your gold, then you will say, "I want a sieve, my hearty." I saw the end completely from the beginning. Get out of here and go somewhere else, and good day to you!'

From the beginning of the enterprise discern the end, that you may not repent upon the Day of Judgment.

78

The hermit who broke his vow

A DERVISH once dwelt in a mountainous place with solitude for his bedfellow and companion; he had grown weary of the breaths of men and women, since the soft zephyr of grace was wafting to him from the Creator.

Now upon that mountain grew many trees and fruits, many mountain pears, innumerable indeed.

'Lord,' the dervish declared, 'I have made covenant with Thee that so long as I live I will not pluck any of these. Excepting those fruits that the wind has caused to fall, I will not pluck any from the upstanding trees.'

For a while he kept faithful to his vow, until the trials of Destiny came upon him. For five successive days the wind caused not one pear to fall; so fierce was the fire of his hunger that endurance deserted him. He glimpsed several pears on a twig, but still he controlled himself with fortitude.

Then the wind came along and bent down the end of the branch, whetting his natural appetite to devour that fruit. Hunger, weakness and the power of Destiny's pull conspired to make the ascetic unfaithful to his vow. He became false to his vow and covenant, and plucked the fruit from the mountain pear. In that same moment God's chastisement descended on him, opening his eyes and tugging his ear.

Twenty thieves and more were mustered in that place dividing among themselves the goods thay had stolen. An informer had apprised the commissioner of police; the police officers fell upon them promptly. The prefect cut off the left foot and right hand of every one of them, and a great commotion arose. By mistake the ascetic's hand was also cut off; the prefect moreover was just about to amputate his foot. At that very moment a high-ranking officer came riding and shouted to the policeman.

'Dog, look what you are doing! This man is Shaikh So-and-so, one of the great saints of God. Why have you severed his hand?'

The policeman rent his uniform and went in haste to the commissioner, reporting the matter at once. The commissioner came barefoot, begging to be excused.

'I did not know,' he said. 'God is my witness. Pray absolve me of this abominable deed, noble saint and headman of the population of Paradise!'

'I know,' said the saint, 'the cause of this injury. I recognize my own sin. I broke the sanctity of God's oaths, therefore His judgment took away my right hand. I broke my covenant knowing it to be evil, so that that ill-omened audacity recoiled upon me. Governor, may my hand and my foot, my brain and my skin be offered in sacrifice to the Friend's decree! This was my destiny. I absolve you. You did not know. It was no fault of yours. He who knows all things knew this too; His command is absolute. Where is the strength to wrestle with God?'

Since the ascetic's hand had been cut off on account of his throat's gluttony, he closed the door of complaint. He became known amongst the people as the Amputated Shaikh; the calamities caused by his gullet made him famous by that name.

A visitor found him in his hut one day weaving a basket with both his hands.

'Enemy of your own life,' the shaikh addressed him, 'you have come poking your head into my hut. Why have you ventured in with such indecent haste?'

'Out of the excess of love and longing,' said the visitor.

The shaikh thereupon smiled.

'Come in now,' he said. 'But see that you keep this thing secret, noble sir. Till I die, tell this not unto any man, neither to a comrade, a loved friend or a worthless nobody.'

Thereafter other people peeping through his window became informed of how he was weaving.

'Thou, Creator, knowest the wisdom in this,' the saint cried. 'For all that I conceal my secret, Thou hast revealed it.'

Divine inspiration came to him, saying, 'There were a number of people who, on account of this affliction, were beginning to disbelieve in thee, saying, "Haply he was an impostor in the Way, so that God has exposed his shame amongst the brotherhood." I do not wish that that flock should become unbelievers and in their evil thoughts go into perdition. Therefore We manifested this miracle, by giving thee a hand at the time when thou art working, so that these luckless men with their real evil thoughts may not be repulsed from the Lord of Heaven. Aforetime indeed without such miracles I was giving thee consolation from My Self; this miracle I have given thee for their sake, and on that account I have committed to thee this lamp. Thou hast transcended the fear of bodily death and the scattering of the members. Dark thoughts of the scattering of head and foot have gone from thee; a shield right strong has come to thee, to ward off dark thoughts.'

79

The mule and the camel, on the soaring vision

THE mule said to the camel, 'My good companion, over hill and dale and on the narrow track never do you come a cropper. You go along merrily, while I am always coming a cropper like a lost soul. Every moment I am falling on my face, whether the place be dry or wet. Declare to me what the cause of this is, so that I may know how one must live.'

The camel said, 'My eye is clearer than yours; moreover it also looks always from on high. Whenever I come to the top of a high hill I espy prudently the end of the pass. Then too, God discloses to my eye every dip and rise of the road, so that I take every step with clear vision and escape from all stumbling and falling. You do not see so far as two or three steps ahead of you; you see the bait, but not the anguish of the snare.'

80

The shaikh who showed no sorrow at the death of his sons

ONCE upon a time there was a shaikh, a guide to men, a heavenly candle upon the face of the earth, as it were a prophet amongst the congregation, opener of the door to the garden of Paradise.

One morning his family said to him, 'Tell us, how is it, with your goodly character, that you are so hard-hearted. We are mourning, our backs bent double, for the death and loss of your sons. Why are you not weeping and lamenting? Is it that you have no compassion in your heart? Since you have no pity within you, what hope have we now of you? We are in hope of you, our guide, that you will not abandon us to perish. When the Throne is arrayed on the Resurrection Day, upon that cruel day you will be our intercessor; on such a merciless day and night we are hopeful of your beneficence. In that hour our hands will clutch your skirt, even in the moment when security remains not to any sinner.'

'Do not think,' said the shaikh to his wife, 'that I have not pity and love and a compassionate heart. I have compassion for all unbelievers, though the souls of them all be ungrateful for God's grace. Even for dogs I have compassion and forgiveness, saying, "Why should they be chastised with stones?" For the dog that bites I offer a prayer, saying, "O God, deliver him out of this evil disposition! Keep these dogs also mindful, that they may not be stoned by the people".'

'Since then you have compassion for all,' said his wife, 'going about this flock like a shepherd, how is it that you do not mourn for your own sons when Death, the cupper, has pierced them with his lancet? Since the witness to compassion is tears in the eyes, why are your eyes untouched by wetness and weeping?'

231

'Old lady,' he turned to his wife and said, 'the season of December is not like July. Whether they be all dead or living, when are they absent and hidden from the eye of the heart? Since I behold them distinctly before me, why should I lacerate my cheeks as you do? Though they are gone without the revolution of Time, yet still they are with me, playing around me. The occasion of weeping is parting or separation; I am united with my dear ones, I am embracing them. Other men behold their dear departed ones in sleep; I see them visibly even when I am awake. I hide myself from this world for a moment; I shake the leaves of sense-perception from the tree.'

Sense-perception, my friend, is captive to the intellect; know too that the intellect is captive to the spirit. The spirit frees the intellect's chained hand; the spirit tunes all the tangled chords.

The senses and thoughts are like weeds upon the clear water, covering the surface. The hand of the intellect sweeps aside those weeds; the water becomes manifest before the reason. When reason becomes your captain and master, the powerful senses submit to your mastery. Such a man, without being asleep, puts the senses to sleep so that the things unseen emerge from the world of the Soul. Even waking he dreams dreams; he opens even the gates of Heaven.

81

Buhlul and the dervish, on
absolute contentment

BUHLUL said to a certain dervish, 'How are you, dervish? Pray apprise me.'

The dervish answered, 'How should such a man be, according to whose desire the work of the world goes on eternally? —according to whose desire torrents and rivers flow, and the stars move after the manner that he wills; according to whose desire Life and Death, his officers, go from street to street. Wheresoever he wills he sends condolences; wheresoever he wills he bestows congratulations. The travellers on the Way proceed according to his pleasure; those that have lagged behind are fallen into his snare. No tooth flashes with laughter in all the world without the consent and command of him whose command is absolute.'

Buhlul said, 'King, you have spoken the truth; so it is. It is evident in your splendour and glorious mien. Truthful one, you are this and a hundred times as much; only explain this mystery to me, and expound it well, in such manner that the man of virtue and the trifler alike, when they hear it, may assent to it. When you discourse, explain the matter so that the understanding of the common folk may derive profit from it.'

The dervish answered, 'This much at all events is evident to the common folk, that the world is docile to the command of God. No leaf drops from a tree without the doom and ordinance of that Sultan of Fortune. No morsel proceeds from the mouth towards the gullet until God says to the morsel, "Enter!" Desire and inclination, the nose-ring of man— its movement obeys the command of the All-sufficient. In all the earths and all the heavens not an atom stirs, not a straw turns save by His eternal and absolute command. This cannot be expounded, and rashness is not good. Who may number completely the leaves of the trees? How shall the Infinite become submissive to speech? Yet hear this much: since every action that transpires only transpires by the command of the Creator, when the doom of God becomes the good pleasure of His servant, that servant becomes the willing slave of His command; not by his taking of pains himself, not for the sake of the reward and recompense, but because his very nature has become thus goodly. Not for himself does he wish for his life, nor to enjoy the life delectable; wherever the fore-eternal Command takes its course, living and dying are both one to him. He lives for God's sake, not for the sake of treasure; he dies for God's sake, not out of fear and pain. He keeps his faith in order to do God's will, not for the sake of Paradise and its trees and rivers; he has abandoned unbelief also for God's sake, not out of fear lest he should go into the Fire. His disposition is such from its origin, not as the result of discipline and conscious striving. He laughs at the very moment he sees God's pleasure; God's doom is sweet to him even as halva.'

82

The miracles of Daquqi

THAT man Daquqi had a fair frontispiece; he was a true lover of God, a worker of miracles, a lord of the spirit. He wandered through the earth as does the moon in heaven, and the spirits of all night-travellers gained illumination from him. He was loth to make his residence in any fixed place, rarely alighting in one village for as long as two days.

'If I dwell for two days in one house,' he said, 'I am fired with love for that dwelling-place. I am wary of the fascination of the dwelling-place: stir yourself, my soul, and travel to independence! I will not accustom my heart's nature to being in one place, so that it may be free of attachment in the hour of trial.'

By day he was on his travels, by night he was at his prayers; himself like a falcon, his eyes were fixed on the King. He was cut off from God's creatures, yet not out of ill-nature; he was in isolation from men and women, yet not out of dualist views. Indeed he was compassionate to all creatures, beneficial to them as water, an excellent intercessor, and his prayers were answered. He was a friendly refuge to good and wicked alike, better than a mother, more affectionate than a father.

With all his piety, his litanies and all-night prayers, he continually sought out the elect of God; his principal objective in travelling was that he might encounter, even for a moment, a privy servant of God.

'O God, make me an associate of Thy elect,' he would pray as he went along the road. 'O Lord, I am a slave to those whom my heart knows; my loins are girded, I am ready to serve them well. As for those whom I know not, O God of the soul, make them loving towards me, who am excluded from their presence.'

'Greatest and chief of men,' the Divine Presence would

answer him, 'what passion is this, what insatiable thirst? Thou hast My love; why seekest thou other? When God is with thee, how seekest thou man?'

'Lord, who knowest all secrets,' he would reply, 'Thou Thyself didst open in my heart the way of petition. If I am seated in the midst of the Sea, yet I have fixed my desire on the water in the pitcher. I am like David; I possess ninety ewes, yet the desire for my competitor's single ewe has arisen in me. Greed for Thy love is glory and grandeur, greed for aught besides Thee is infamy and ruin.'

Daquqi (God's mercy be upon him) said, 'A long space I travelled between God's twain horizons. Months and years I journeyed for love of the Moon, uninformed of the way, distraught in God.'

'Why do you go barefoot over thorns and stones?' someone asked him.

'I am bewildered and beside myself and confounded,' he replied.

'One day,' he continued, 'I was going along like one distraught with passion, seeking to see in man the radiance of the Beloved, seeking to see in a drop of water an ocean, a sun enfolded within a mote. The day was far spent and evening was at hand when I arrived on foot at a certain shore. Suddenly from afar I descried seven candles, and made haste along the shore towards them. The light of the flame of each of the candles mounted in beauty to the lofty reaches of heaven. I became amazed; even amazement became amazed; the waves of bewilderment passed over the head of my reason. "What manner of candles are these that He has lighted," I asked myself, "so that the eyes of His creatures are sewn up from seeing them?"

'Again I looked, and behold, the seven had become one, its light splitting the bosom of the sky. Then again that one became seven once more; my intoxication and bewilderment grew immense. There were between the candles communications such as transcend the range of my tongue and speech.

'I ran on further, wondering what thing those candles might be, surely a sign of the majesty of God. So I proceeded, out of myself, dumbfounded, deranged, till in the impetuousness of my haste I fell down. So I lay in the dust awhile, lost to sense and reason. Then I returned to my senses and rose up; as I strode, it was as though I had neither head nor feet. The seven candles seemed to my regard as seven men, their light ascending up to the azure roof. Before those lights the light of day was as dregs in a cup; by their intensity they were blotting out all other lights.

'Then each man took on the shape of a tree; their greenness was a delight to mine eye. So dense were their leaves that no bough was visible; the leaves too were lost in the abundance of the fruit. Each tree had lifted its boughs above the Lote-tree; the Lote-tree, said I? Indeed, they had reached beyond the Void. The root of each tree descended into the bottom depths of the earth, certainly lower than the Ox and the Fish. Their roots were even more smiling of face than the boughs; the reason was turned topsy-turvy by their shapes. Out of the fruit, that was splitting by main force, flashes of light leaped forth, like juice.

'More wonderful still, countless multitudes of people were passing by desert and plain beside them, gambling their lives in the desire for shade, fashioning parasols out of woollen gowns, not seeing the shade of those trees at all. Fie, fie, fie upon those twisted eyes! The wrath of God had sealed their eyes, so that they should see not the moon, but only the dim star Suha.

'From every tree was issuing the cry, "Come unto us, unhappy people!" The Divine jealousy thundered back to the trees, "We have bound their eyes. *No indeed, not a refuge!*" If any had said to them, "Come hither, that you seek happiness from these trees," they would all have answered, "This poor drunkard by the doom of Allah has become quite mad. The brain of this poor wretch through long melancholy and austerity has turned rotten, like an onion." And he that summoned them would have remained marvelling, "Lord, what is amiss? What is this veil, this misguidance blinding the people?"

'I, the fortunate one, pushed on forward. Once again those seven trees, all became one. Every moment they were becoming now seven, now one: picture the state I was in in my bewilderment!

'Then I beheld the trees engaged in prayer, drawn up in

237

ranks and duly mustered like the congregation; one tree in front like the Imam, the others standing behind him. Very marvellous to me was that standing, that kneeling, that prostrating of the trees. In that moment I remembered the words of God, "And the stars and the trees bow themselves." Inspiration came to me from God, saying, "Illumined one, wonderest thou still at what We work?"

'After a long while those trees became seven men, all seated in meditation for the sake of the One God. I kept rubbing my eyes, wondering who those seven lion-hearts might be and what place they had in the world. When I drew near them on the road, I hailed them alertly, and the company answered my salutation: "Greetings to thee, Daquqi, pride and crown of the noble!"

'I said to myself, "How then did they recognize me? Until this moment they never set eyes on me." Immediately they knew of my thoughts, and looked covertly at one another. Then they answered me with a smile, "Honoured sir, is this hidden from thee even now? How should the mystery of left and right be hidden from the heart bewildered in the presence of God?"

'I said to myself, "If they are open to receive the eternal realities, how are they apprised of names made up of letters in writing?" One of the seven replied, "If a name vanishes from the mind of a saint, know that that transpires out of absorption, not out of ignorance."

'Then the seven said, "We desire to follow behind thee, holy friend." I replied, "Surely. But wait a little, for I have certain complications involved in the revolution of Time. Wait until they are solved through holy companionships; it is by companionship that the grape grows from the earth. First, a pithy seed graciously consorted in solitude with the murky earth and effaced itself utterly in the earth, so that there remained to it neither scent nor colour, be it red or yellow. After that effacement its constriction ceased; it opened its wings, expanded, and speeded away. Inasmuch as it became selfless before its origin, the form departed, its real meaning was displayed."

'They nodded to signify, "Give heed! The command is thine." At their nodding so, a flame burst forth in my heart.

'When I had been contemplative awhile with that elect company, parted from my self, in that very hour my soul was delivered out of Time; for it is the passing hours that make the young man old.

'Then they cried, "Make haste, Daquqi! The hour of prayer is come. Stand forward! Unique one, come now, perform the twofold prayer, that Time may be adorned by thee. Clearsighted Imam, the leader in prayer must always be clearsighted." '

Daquqi made ready to act as Imam; he began to perform the ritual prayer on that shore, while that company were upstanding behind him—a goodly congregation, and a chosen Imam!

Suddenly he heard a cry for help coming from the sea, and he turned his eyes towards it. Amidst the waves he saw a ship, cruelly buffeted and in its hour of doom; night, and clouds, and mighty waves—triple darkness, and the dread of the whirlpool. A hurricane arose, ruthless as Azrae-l; the waves surged to left and right. The people in the ship were fordone with terror; shouts of woe rose amain. They beat their heads in lamentation; infidel and heretic, all had turned true believers, pouring out promises and vows to God with all their hearts, humbling themselves a hundredfold in that hour. Bareheaded they were as they bowed prostrate, men perverse who had never before turned their faces to Mecca. They had given up hope entirely of ever seeing again friends, uncles, fathers and mothers. In that moment ascetic and godless alike had become godfearing, even as the sinful man in the time of giving up the ghost.

When Daquqi beheld that commotion compassion surged in him, and his tears ran.

'Lord, consider not what they have wrought,' he cried. 'Take them by the hand, most noble King! Bring them back safe and sound to shore, O Thou whose hand extends over both sea and land! All-gracious, All-merciful, Thou the Eternal, pass over the wickedness of these wicked men. Thou who hast given, gratis, a hundred eyes and ears, and dispensed, without bribe, reason and understanding, who hast bestowed gifts on us before ever we merited, and who hast suffered from us all ingratitude and transgression; O most

Mighty One, Thou art able to pardon privily our great sins. We have burned ourselves through and through out of lust and avarice; even this prayer we have been taught by Thee. We beseech Thee in veneration for that Thou hast taught us to pray, and that Thou hast lighted a lamp to light us in so great darkness.'

Such was the prayer Daquqi uttered at that time, a prayer like the petition of true mothers. From his eyes tears were flowing; out of him, unconscious, this prayer mounted up to Heaven.

Daquqi continued his story. 'The ship was saved, and all turned out well. The prayer of that congregation too was completed. Then a murmur broke out amongst them. "Father, which of us is the meddlesome one?" Each one whispered to the other, hidden behind Daquqi's back. Each one said, "I did not make this invocation just now, neither outwardly nor inwardly." One of them said, "It would seem that our Imam here, moved by anguish, meddlesomely offered up a litany." Another answered, "O companion of certainty, to me too so it appears. He was the meddler; out of distress he set himself up against God, the Absolute, who chooses as He wills."

'When I glanced behind, to see what those noble ones were saying, I saw not one of them in his place; they had all departed from their place. They were neither to left nor to right, neither above nor below; my keen eye could not descry the company anywhere. They were pearls, you might say, that had turned into water; not a footprint, neither dust of their track showed in the desert. Into God's tabernacles they had all gone at that moment; into which meadow had that saintly flock departed? I remained in amazement, how God had concealed that company from my eyes.'

So they vanished from his eyes, even as when fish dive in a stream. Many years he continued to sorrow for them; many lifetimes he shed tears of yearning after them.

Daquqi of the streaming eyes, come, do not give up hope: seek, and seek ever! Seeking is the cornerstone of felicity. Fixing the heart on the goal ensures its attainment.

83

How Jesus fled from a fool

JESUS the son of Mary was fleeing to a mountain, just as though a lion wanted to shed his blood.

'Is all well?' asked a man, running after him. 'No one is after you. Why are you fleeing like a bird?'

Jesus continued to run with haste, so fast that out of his haste he gave the man no answer. The man pushed on after Jesus for one or two fields, then called to Jesus with extreme earnestness.

'To please God, halt one moment,' he cried. 'I have a problem regarding your flight. From whom are you fleeing hitherwards, noble one? No lion, no adversary is after you, no fear or peril.'

'I am fleeing from a fool,' answered Jesus. 'Go! I am saving myself; do not impede me.'

'But,' said the man, 'are you not that Messiah by whom the blind and the deaf are made whole?'

'Yes,' said Jesus.

'Are you not that King,' said the other, 'in whose keeping are all the spells of the world unseen? When you recite those spells over a dead man, leaps he not up like a lion that has caught his prey?'

'Yes, I am he,' said Jesus.

'Do you not make birds out of clay, beauteous one?' asked the other.

'Yes,' answered Jesus.

'Then, pure Spirit,' said the man, 'seeing that you do whatsoever you will, of whom are you afraid? With such proof, who is there in all the world who would not be among your slaves?'

'By the holy Essence of God,' said Jesus, 'who fashioned forth the body and created the soul aforetime, by the sanctity of His pure Essence and Attributes, with rapturous love for whom Heaven itself is possessed, the spells and the Name Most Great which I chanted over the deaf and the blind were of good effect. I recited them over the rocky mountain and it was split, rending upon itself its mantle even to the navel. I chanted them over the dead body and it was quickened; I chanted them over nonentity and it became entity. I chanted them lovingly over the heart of the fool a myriad times, but it proved no cure; he became hard rock and did not change from that character; he became sand out of which no herb grows.'

'What then is the wisdom,' the man asked, 'that in the former cases God's Name bore profit, whereas in the latter it had no advantage? Deafness and blindness are a disease, foolishness is also a disease; why did God's Name prove a cure for the former and none for the latter?'

'The disease of foolishness is the wrath of God,' said Jesus. 'Sickness and blindness are not wrath; they are a proving.'

Flee from fools as Jesus fled. Association with fools has shed how much blood! Little by little the air steals away water; even so the fool too steals away religion from you.

84

The story of the people of Saba, in illustration of the foregoing

I AM reminded of the story of the people of Saba, how their refreshing zephyr was turned into pestilence by the utterance of fools.

Saba was like that huge, huge city which you hear mentioned by children in their fairy-tales. Children tell fairy-tales, but wrapped up in their stories is much mystery and wisdom. They say foolish things in their legends: search for the treasure in every ruin.

Once upon a time there was a huge, enormous city, only its size was no more than the size of a saucer. Very huge it was, very wide and very long, really tremendous, tremendous as an onion. The people of the ten townships were gathered together in it, but all together they were three bodies with unwashed faces. It was crowded with men and women innumerable, but all together they were three beggarly idiots.

One of the three was far-sighted and blind of eye—blind to Solomon, but he could see the leg of the ant. The second was very keen of hearing and stone-deaf—a treasure containing not a grain of gold. The third was bare and naked, you could see everything, but the skirts of his clothes were long.

The blind man said, 'See, an army is arriving! I see what people they are, and how many.'

The deaf man said, 'Yes, I heard their voices, what they are saying openly and in secret.'

The naked man said, 'I am afraid they will cut off some of my long skirt.'

The blind man said, 'See, they have come near! Up, let us flee before they beat and bind us!'

The deaf man said, 'Yes, the hubbub gets nearer. Hurry, my friends!'

The naked man said, 'Alas, they will covet my skirt and cut it, and I have no protection.'

They left the city and came without. In the flight they entered a village, and in that village they found a fat bird, only it was skinny with not an atom of flesh on it—a shrivelled, dead bird, its bones thin as threads through being pecked by crows. They set to and devoured it as a lion devours its prey; they ate till each was as full as an elephant. All three ate of it and became very fat, they became like three huge and mighty elephants; so fat did each of those three lads become that he was far too stout to be contained in the world. Despite their tremendous size and bloated bodies, they slipped through a crack in the door and were off again.

The people of Saba were fundamentally evil; they shied away from the means of encountering God. God gave them so many farms and orchards and meadows, left and right, to entertain themselves withal. The ripe fruit was dropping in such abundance that it choked the road, and nobody could pass. The scatter of the fruit blocked the way completely; the wayfarer marvelled at the abundance of the fruit. In their groves a basket on the head would be filled unasked-for by the tumbling of the fruit. No hand, but the breeze would scatter the fruit; many skirts would be filled by that fruit. Huge clusters hanging low would strike the head and face of the passer-by.

So abundant was the gold that even the man who stoked the public baths might have tied a golden belt round his waist. The dogs would trample buttered scones underfoot; the desert wolf would get indigestion from the rich food. City and village were safe from thieves and wolves; the goat was not afraid even of the ravening wolf.

Thirteen prophets came to that place, all eager to guide those who had lost the way.

'Lo, the blessing has increased,' they cried. 'Where is gratitude? If the steed of thanksgiving slumbers, stir it on! Reason argues the obligation of giving thanks to the Benefactor, else the door of wrath everlasting will be opened. Give heed! Behold the munificence of God: would any but God be satisfied with a single thanksgiving for blessings such as these?'

244

'The ghoul has snatched away our thanksgiving,' the people answered. 'We have become weary of thanksgiving and of blessing alike. We have become so worn out with bounty that we find no pleasure anymore in devotion or in sin. We have no desire for blessings and orchards; we have no desire for amusements and leisure.'

'There is a sickness in your hearts,' the prophets said, 'that has produced a blight in your natural gratitude. Thereby the blessing is altogether turned into sickness. Do tasty morsels give strength to the sick? So many sweet things have come before you, unregenerate sinner, and they have all turned sour; their purity has become defiled. You have come to be an enemy to these sweets; whatever you laid your hand upon has become sour. Whosoever was in truth your familiar and friend became mean and contemptible in your sight; whosoever may be a stranger to you likewise is mighty and mightily worshipful in your eyes. This too is the effect of that sickness; its poison permeates all associated with it. You must speedily shake off that sickness which will make sugar to appear as dung. Every sweet that comes to you turns sour; if the Water of Life itself should arrive, it would turn to fire. That quality is the alchemy of death and disaster, converting your life at last to death.

'Many a food there was whereby your heart was revived, but when it entered your body it putrified. Many a beloved one was hunted by you with all blandishments, but when he became your prey you accounted him contemptible. When intellect with intellect sincerely becomes familiar, every moment that passes their loyalty increases; when carnal soul becomes familiar with base carnal soul, know for certain that from moment to moment their friendship diminishes, for that carnal soul hovers around sickness and very soon corrupts the acquaintance. If you do not desire your friend to turn away from you tomorrow, make friends with the intelligent and with intellect.

'Since you are sick of the simoom of the carnal soul, whatever you take you infect with the same disease. If you take a gem, it turns into a common stone; if you take a heart's affection, it converts to hostility. If you take a fine and original saying, after you have comprehended it it becomes vapid and

245

coarse: "I have heard this times enough; it is old stuff; tell me something different, my trusty." Let that something different be new and never said before, by tomorrow you will have become sick and tired of it.

'Get rid of the sickness: once the sickness is rooted out every ancient tale will become new to you. The old tale will bring forth new leaves; the old tale will cause a hundred clusters to blossom out of the ditch.

'We are the true physicians, the disciples of God; the Red Sea beheld us and clave apart. The natural physicians are different, for they look into the heart by way of the pulse. We look well into the heart without any intermediary; through intuition we stand on a high vantage-point. The others are the physicians of food and fruit; by them the animal soul is made strong. We are the physicians of deeds and words; our inspirer is the ray of the light of the Most High, so that we know that such and such an act will benefit you while such and such an act will cut you off from the Way; that such and such a saying will lead you aright, while such and such a saying will bring suffering upon you. To the other physicians urine provides the proof; our proof is the inspiration of the Almighty. We do not look for a fee from anyone; our fee comes from a Holy Place. Come hither, attend, ye that have sickness incurable! We are a medicine successive for them that are sick.'

'Gang of impostors,' the people cried out, 'where is the evidence of your medical knowledge and beneficialness? Since you are bound up with the same sleep and food as we, grazing the same pasture, trapped likewise in this snare of earth and water, how should you be huntsmen of the simurgh of the heart? It is love of office and leadership that induces a man to count himself among the prophets. We will not stuff our ears with such bragging and lies, and so fall into deception.'

'Your attitude springs from that old sickness,' answered the prophets. 'The root of your blindness is the veil over your vision. You have heard our summons, and yet you do not see this jewel in our hands. This jewel is a test for the people; we turn it round about before their eyes. Any man who says, "Where is the evidence?" his words are evidence that he does not see the jewel, being the prisoner of blindness.'

'All this is fraud and humbug,' said the people. 'How should God appoint as His deputy Tom, Dick and Harry? Every king's messenger must be of the king's own kind; where are clay and water in comparison with the Creator of the skies? Have we eaten ass's brain, that we should deem a gnat like you to be the confidant of the phoenix? The phoenix and the gnat, clay and God—what is the comparison between between them? Where stands the mote in relation to the sun in heaven? What relationship is this, what connexion, that it should enter into any mind and brain?

'It is like what a hare once said. "I am the moon's ambassador," said the hare, "the mate of the moon."

'For all the beasts of the chase were in sore straits because of a herd of elephants inhabiting the crystal-clear spring. All were suffering deprivation, and out of fear kept far from the spring. Since their strength was inferior, they concocted a plot. From the top of the mountain the old hare shouted to the elephants on the first night of the new moon, "Come on the fourteenth, king elephant, so that you may find within the spring the proof of what I say. King elephant, I am the ambassador: stand at attention! Ambassadors are immune from arrest and hindrance and violence. The moon says, 'Elephants, be gone! The spring is mine; go aside from it, else I will blind you. I have warned you of your trespass; whatever follows is not my responsibility. Leave this spring and be gone, that you may be safe from the striking of the moon's sword.' The token of my veracity is that in the spring the moon will be all a-quiver on account of the elephant seeking water. Present yourself on such and such a night, king elephant, that you may find within the spring the proof of what I say."

'When seven plus eight nights of the month had passed the king elephant came to lap at the spring. When he put his trunk in the water, the water quivered and the moon likewise quivered. The elephant, seeing the moon a-quiver in the spring, believed what the hare had told him.

'Gang, we are not gullible elephants to be terrified when the moon goes a-quiver.'

'Alas!' cried the prophets. 'Our spiritual counsel has only made your bonds firmer, you fools! Alack, in the disease from which you suffer the remedy has turned into the poison of wrath wringing from you your souls. This lamp has increased the darkness of those eyes, God having set over them the veil of anger. What leadership forsooth should we crave from you, seeing that our leadership is greater than the heavens?'

'Good counsellors, what you have said is enough,' said the people, 'if there is anyone in this village who will heed you. God has fastened a lock upon our hearts; no man can win against the Creator. This is the picture the Artist has made of of us, and it will not be altered by any amount of talking. Tell the pebble for a hundred years, ''Become a ruby''; tell the old for a hundred years, ''Become new''; tell the earth, ''Take on the qualities of water''; tell water, ''Become honey or milk''—vain will be your talking: He is the Creator of the heavens and the celestials, He is the Creator of water and dust and the terrestrials. He gave to the heavens circular motion and purity, to water and clay darkness and generation and corruption; how can the heavens choose for themselves turbidity, or how can water and clay purchase clarity? He has allotted a certain way for every one; how shall a mountain by striving become as a straw?'

'That is so,' said the prophets. 'He has created certain qualities of which it is impossible to get rid; and He has created also accidental qualities—thus, a well-hated man may become well-pleasing. Say to a stone, ''Become gold,'' and you waste your breath; say to copper, ''Become gold,'' and a way exists. Say to sand, ''Become clay,'' and it is incapable of that; say to earth, ''Become clay,'' and that is possible. He has given distempers for which there is no remedy, such as lameness, having a flat nose, and blindness; He has also given distempers for which there is a remedy, such as facial palsy and the headache. These medicines He has fashioned for the sake of restoring concord; these distempers and medicines are not at random. On the contrary, most distempers have a remedy; if you seek it earnestly it will come to hand.'

'Gang,' replied the people, 'this distemper of ours is not of the kind that is susceptible of cure. Many long years you have uttered spells and counsels like these, and our bonds have become firmer every moment as a result. If this disease were amenable to cure, surely by now a particle of relief would have been procured. In cases of hepatitis water does not penetrate the liver; though the sufferer should drink up the sea, it would pass somewhere else; inevitably the hands and feet swell up, and all that intake of water does not overcome the thirst.'

'Despair is wicked,' the prophets rejoined. 'God's grace and compassion are infinite. It is not seemly to despair of such a Benefactor: hold fast to the saddle-strap of this compassion. Many a situation is difficult at the beginning, but after a while it is resolved and the hardship passes. After despair many hopes emerge; after darkness many suns arise. I concede that you have become hard as stone, that you have fastened locks upon your ears and hearts; it is no affair of ours whether we are accepted by you, our affair is to resign ourselves to God and to do His bidding. He has commanded us to perform this service; this spokesmanship is not of ourselves. We possess life only to obey His command; if He bids us sow in sand, we sow in sand. The prophet's soul has no friend but God; it is no affair of his whether he is received or rejected by men. The reward for delivering His messages comes from Him; we have become hard and hostile of feature for the sake of the Friend. We are not weary of this portal of God, that we should halt anywhere because the road is far.

'That man is truly downcast of heart and weary who languishes in prison, being parted from the Friend. Our Darling and only Desired is here with us; our souls give thanks in the scatter of His mercy. In our hearts anemones and roses bloom; age and decay cannot enter our garden. We are forever fresh and young and graceful, tender and sweet, laughing and gay. To us a hundred years are the same as one hour; length and shortness of time are dissevered from us. Such length and shortness are in bodies only; where are length and shortness in relation to the soul? The three hundred years and nine that those Men of the Cave dwelt in darkness seemed to them as one day passed without grief and sorrow; it appeared to them as only one day, when at last their spirits returned out of non-existence into their bodies. When there is neither day nor night, month nor year, how should there be satiety and old age and weariness? Naughted to self in the rose-garden of non-existence, we are drunk of the goblet of the grace of God. What knows he of that joy who has never tasted that cup?

How should the dung-beetle ever imagine the fragrance of the rose? God's grace is inconceivable; were it conceivable, then like all things that are conceived it would become non-existent. How should Hell imagine Paradise? Does a lovely countenance radiate from a hideous swine? Give heed, do not cut your own throat! Contemptible one, beware when such a morsel has reached your mouth! We have endured to the end the ways of tribulation; we have made easy the way for our own people.'

'If you bring luck to yourselves,' said the people, 'to us you are ill-omened; we oppose you and reject you. Our souls were carefree; you have cast us into grief and trouble. The delightful solidarity and concord that obtained between us have been converted into a hundred divisions, thanks to your evil presage. We were parrots cracking sugar for dessert; you have turned us into birds meditating upon death. Wherever there is a tale scattering gloom, wherever there is an ugly rumour, wherever in the world there is an evil presage, wherever there is a monstrous metamorphosis, a dreadful punishment, a terrible taking to task, all these are incorporated into the parable of your story and your presage. You have a positive appetite for provoking gloom.'

'The hideous evil presage,' retorted the prophets, 'is reinforced from within your souls. If you should be asleep in a hazardous place and a dragon stalks you from near at hand—if a well-disposed person apprises you of the danger, saying, "Jump up quickly, or the dragon will devour you"; if you reply, "Why do you utter an evil presage?" "What presage?" he will answer. "Jump up, and see in broad daylight! I will rescue you myself from the midst of the evil presage. I will take you home." Such a man, who apprises you with hidden things, is the prophet who has seen what the worldlings have not seen. If a doctor says to you, "Do not eat unripe grapes, the sickness they cause leads to serious trouble," and if you reply, "Why do you utter an evil presage?" then you are making out your good counsellor to be a criminal. If an astrologer says to you, "Do not by any means embark on such an enterprise today," though you see the falseness of the star-man a hundred ways, let him be right once or twice and you will swear by him. Our stars are never at variance with the truth: how has their veracity remained hidden from you? The doctor and the astrologer apprise you out of surmise; we apprise you out of direct vision. We descry the smoke and the fire already rushing upon the unbelievers from afar. Yet you say, ''Be silent, speak not so! Words of evil presage do us no good at all.''

'How long,' said the prophets in their hearts, 'shall we continue to give exhortation and counsel to this one and that one? How long shall we misguidedly hammer upon cold iron? How long shall we go on blowing into a cage?'

85

The prince and the slave, each a captive

A CERTAIN prince desired early one morning to go to the baths. He shouted to his slave, 'Sunqur, bestir yourself! Get the basin, the towel and the clay from Altun, my indispensable one, that we may go to the baths.'

Sunqur at once seized the basin and a fine towel, and set off with his master. On the way there was a mosque, and the sound of the congregation at prayer came clearly to Sunqur's ears.

Now Sunqur was exceedingly fond of prayer. So he said, 'Indulgent master, wait patiently awhile on this bench here, so that I may do my duty, pray and recite the Credo.'

Presently the Imam and the people came out, having finished the prayers and the litanies. Sunqur remained in the mosque till nearly forenoon. The prince waited for him some time.

Then the prince called out, 'Sunqur, why do you not come out?'

Sunqur replied, 'Accomplished master, He will not let me. Be patient. See, I am coming, light of my eyes! I am not inattentive. I hear and obey.'

Seven times the prince contained himself, and then shouted. At last he could not endure the slave's prevarications any longer. It was always the same answer—'He will not let me come out yet, your reverence.'

'Why,' shouted the prince, 'no one is left in the mosque. Who is keeping you back there? Who is restraining you?'

'The same One who has chained you outside,' Sunqur answered, 'has chained me inside. He will not let you in, and He will not let me out. The One who will not let you set foot in this direction has chained the foot of your slave so that he cannot stir from here.'

86

The miracle of the napkin

IT is related that a certain man once enjoyed the hospitality of Anas son of Malik. He afterwards reported that at the end of the meal Anas noticed that the napkin was yellow, dirty and stained. He said to the servant-girl, 'Throw it into the oven at once!'

The prudent girl immediately threw the napkin into the oven, which was full of fire. All the guests were astonished at that, expecting to see the smoke of the burning napkin. After a little while she took it out of the oven, clean and white; the dirty marks had vanished.

'Noble companion of the Prophet,' the people cried, 'how is it that it did not burn? How did it become cleansed too?'

Anas replied, 'Because the Chosen Prophet wiped his hands and mouth in this napkin.'

The guests afterwards questioned the servant-girl.

'Will you not tell us how you felt about this? How did you come to throw the napkin in the oven so promptly when he told you to? I take it your master knew its miraculous properties; but why, mistress, did you throw such a precious napkin into the fire?'

'I have confidence in the reverend ones,' she answered. 'I do not despair of their beneficence. What is a mere strip of linen? If he told me to go without compunction into the heart of the fire I would throw myself in, so complete is my confidence; I have very great hope of the servants of God. I would throw myself in bodily, not merely this napkin, such is my reliance upon every one of those reverend masters of God's mystery.'

Brother, make trial of this elixir: a man's faith should not be less than the faith of a woman.

87

The miracles of the water-skin and
of the negro who was made white

A PARTY of Bedouins were travelling in a certain wadi,
and their water-skins had become dry for lack of rain—a
caravan stranded in the midst of the desert reciting their own
death-dirge. Suddenly that succourer of both worlds, the
Chosen Prophet, appeared upon the path, come to give help.
He saw there a very great caravan on the burning sands, upon
an arduous and dreadful journey, the tongues of their camels
hanging out, the people spilled in all directions over the sand.

Compassion overcame him, and he said, 'Listen! Go as
quickly as you can, some of your party, run to those sandhills
yonder. A negro will bring a water-skin upon a camel; he is
carrying it at top speed to his master. Bring me that negro
camel-driver, by force if need be.'

The scouting party reached the sandhills, and after a little
while saw this very thing come to pass. A negro slave was
going along with a camel, the water-skin full of water, like
one bearing a gift.

They said to him, 'The pride of mankind and the best of
mortals calls upon you to come this way.'

'I do not know him. Who is he?' the negro asked.

'Face fair as the moon, temper sweet as candy, that is he,'
came the reply.

They expounded to him the Prophet's diverse qualities.

'Belike,' said the negro, 'he is that poet who overcame by
magic a multitude. I will not come half a span towards him.'

Thereupon they dragged him along that way; he shouted
and screamed in rage, uttering vehement reproaches. So they
haled him before that lordly one.

'Drink the water, and carry it with you too,' the Prophet
cried.

He satisfied the thirst of them all from that one water-skin; the camels and every man in the caravan drank of that water. He filled water-skins large and small from the negro's water-skin; the clouds in the sky looked on in amazement, envying him. The people of the caravan were astonished at what the Prophet had wrought.

'Muhammad, you whose bounty emulates the sea, what is this?' they exclaimed. 'You have made a little water-skin into a veil. You have flooded out Arabs and Kurds together.'

'Slave,' said the Prophet to the negro, 'see your water-skin is full now, lest you should say aught good or ill in complaint.'

The negro was amazed at this proof of the Prophet's powers. Out of the world where space is not his faith was dawning. He saw that a fountain was cascading out of the air, and his water-skin had become a veil for that outpouring of grace. By his entranced gaze the veils too were rent apart, so that he saw distinctly the fountain of the Unseen.

In that moment the eyes of the slave filled with tears. Forgotten to him were his master and home. He could stir neither hand nor foot; God cast into his soul a mighty commotion. Then the Prophet drew him back again for the good of his soul.

'Come back to your senses. Begone, student of the heavenly science! This is not the time for bewilderment; bewilderment lies ahead of you. Advance now on the Way, briskly and nimbly!'

The negro placed the hands of the Prophet on his face, showering them with loving kisses. Then the Prophet rubbed his blessed hand on the negro's cheek, imparting to it his blessing. That Ethiopian negro became white as the full moon; his night turned to bright day.

He went along intoxicated, as though without head or foot; in truth, as he fared he could not tell apart foot from hand. Leaving the caravan, he came to his master with two full water-skins.

His master espied him from afar, and stood rooted in amazement. In astonishment he called the people of the village to come to him.

'That is my water-skin,' he said, 'and that is my camel.

Where then has my swarthy-browed slave vanished? This man approaching from afar is white as the moon at the full; the light of his countenance contends with the light of the day. Where is my slave? Haply he has lost his way, or a wolf has waylaid him and he has been killed.'

When the slave came before him, the master said, 'Who are you? Are you a native of Yemen, or are you a Turkoman? Tell me, what have you done with my slave? Tell the truth! If you have killed him, declare it! Do not seek to deceive me.'

'If I have killed him, how is it I have come to you?' replied the slave. 'How have I walked on my own feet to my own destruction?'

'Where is my slave?' his master repeated.

'See, I am he,' the slave answered. 'The hand of God's grace has made me bright.'

'Ha, what are you saying? Where is my slave?' his master demanded once again. 'Pay heed, you will not escape from me except by telling the truth.'

The slave said, 'I will disclose all your secret dealings with that slave you speak of, one by one to the end. I will declare what has happened, from the time you purchased me down to the present, so that you may know that spiritually I am the same, though out of my dusky body a bright dawn has broken. The colour is changed, but the pure spirit is free of colour, of the elements of the dust.'

88

The miracles of the baby who spoke and
of the eagle and the snake

A WOMAN of the selfsame village, one of the unbelievers,
came running to the Prophet to test him. She entered the
Prophet's presence veiled, a two months' infant at her breast.

'God's peace be upon you,' the infant said. 'Messenger of
Allah, lo, we have come to you.'

'Hold your peace!' cried the mother angrily. 'Who put
this attestation in your ear? Little child, who taught you,
that your tongue became loosed in infancy?'

'God taught me, then Gabriel,' said the child. 'In this
declaration I stand in with Gabriel.'

'Where is Gabriel?' asked the woman.

'Above your head,' said the child. 'Do you not see? Turn
your gaze aloft. Gabriel is standing over you. He has been a
guide to me in a hundred ways.'

'Do you see him?' asked the mother.

'Yes,' said the child. 'Shining over you like a moon perfectly full. He is teaching me the description of the Prophet,
by that sublimity delivering me out of this degradation.'

Then the Prophet said to the child, 'Sucking child, what
is your name? Declare it, and obey my command.'

'With God,' replied the infant, 'my name is the Servant of
the Almighty. With this handful of catamites my name is
Servant of 'Uzza. I declare I am innocent and free and quit of
'Uzza, I swear it by the truth of Him who gave you this prophet-
hood.'

The two months' child, illumined as the full moon, dis-
coursed as an adult man, even as those who sit on the dais.

In that instant sweet herbs rained out of Paradise; the
nostrils of mother and child drew in the scent.

R   257

'Better it is, for fear of falling from grace,' both said, 'to surrender the soul to this fragrance of sweet herbs.'

They were so occupied, when Muhammad heard from aloft the call to prayer. He asked for water and made ablution anew. He washed his hands and face in the cold water, then he washed both his feet, and was about to take his shoe when a shoe-thief snatched his shoe. The eloquent one reached out his hand towards the shoe, and an eagle snatched the shoe out of his hand and bore it up in the air as swiftly as the wind, then turned it upside down, and a snake fell out of it. Out of the shoe fell a black snake; by Divine providence the eagle had become the Prophet's well-wisher.

Then the eagle brought back the shoe, saying, 'Come, take it and go to prayers. It was of necessity that I acted so brusquely; naturally I am humbled and bow my wing in reverence to you. Woe to him who comports himself impertinently without necessity, following the dictates of desire.'

The Prophet thanked the eagle, saying, 'I thought your act rudeness, but it was really kindness. You snatched off the shoe, and I was put out; you took away my grief, and I was aggrieved. Though God has shown me every unseen thing, in that moment my heart was occupied with self.'

'Far be it from you,' said the eagle, 'that inattention should arise in you. My seeing that unseen thing was a reflexion from you. If while in the air I see a snake in your shoe, that is not of myself; it is a reflexion from you, Chosen of God.'

The reflexion of the man of light is all luminous; the reflexion of the man of darkness is all dim as a slag-heap. The reflexion of the servant of God is all of light; the reflexion of the stranger to God is all blindness.

Know the reflexion of every man; my soul, see clearly, then sit ever beside the class of man that you desire.

89

The man who asked Moses to teach him the language of beasts and birds

A CERTAIN youth said to Moses, 'Teach me the language of the animals that haply from the speech of living creatures and wild beasts I may obtain a lesson concerning my religion. Since the tongues of the sons of Adam are all in quest of water, bread and renown, it may be that the animals have another preoccupation, how to prepare for the hour of passing out of this world.'

'Depart!' said Moses. 'Give up this vain desire, for it holds much danger before and behind. Seek your lesson, and a wakeful mind to heed it, from God, not from books and speeches, letters and lips.'

The man became more eager because of Moses' refusal; a man always becomes more eager when he is refused.

'Moses,' he resumed, 'since your light shone forth everything has found its proper value from you. It does not befit your gracious goodness, generous one, to frustrate me in this wish of mine. You are God's vicegerent in this present time: if you should deny me, then there is nothing but despair.'

'Lord,' cried Moses, 'surely the accursed Satan has overmastered this simple-minded man. If I teach him, it will be harmful to him; if I do not teach him, he will lose heart.'

'Teach him, Moses,' said God. 'We in our generosity have never turned away prayer.'

'Lord,' said Moses, 'he will repent of it, gnawing his hands and rending his garments. Power is not suitable for everyone: impotence is the best capital of the pious.'

'Accord him his need,' said God. 'Give him a free hand to choose in this matter. Place a sword in his hand: wrest him out of impotence: so that he may become either a fighter for

259

the Faith or a highwayman. For We have honoured Man by the gift of free will; he is half honey-bee and half snake.'

Once more Moses gave the youth loving counsel.

'What you desire will cause your face to grow pale. Give up this melancholy passion and be fearful of God. The Devil has taught you to ask for this for his own cunning purpose.'

'At least teach me the speech of the dog at the door,' pleaded the youth, 'and the speech of the winged domestic fowl.'

'Well, you know best,' answered Moses. 'Go: your wish is fulfilled. The speech of both will be patent to you.'

Next morning at dawn the youth stood waiting on his threshold to make trial. The maid shook out the table-cloth and a piece of bread, left over from the previous night's meal, fell out. A cock snatched it up as though it were a wager.

The dog said, 'You have done us wrong. Off with you! You are able to eat a grain of corn, while I am incapable of eating grain in my home. You can eat corn, barley, all the rest of the grains: I cannot, joyous rooster! This crust of bread which is our allotment—you are snatching away from the dogs such a little amount!'

'Hush, do not fret,' answered the cock. 'God will give you something to make amends for this. This gentleman's horse is going to drop dead; tomorrow eat your fill, and do not sorrow. The death of the horse will make a feast-day for the dogs; there will be plenty of provender without any trouble or toil.'

When the youth heard this he sold his horse. The cock was put to shame in the eyes of the dog.

Next day the cock snatched the bread in the same manner, and the dog opened his lips to address him.

'Tricky cock, how long will you be telling these lies? You are a malefactor, a liar, a lack-lustre. Where is the horse you said would die? You are a blind star-reader, utterly deprived of truth.'

'The horse dropped dead somewhere else,' replied the artful cock. 'He sold the horse and escaped from loss; he cast the loss upon others. But tomorrow his mule is going to die. That will be a blessing—only for the dogs!'

260

The greedy man immediately sold the mule, finding instant refuge from sorrow and loss. On the third day the dog spoke to the cock again.

'Prince of liars, with your drum and kettledrum!'

'He sold the mule in haste,' said the cock. 'But tomorrow his slave will be struck down. When his slave dies, his next of kin will scatter loaves for the dogs and the beggars.'

The master heard this and sold his slave; he escaped from loss, and his face shone with joy. He kept uttering thanks and making merry.

'Now I have escaped from three disasters together. Since I learned the speech of fowl and dog I have sewn up the eye of evil destiny.'

'Gibbering cock,' said the disappointed dog next day, 'where are the odds and evens that you promised me? How long, how long pray will you continue your lying tricks? Surely nothing but lies flies out of your nest.'

'Far be it from me and my kind,' said the cock, 'that we should become afflicted with falsehood. We cocks tell the truth, like the muezzin; we keep watch on the sun, seeking for the right time. We keep watch upon the sun inwardly, even though you may invert a basin over our heads. God bestowed our stock as a gift to man to call him to prayer and to prepare him. If we make a mistake and call to prayer at the wrong time, that will be the death of us. To cry at the wrong time "Come to salvation!" makes our blood forfeit and lawful to shed.'

The man's slave died in the house of the purchaser; the loss fell entirely upon the purchaser. The master saved his money, but mark this well, he shed his own blood.

'Tomorrow, however,' the cock continued, 'he will die for sure. His sorrowing heir will slaughter a cow. The master of the house is going to die and be done with. Tomorrow you will be getting plenty of titbits. People of high estate and low will find in the middle of the street pieces of bread and scraps from the feast, victuals for all. Meat from the cow slaughtered in sacrifice and thin breads will speedily be scattered for the dogs and the beggars.'

When the man heard these things, he ran hot-foot to Moses' door.

'Save me from this doom, man of God,' he cried, rubbing his face in the dust out of fear.

'Go, sell yourself, and escape!' answered Moses. 'You have become an expert; now leap out of this pit! Throw the loss upon true believers; double the size of your purses and money-bags! In the brick I descried this destiny which only became visible to you in the mirror. The intelligent man sees in his heart the end at the beginning; the man scant in wit sees it only at the end.'

'Do not beat me on the head, virtuous sir,' wailed the man again. 'Do not rub it into my face. I acted so because I was unworthy; grant to my unworthy action good recompense.'

'My son,' said Moses, 'an arrow sped from the thumb-stall cannot return to base—that is against all the rules. Nevertheless I will petition God's good governance that when you die you may die in faith. If you die in faith, you will truly live; if you depart with the faith, you will endure for ever.'

In that same moment the master fell sick; his heart fluttered, and they brought the basin. Four men carried him to his dwelling, the while he rubbed one leg against the back of the other leg. At dawn Moses began his litany.

'O God, take not the faith from him, bear it not away! Act like the King Thou art and pardon him, for he has erred shamefully and exceedingly. I said to him, "This knowledge is not meet for thee"; he deemed my words foolish and a thwarting of his desire. He plunged into the sea, not being a water-fowl. He sank: take his hand, God of Love!'

God answered, 'Yes, I have bestowed on him the Faith. If thou desirest, I will bring him to life this moment; indeed, for thy sake this moment I will bring to life all the dead in the earth.'

Moses said, 'This world is the world of death. Raise them to the world beyond, for there all is light.'

90

The woman whose children died, on the virtue of fortitude in sorrow

A CERTAIN woman bore a son every year, but the child never lived more than six months; he would perish within three months or four.

The woman lamented, saying, 'Alas, O God, for nine months I carry the burden and for three months I have joy. My bliss is swifter sped than the rainbow.'

On account of the fearful agony she suffered the women shrilled her complaint before the men of God. Twenty sons in this manner went into the grave; their lives were consumed by a swift fire.

Then one night she had a vision of a garden everlasting, verdant, delectable, ungrudged. Seeing that, the woman became intoxicated; the frail creature fainted to behold that revelation. She saw her name inscribed upon a palace; being of goodly faith, she knew that that was hers.

Thereafter they said to her, 'This blessing is reserved for such as dedicated their lives truly to the service of God. Much service you must have performed to be worthy to partake of this repast. Since you were dilatory in taking shelter with God, God instead bestowed upon you these afflictions.'

'Lord,' she cried, 'give me such afflictions for a hundred years and more! Shed Thou my blood!'

When she drew nigh unto that garden, she beheld there all her children.

'They were lost to me,' she cried, 'but they were not lost to Thee.'

91

How Hamza in old age went into battle unarmed

AT the end, whenever Hamza went into the ranks of battle he came into the combat as one intoxicated, without a coat of mail; moving forward bare of body, breast open, he would fling himself into the serried ranks of swords.

The people asked him, 'Uncle of the Prophet, Lion shattering the ranks, Prince of stallions, have you not read in the Message of God, "Cast not yourselves by your own hands into destruction"? Then why are you casting yourself into destruction thus upon the battlefield? When you were young and strong and toughly strung, you never entered the ranks of battle without a coat of mail. Now you have become old and infirm and bent, you comport yourself with utter recklessness. Recklessly you grapple and wrestle and make trial with sword and lance. The sword has no respect for age; how should sword and arrow possess discrimination?'

Hamza replied, 'When I was a young man I used to regard bidding farewell to this world as death. How should any man go to death eagerly? How should he come before the dragon naked? But now, through the Light of Muhammad, I am not subject to this city that passes away. Beyond the world of the senses, I descry the camp of the King thronged with the army of the Light of God, tent upon tent, tent-rope upon tent-rope. Thanks be to Him who awakened me out of slumber!'

92

How Bilal died rejoicing

WHEN Bilal became thin as the new moon from weakness, the colour of death overtook his face.

'Ah, woe!' cried his wife, seeing him in this state.

'No, no. Ah, joy!' answered Bilal. 'Till now I have been in woe from being alive. How should you know what delight death truly is?'

As he said these words, his cheeks bloomed with narcissi, rose-petals and anemones; the glow in his face and the light filling his eyes bore testimony to the truth of what he was saying.

'This then is the parting, virtuous husband,' said his wife.

'No, no. It is the union, the union,' Bilal replied.

'Tonight,' said his wife, 'you go to a strange country, vanishing from the ken of your kin and family.'

'No, no,' said Bilal. 'On the contrary, tonight my soul arrives home from a strange country.'

'Where shall we see your face?' asked his wife.

'In God's chosen circle,' Bilal replied.

'Alas,' cried his wife, 'this house has been ruined.'

'Look on the moon, not on the cloud,' said Bilal. 'God has ruined it in order to make it more prosperous. My people were a multitude, and the house was small. Formerly I was the prisoner of grief, like Adam; now East and West are filled with the offspring of my spirit. I was a beggar in this well-like house; now I have become a king, and a palace is needed for a king. The body is a narrow house, and the soul is cramped in it. God ruined that house, to make a palace fit for kings. I am cramped like the embryo in the womb; I have become nine months old; this migration is pressing. Unless the pangs of birth overtake my mother—in this prison I am in the midst of the fire. My mother, my natural body, out of the throes of its death is giving birth, that the lamb may be delivered from the ewe, that the lamb may pasture in the green plain. Come, open the womb, for the lamb has grown great.'

93

The Virgin Mary and the Archangel

MARY, being privately in her chamber, beheld a life-augmenting, heart-ravishing form: the Trusty Spirit rose up before her from the face of the earth, bright as the moon and the sun. Beauty without a veil rose up from the earth, even like as the sun rising in splendour from the East. Trembling overcame Mary's limbs, for she was naked and feared corruption. Mary became unselfed, and in her selflessness she cried, 'I will leap into the Divine protection.'

For she of the pure bosom was wont to take herself in flight to the Unseen. Seeing this world to be a kingdom without permanence, prudently she made a fortress of the Presence of God, to the end that in the hour of death she might have a stronghold which the Adversary would find no way to assail. No better fortress she saw than the protection of God; she chose a camping-place nigh to that castle.

That Proof of the Divine bounty cried out to her, 'I am the trusty messenger of the Presence. Be not afraid of me. Turn not you head away from the lordly ones of the Majesty, do not withdraw yourself from such goodly confidants.'

As he spoke, a candlewick of pure light spiralled up from his lips straight to the star Arcturus.

'You are fleeing from my being into not-being. In not-being I am king and standard-bearer; verily, my house and home are in not-being, only my graven form is before Our Lady. Mary, look well, for I am a form hard to apprehend; I am both a new moon and a fantasy in the heart. I am of the light of the Lord, like the true dawn, for no night encompasses my day. Daughter of Imran, cry not to God for refuge against me, for I have descended from the refuge of God. The refuge of God has been my origin and sustenance, the light of that refuge which was before ever word was spoken. You are taking refuge from me with God; yet in pre-eternity I am the portrait of that Refuge. I am the refuge that oft-times has been your deliverance; you are taking refuge, and I myself am that refuge. There is no bane worse than ignorance: you are with the Friend, and know not how to love. You suppose the Friend to be a stranger; you have bestowed the name of sorrow upon joy.'

94

The chamberlain of Bukhara,
a story on the power of love

THE servant of the prince of Bukhara fell under suspicion and hid from his highness, He wandered about hither and thither ten years long, now in Khurasan, now in the mountains, now in the desert.

After ten years he could not endure the days of separation any longer. Yearning overcame him, and he said, 'Henceforth I cannot bear to be parted from him further. How should fortitude assuage the sense of being cast off? I will arise now and return thither. If I became an infidel, I will believe once more. I will return thither and fall before him, before that benevolent prince. I will say, "I throw myself before you. Either revive my soul, or cut off my head like a sheep! Better it is to be slain and dead at your feet, O moon, than to be king of the living in another place. I have made trial more than a thousand times; I do not hold my life sweet without you. Sing to me, O my desire, the melody of resurrection! She-camel of mine, kneel and let me away! Joy is complete. Earth, swallow up my tears, for they have flowed enough. Drink, my soul, a draught that is now pure! You have returned to us, my day of festival: welcome, I cry! What goodly refreshment you have brought, zephyr wind!

'Friends, farewell! I am on my way to the prince who commands and is obeyed. Every moment I am roasting in the fire; come what may, thither I will go. Though he is making his heart hard as rock, my soul is bound for Bukhara, for it is the friend's dwelling-place, the city of my king. In the lover's eyes, this is true patriotism.'

'Unwary man,' a sincere counsellor said to him, 'if you have the wit, think upon the consequence. Apply your reason;

269

consider the past and the future; let not yourself be burned
like a moth. How is it that you are going to Bukhara? You are
mad, fit for chains and prison. He is gnawing iron in his fury
against you; he is searching for you with twenty eyes. He is
whetting the knife for you; he is like a starving dog, with
yourself the bag of flour. After having escaped, God opening
the way for you, now you are making for prison! What has
happened to you? If ten kinds of guardians had been watching
over you, you would have needed intelligence to shake clear
of them. Now that not a single guardian is set over you, why
have the future and the past become closed to you?'

'Counsellor, be silent! How long will you rail at me?' the
chamberlain replied. 'Keep your advice to yourself; my bonds
are hard to bear, harder to bear than your advice. Whoever
taught you knew nothing of love. Bu Hanifa and Shafi'i gave
no instruction touching love's augmentation of pain. Do not
threaten me, that I shall be slain; I thirst grievously for my
own blood.'

Heart throbbing, that lover, his tears suffused with blood,
set forth for Bukhara in hot haste. The sands of Amun seemed
to him like silk, the waters of Oxus seemed to him as a pool.
To him that desert was like a rose-garden; he was falling
supine with laughter like a full-blown rose. When he espied
the blackness of his prince's Bukhara a whiteness shone upon
the blackness of his grief. For a while he lay at full length,
senseless; his reason winged away into the garden of mystery.

At last, full of joy, he entered Bukhara, the presence of his
his beloved and the abode of security. Everyone who saw him
in Bukhara shouted, 'Before you let yourself be seen, rise and
flee! Do not tarry! The prince is seeking you in fury, to
wreak his ten years' vengeance on your life. For the sake of
Allah, do not plunge into your own blood. Do not rely upon
your own powers of spellbinding. You were the prince's
constable, a peer of the realm; you were his trusted minister,
his master-engineer. You acted with treachery, and fled from
punishment; you had got clean away; how have you got into
the toils again? You fled from disaster by a hundred artful
dodges; is it folly, or fate, that has brought you here? You
whose intellect teases Mercury himself, doom makes a fool of
intellect and the intelligent. Unlucky is the hare that seeks

to challenge the lion! Where now is your cleverness, your intelligence and nimble wit? Destiny's wiles are a hundred times as many as yours; the Prophet said, "When Destiny comes, the wide spaces are narrowed." A hundred ways and asylums may lie to left and right; yet they are all barred by Destiny, the invincible dragon.'

'I am as a man with dropsy, drawn on by water,' said the chamberlain. 'The water draws me, though I know full well it will kill me. Though my hands and my belly be swollen, yet my passion for water will not abate. Let them ask me how I am faring within me, I answer, "Would that the sea were flowing in me!" Let the water-skin of my belly be burst by the waves of the water; if I die, death is sweet to me. Hands huge as a tymbal, belly swollen as a drum, I drum my love for the water, like a rose. If that Trusty Spirit spills my blood, like the thirsty earth I will drink gout on gout of blood. I am a drinker of blood, like the earth and the child in the womb; ever since I became a lover, this has been my occupation. By night I boil on the fire like a cauldron; all day, till night, I drink blood like the sand.

'I repent that I ever contrived and plotted and fled from that which his wrath desired. Let him loose his wrath against my intoxicated soul; he is the Feast of the Sacrifice, and his lover is the buffalo. Whether the buffalo is sleeping or eating, he fattens it up for the Feast and the slaughter.

'Noble friends, slaughter this cow of the flesh, if you desire to raise up spirits endowed with vision. I died to the mineral, and became a plant; I died to plant, and attained to the animal. I died to the animal, and became a man. Why, then, should I fear? When have I become less by dying? At the next onset I shall die to man, that I may soar on wings and stand among the angels. And I must transcend even the angels: "All things perish, except His Face." Once more I shall be sacrificed, and die to the angel; that which enters not into the imagination, that I shall become. Then I shall become not-being; like an organ, not-being proclaims to me, "Surely to Him we return." Know that death is as the community of the faithful are agreed: the Water of Life hidden in the Darkness. Like the water-lily, grow out of this river-bank, greedy and eager for death as a man with dropsy. Though the water is death to

271

him, yet he seeks after the water and drinks; and God knows the right course. O frozen lover hugging your robe of shame, fleeing from the Beloved for fear of your life! Disgrace even to women, behold the multitudinous souls rushing towards the sword of His love, clapping their hands! You have seen the river; pour your pitcher into the river. How should water be a fugitive from the river? When the water in the pitcher goes into the water of the river it vanishes into it, and itself becomes the river. The lover's attributes have passed away, and his essence continues; thereafter he becomes not less, neither ill-favoured. I have hanged myself upon His palm-tree in contrition for having fled from Him.'

Bowing low on his face like a ball, with eyes streaming he went towards the prince. All the people were waiting, head in air, to see whether he would burn him or hang him.

'Now he will show this utter fool,' they muttered, 'what Time shows to the luckless. Like the moth, he took the sparks for light; like a fool he fell into the flame and was severed from life.'

That man of Bukhara flung himself upon the candle; passion had made that agony easy for him to bear. His burning sighs mounted to heaven; loving kindness entered the heart of the prince, who communed inwardly at dawn.

'O Thou who art One, how fares that wandering lover of ours? He committed a sin, and we saw it; but he knew not well our mercy. The heart of the sinner becomes afraid of Us, but mingled with his fear are a hundred hopes. I terrify the impudent and abandoned, but how should I terrify him who is afraid? Fire is put under the cold pot, not the pot which is boiling over. I terrify the secure by the knowledge of Me; I take away the fear of the fearful by My clemency. I am a patcher; I put a patch where it is wanted. I give to every man drink as suits his capacity.'

When that man beheld the face of the prince it was as though the bird of the soul flew out of his body. His body dropped like dry wood; he became cold from the crown of his head to his nails. However much they censed him and sprinkled him with rose-water, he neither stirred nor spoke.

When the prince saw his face pale as saffron he dismounted from his steed and came towards him.

'The lover seeks the beloved in hot haste,' he said. 'When the beloved is come, the lover is gone.'

Gently, little by little, the prince drew him out of senselessness to understanding.

'O beggar,' the prince cried into his ear, 'I bring you scatter of gold: open your skirt! Your spirit, which quivered in separation from me, now that I have come to defend it how it has fled away! You who have suffered both heat and cold in separation from me, return, come back to yourself out of selflessness!'

The prince took him by the hand.

'This man, whose breath has departed,' he said, 'will only come to when I give him breath. When he whose body is dead becomes living through Me, it will be My spirit that turns to Me. Through this spirit I bestow dignity on him; only the spirit that I give sees My munificence. The unadmitted spirit sees not the face of the Beloved, only that spirit beholds Him who springs from His dwelling-place. Like a butcher, I breathe upon this friend of Mine so that his delicate essence may freely relinquish the skin.

'Spirit fled out of great tribulation, We have opened the door to union with Us: welcome! You whose selflessness and intoxication derive from Our Self, you whose being is ever more drawn from Our Being, now, without lip, I will tell you anew the ancient mysteries: hearken! For those bodily lips flee away from this Breath, which is breathed on the bank of the secret River. Open this moment the ear of earlessness to receive the mystery, "God does what He will".'

Little by little, as he began to hear the summons to union, the dead man began to stir. He leaped up quivering and joyously whirled once or twice, then fell prostrate in adoration.

'Simurgh of God,' he cried, 'place of the spirit's circling flight, I give thanks that you have returned from the far Mountain of Qaf. Seraphiel of Love's resurrection-place, Love of love and Heart's desire of love, I desire, as the first robe of honour you shall give me, that you will lay your ear against my window. Though in your purity you know well my state, cherisher of slaves, accord your ear to what I say. A myriad times, Prince unique, my wits flew away yearning for your ear, that hearing of yours, that heeding of yours, those life-quickening smiles of yours, that hearkening to my trivial and greater matters, even the beguilement of my evil-thinking soul. Then you accepted as genuine coin my counterfeit pieces, though you knew them well, for the sake of the impudence of one bold and deluded—Thou beside whose clemency all clemencies are but a mote. Hear first, that when I abandoned Thy net both the former and the latter world were lost to me; hear secondly, O loving Prince, that long as I sought I found no second to Thee; thirdly, since I went forth from Thee it is as though I have declared, "God is the third of three"; fourthly, inasmuch as my cornfield is all burnt up I cannot tell apart the fifth from the fourth. Wherever you may find blood upon the furrows, track well and it will surely prove to be blood from my eyes. My words are thunder, and the roar of my lamentation demands of the clouds to rain upon the earth. I weave between words and weeping, whether I shall speak or weep: how shall I do? If I speak, the weeping will be lost; and if I weep, how shall I offer thanks and praise? Prince, from my eyes the heart's blood is falling; see what has befallen me from my eye!'

So he spoke, that emaciated man, and began to weep so that all men, commoners and nobles, wept over him. So many cries of ecstasy mounted from his heart that the people of Bukhara formed a circle around him. Speaking crazily, weeping crazily, laughing crazily—men and women, small and great, were struck with bewilderment. The whole city shed tears in concord with him, men and women mingled together as at the Resurrection.

Heaven that moment was saying to the earth, 'If you never saw the Resurrection, behold it now!'

'What is love and what is ecstasy?' bewildered reason was saying. 'I know not whether separation from Him or union is the more wonderful.'

95

Satan and the tribe of Quraish

SATAN enlisted Number 101 in the army of the Quraish.
'I will be your protector,' he promised guilefully.

Quraish fell in at his command, and the two armies ranged against each other.

Then Satan espied a host of angels stationed upon a road towards the ranks of the believers, those 'legions you did not see' drawn up in battle-order. In terror his soul became as it were a temple of fire. Turning on his heel, he began to retreat.

'I behold an amazing host,' he cried. ' "I fear God"; I have no succour from Him. Depart! "I see what you do not see".'

Harith said, 'You who have taken the likeness of Suraqa, why did you not say such things as these yesterday?'

Satan answered, 'This moment I see disaster facing me.'

Harith said, 'You see the meanest dwarfs of all the Arabs; that is all you are seeing. But, scandal that you are, yesterday was the time of boasting, today is the time of battle. Yesterday you proclaimed, "I go bail that yours shall be the victory God-given constantly." Yesterday you were the great chief of the army, accursed one; now you are a coward, a nothing, contemptible. Having got us to swallow your words and come into battle, off you went to the stokehole, and we became the fuel.'

When Harith had said these words to Suraqa, the accursed one became enraged at his reproach; angrily he snatched his hand from Harith's hand, for the words he had spoken pained his heart sorely. Satan smote Harith upon the breast, and fled. By this trick he shed the blood of those miserable men. Having destroyed so great a multitude, he said, 'I am quit of you!'

The carnal soul and Satan have ever been one person, though

275

they have shown themselves forth in two forms; even as the angel and reason, which were truly one, in God's inscrutable wisdom became two separate forms.

Such an enemy as this you have in your inmost part, impeder of reason, adversary to spirit and faith.

96

*The chickpea in the pot compared
with the believer*

CONSIDER a chickpea in the pot, how it leaps up when it is at the mercy of the fire. Constantly, as the water boils, the chickpea rises to the top of the pot with a hundred outcries.

'Why you do set the fire on me? Seeing you have given good money for me, why are you now turning me upside down?'

The housewife goes on hitting it with the ladle.

'Boil nicely now,' she says. 'Do not leap away from the one who made the fire. I am not boiling you because I detest you; on the contrary, it is so that you may get taste and flavour, so that you may become fit to eat and mingle with the spirit. You are not being afflicted because of being despised. When you were green and fresh, you drank water in the garden; that water-drinking was a preparation for this fire. Chickpea, you pastured in the springtime. Now pain has become your guest; look after him well so that your guest, when he returns home, may give thanks for your hospitality, telling of your devotion in the presence of the King. Then, in lieu of the blessing, He who blesses will come to you, and all blessings whatever will envy you!

'I am Abraham and you are my son. Lay your head before the knife; "I see in a dream that I shall sacrifice thee." Lay your head before my wrath with a tranquil heart, so that I may cut your throat as Abraham did to Ishmael. I will cut off your head; but this head is the head that is immune from being cut off and dying. Yet your self-surrender is God's eternal purpose; good Muslim, you must seek to surrender yourself.

'Boil on, chickpea, in tribulation, that neither being nor self may remain to you. If you have laughed in that terrestrial garden, yet you are the rose of the garden of the spirit and of vision. If you have been parted from the garden of water and clay, yet you have become food fit to enter into the living. Become nourishment and strength! Become pure thought! You that were a milksop, become now a lion in the jungle! In the beginning you grew out of God's attributes; return now swiftly and nimbly into His attributes. From cloud and sun and sky you came; then you became divers attributes, and ascended to the sky. You came down in the form of rain and heat; you will go back in the goodly attributes of God. You were a part of sun and cloud and stars; you have become soul and act and speech and thought.

'The caravan is ever arriving from heaven, to traffic here below and then to return. Go then, sweetly and gladly and of free will, not like a thief with bitterness and unwilling. I am speaking bitter words to you, that I may cleanse you of all bitterness. The frozen grape is thawed by cold water and lays aside its coldness and frozenness. When out of bitterness your heart is filled with blood, then you will get away from all bitterness.'

'Since that is so, lady, I will gladly boil,' said the chickpea. 'Help me truly! You are my architect, so to speak, in thus boiling me; smite me with the ladle, for you smite most sweetly. I am as the elephant; strike, and brand my head, that I may no longer dream of the gardens of India. Smite on, that I may surrender myself to the boiling, that I may find a way to the Beloved's bosom. Man in his independence waxes rebellious and becomes hostile, like the dreaming elephant; when the elephant dreams of India he will not heed the driver, and manifests treachery.'

'Formerly I too was like you, a part of earth,' said the housewife. 'When I had quaffed the cup of fiery discipline I became suitable and acceptable. For a space I boiled in Time, for another space in the pot of the body. By this double boiling I became strength to the senses; I became spirit; then I became your teacher. In the inanimate state I used to say, "You are running to and fro that you may attain knowledge and spiritual qualities." Since I have become spirit, once again let me boil and transcend the animal.'

278

97

The foal that would not drink

A FOAL and a mare were once drinking the water. All the time the stablemen were coaxing the horses, 'Come on now, drink!'

The foal heard their clucking. It lifted its head and refused to drink.

'Foal, why do you all the time refuse to drink this water?' asked the mare.

'That mob keep on clucking,' replied the foal. 'Their sudden noise terrifies me, so that my heart trembles and jumps about. It is the suddenness of the sound that makes me afraid.'

'Ever since the world existed,' said the mare, 'there have been busybodies like these on the earth.'

Attend to your own business, my good man; the busybodies will soon be plucking our their beards in vexation.

98

The guest in the enchanted mosque

THERE was once a mosque on the outskirts of Rayy in which nobody ever slept, but that very night he expired of fright and his children became orphans. Many a destitute stranger entered it to go down at dawn like the stars—into the grave.

Everyone said it was inhabited by fierce genies who butchered the guests with blunt swords.

Said another, 'It is the magic, the talisman. This kind of sorcery is the foe and enemy of life.'

Said another, 'Post up a notice on the door stating clearly, "Guest, do not stay here. If you want to stay alive, do not sleep the night here; otherwise, death will spring an ambush for you here".'

Said another, 'Bolt the door at night. Deny admission to the unsuspecting visitor.'

One night a guest arrived who had heard tell of the amazing rumour. Being a very brave man and surfeited with life, he was determined to put it to the proof.

'I set small store by one sheep's head and paunch,' he said. 'Even suppose one grain is gone from the spirit's treasure, what does that matter? Bid the body's form be gone: who am I? Is not the figure of small account, since I am immortal? Since by God's grace the spirit was breathed into me I am the breath of God, apart from the body's pipe. So it is, that the sound of His breathing may not be wasted here, and that the pearl of great price may escape from its narrow shell. God says, "Long for death, if you speak truly." I am a truthful man; I will spill my life for this.'

'Beware!' shouted the people. 'Do not sleep here, lest the Soul-snatcher pound you like the dregs of sesame-seed. You are a stranger and do not know the facts, how that whoever sleeps here passes away for sure. This is no isolated incident;

we, and all men of good sense, have seen it time and time again. Whoever has lodged in this mosque for a single night, sure enough venomous death has come for him at midnight. If we have seen this once, we have seen it a hundred times; what we are telling you is not mere hearsay. The Prophet said, "Religion is sincerity." Linguistically, sincerity is the opposite of deceitfulness. Sincerity means being a true friend; when you are deceitful, you are treacherous and a cur. This sincerity we are showing you springs of love and is innocent of treachery. Do not turn away from reason and justice!'

'My sincere counsellors,' the man replied, 'I have become impenitently satiated with the world of life. I am a vagabond, seeking blows and courting blows; do not look for salvation in the vagabond of the road. I am not the vagabond who looks for a crust here and there; I am the reckless vagabond who is looking for death. I am not the vagabond who grabs at a penny; I am the nimble vagabond who hurries to cross this bridge. I am not the vagabond who haunts every shop; I am the one who leaps away from material being and strikes the true mine. Death and departure from this earthly dwelling-place has become as sweet to me as to the bird to burst out of its cage and fly free. Even though that cage is in the heart of the garden, so that the bird beholds the rose-beds and the trees, outside, all around the cage, a choir of birds is sweetly chanting tales of liberty. The bird, beholding that verdant place, no more craves for food; impatient and restless, it puts out its head through every hole, hoping that somehow it may wrest this fetter from its foot. Inasmuch as its heart and soul are already out of the cage, how will it be when you open the cage?'

'Do not act rashly,' the people warned the stranger, 'lest your bodily garment and your soul become a pawn to destruction. Do not act rashly, father of generosity: do not expose the mosque and us to grave suspicion. For some enemy, inspired by enmity, will speak and tomorrow meanly kindle a fire against us, saying, "Some criminal strangled him, knowing he would be safe because of the mosque's reputation. Since the mosque had a bad name, he plotted to impute the murder to the mosque and so to escape." Hardy spirit, lay not suspicion upon us, for we are not secure from the machinations of our enemies. Pray be gone! Do not act rashly; en-

281

tertain no insane desire; Saturn cannot be measured by the cubit. Many like you have boasted of their luck, and have afterwards plucked out their beards in handfuls. Now be gone! Cut short this argument. Fling not yourself and us into disaster.'

'Friends, I am not one of those devils,' said the man, 'that my sinews should weaken at a single "God help us!" A boy who kept watch over a cornfield used to beat a kettledrum to scare off the birds; the birds hearing the kettledrum, were startled away from the field, so that the corn was safe from mischievous birds. Now it happened that the noble monarch Sultan Mahmud, passing by, pitched a great tent in the environs of that field. With him was an army multitudinous as the stars in heaven, close-packed, victorious, rank-shattering, empire-wresting. Now a camel was there carrying a drum, a Bactrian beast striding in front proud as a cock. The driver beat the drum and tymbal day and night, setting out and returning. The camel entered that field; the boy beat his kettledrum to guard the corn. A shrewd bystander said to the boy, "Do not beat your kettledrum; the camel is used to the drum, well-seasoned to it. What is your little tambourine to him, boy, seeing that he carries the Sultan's drum twenty times its size?"

'I am a lover, slain in the sacrificing of self-naughting; my soul is the bandstand for the drum of tribulation. The threats you utter are but a tambourine to what my eyes have witnessed. Comrades, I am not the man to be halted on this Way by vain imaginings. Like the Assassin I am without fear; nay, like Ishmael of old, I care nothing for my life. I have done with ostentation and idle show. "Say, come now," He has said to my soul, "hither come!"

'I will sleep in this mosque tonight,' went on the aspiring stranger. 'O mosque, if you should be my Karbala, then you will be my Kaaba granting my inmost need. Grant me leave, chosen House of God, that like Mansur I may dance on the rope. Though you should emulate Gabriel in good counsel, Abraham in the fire does not crave for succour. Gabriel, be gone! I, who have been kindled in love's flames, like aloeswood and ambergris am better burnt. Gabriel, though you succour me and protect me like a brother, brother, I am eager for the fire; I am not such a spirit as to grow greater and then diminish.'

The stranger slept in the mosque; yet where indeed should he sleep? How should a man drowned in the Sea of God slumber in a river? At the midnight hour came a terrible voice.

'I come, I come upon you, disciple!'

Five times came the dreadful voice, and his heart was torn to pieces. Yet that blessed man was not discomfited by that dreadful sound.

'Why should I fear?' he said. 'This is the drum of the Festival. Let the drum fear, for it is being buffeted. Empty drums without hearts, your portion of the spirit's festival is to be beaten with sticks! The Resurrection is the Festival, and the irreligious are the drum; we, like the people holding festival, are laughing as the rose.

'Beware!' he said to himself. 'Let not your heart tremble; only the faint-hearted and faithless souls have died at the sound of this drum. The time has come for me, like Ali, to seize a kingdom or abandon the body.

'Prince, behold, I am here!' he cried, springing to his feet. 'If you are a true man, come!'

At the sound of his voice the talisman was immediately broken. Gold of every species poured down on every side. Such an abundance of gold poured down, that the youth feared that its mass would block the doorway.

Then the intrepid lion rose up. All that night till dawn he was dragging out the gold, burying it, and then returning once more to the gold with sack and satchel.

99

The elements converse with the body

EARTH says to the earth of the body, 'Return! Abandon the spirit, come to me like the dust. You are my congener, you are more proper with me. It is better that you escape from that body and that moisture.'

It replies, 'Certainly. But I am fettered, though like yourself I am weary of being parted.'

The waters are seeking the moisture of the body, saying, 'Moisture, return to us out of exile.'

The aether is calling the heat of the body, saying, 'You are of fire. Take the way to your origin.'

In the body are seventy and two disorders, the elements tugging, though without cords. Disorder comes to shatter the body, that the elements may let go one of another.

The elements are four birds tied leg to leg; death, sickness and disorder release their legs. When death has freed their legs one from another, of a certainty every bird-element flies away.

The tug of these roots and of their branches every moment implants some pain in our bodies, seeking to rend asunder these compositions so that each part, as a bird, may fly away home.

God in His wisdom prevents this hastening, holding them together in health till the appointed time. God says, 'You parts, the term is not foreseen by you. It is useless for you to fly before the appointed time.'

The soul says, 'Base earthly parts of mine, my exile is more bitter than yours: I am celestial.'

100

The gnat appeals before Solomon

THE gnat came in from the garden and the pasture and began to demand justice from Solomon.

'Solomon, you dispense justice to devils and genies and to the children of men. Birds and fishes are under the protection of your justice. Who is the lost soul whom your bounty has not sought out? Grant justice to us, for we are very wretched; we are denied our portion of the orchard and the rose-plot. You find a solution for every weakling's difficulties. Now the gnat is a by-word for weakness; we are proverbial for feebleness and frailty, and you are proverbial for kindness and caring for the poor. You have reached the limit in the reaches of power; we have reached the limit in smallness and futility. Grant justice; relieve us of this misery; take our hand, you whose hand is the hand of God!'

'Tell me,' answered Solomon, 'you seeker of equity, against whom are you demanding justice and equity? Who is the oppressor that in his bluster and arrogance has done you injury and scratched your face? O wonder! Where in this age of ours is the oppressor who languishes not in our prison and chains? When we were born, on that same day oppression died; who then in this age of ours has produced an act of oppression? When the day dawns, darkness vanishes away; darkness is the origin and right arm of oppression. Behold, devils labour and serve me; others are bound in shackles and bonds. The root of the oppression of all oppressors was from the devil; the devil is in bonds; how then did tyranny arise? The Divine fiat bestowed the kingdom on us to the end that the people might not lament to Heaven, that burning sighs might not mount upwards, that the sky and the stars might not be set in commotion, that the empyrean might not tremble at the orphan's lamentation, that no living soul might be

285

maimed by injustice. For this purpose we established a law throughout the kingdoms, that no cry of "O Lord!" should go up to the skies. Oppressed one, look not to Heaven; you have a heavenly king in Time.'

'I appeal for justice against the wind's might,' the gnat replied. 'He has opened the two hands of oppression against us. We are in sore straits because of his oppression; lips tight, we are drinking the blood of his tyranny.'

'How prettily you hum!' said Solomon. 'But it behoves you to heed with all your soul the commandment of God. God has said to me, "Judge, beware! Hear not one litigant without the other party. Until both litigants stand before him, the truth is not manifest before the arbitrator. If one litigant alone raises a hundred shrills, be on your guard! Take not his word without hearing his opponent." I do not dare to turn my face from God's command. Go, bring before me your adversary.'

'What you say is proof binding and correct,' said the gnat. 'The wind is my adversary, and he is under your jurisdiction.'

'Zephyr wind,' cried King Solomon, 'the gnat complains of your oppression. Come hither! Give heed! Stand face to face with your adversary. Answer your adversary, rebut your opponent!'

When the wind heard this summons he came with all speed. The gnat immediately took to flight.

'Gnat,' said Solomon, 'where are you going? Wait, that I may pass judgment upon you both.'

'O king,' cried the gnat, 'my death is of his being. Why, my very day is black with his smoke. Now he has come, where shall I find rest? He wrests the very breath out of my body.'

So it is with him who seeks the Court of God; when God comes, the seeker is naughted.

NOTES

(1) The opening verses establish the poem as an allegory and announce its great theme: the individual human soul, yearning for reunion with its creator God, is compared with the reedpipe and its plangent music, accompaniment of the Mevlevi ritual dance. Rhymed English versions of this sequence have been made by, among others, Sir William Jones (see my *Persian Poems*, pp.118-9), E. H. Palmer (*The Song of the Reed*, pp.3-7) and R. A. Nicholson (Rumi, *Poet and Mystic*, p.31).

(2) The source of this story seems to have been a passage in Avicenna's *Canon of Medicine*; the medical episode occurs in Nizami 'Aruzi, *Chahar Maqala* (transl. E. G. Browne), p.88. For a verse paraphrase see E. H. Palmer, *op.cit.*, pp.8-14.

(3) For other versions of this widely disseminated folk-story see W. A. Clouston, *Flowers from a Persian Garden*, pp.115 ff.; A. Christensen, *Contes persans*, p.64. For a verse paraphrase see E. H. Palmer, *op.cit.*, pp.15-21.

(4) Turkish commentators identify the vizier in this remarkable story with St Paul. E. G. Browne pointed to the likely source as a Persian book of *Tales of the Prophets*. 'Historians say that after God Most High had brought Jesus into Heaven, the Christians followed a good path until Paul misled them. Now he was a man of the Jews who was evilly disposed towards Jesus and those of His Church, and was ever speaking ill of them and showing enmity towards them. Now when he was grown old he said: "I do not wish that my malice should be cut off from them." So he put out one of his eyes and asked the Christians: "Do you recognize me?" They answered: "Yes, thou art the worst of God's creatures." He replied: "Last night I saw Jesus in a dream. He struck me a blow on the eye, which blinded me, and said: 'How long wilt thou afflict my church?' I leapt up trembling from sleep. One of my eyes was out of action. I have come to you to adopt your Faith and Church, so that Jesus may be satisfied with me, for I cannot bear His reproaches." So the Christians received him

287

and took him into a house of theirs, and he adopted the monastic life, fasting all day and praying all night, so that the people were charmed with him.' The story goes on to depict St Paul as approaching various groups of Christians, using plausible arguments to corrupt their beliefs, and sowing dissension among them. Finally he summons three leading doctors of the Faith, and having imparted to each of them in private a different doctrine concerning the nature of Christ, commits suicide. Other versions of this anti-Pauline story are summarized in R. A. Nicholson's annotations on the *Masnavi*, VII, p.36. For a verse paraphrase see E. H. Palmer, *op.cit.*, pp.22-32.

(5) Rumi's immediate source for this story of ultimately Indian origin was Ibn al-Muqaffa', *Kalila wa-Dimna* (ed. L. Cheikho, pp. 72 ff.).

(6) This famous story occurs in many places; Rumi may have taken it from al-Ghazali. For a verse paraphrase see R. A. Nicholson, *Rumi, Poet and Mystic*, pp.66-7.

(7) The source was Farid al-Din 'Attar, *Asrar-nama*, p.90.

(8) This long story, one of the finest and wittiest in the poem, is based upon a tale related by Muhammad 'Aufi in his famous but still as yet unpublished collection of anecdotes, the *Jawami' al-hikayat*, completed in 1228. R. A. Nicholson summarized that version as follows. 'It is related that when Ma'mun succeeded to the Caliphate the fame of his munificence reached all parts of the world. At that time there was a Bedouin living in a barren wilderness. His tribe had only one spring of briny water, and any water that fell from the clouds soon turned bitter by reason of the saltiness of the soil. It so happened that a severe drought and famine forced the Bedouin to leave his home. He resolved to journey to the imperial court in hope of obtaining the Caliph's bounty. When he had passed beyond the habitations of his tribe, he came to a pool of stagnant water, in which the brine had been absorbed by particles of earth. On tasting it, he was astounded, for the poor fellow had never drunk sweet water and did not know that there was such a thing in the world. "By God," said he, "this is nowhere to be found but in Paradise: the Creator of the world has sent it down to me from Paradise in order to relieve my distress. I must put some of it in a skin and carry

it as a gift to the Caliph. Since he can never have tasted water like this, he will certainly bestow on me a fine robe of honour and a splendid donation." Taking some of the water with him, he went on his way. The Caliph, with a cavalcade in attendance, was hunting in the neighbourhood of Kufah when the Bedouin arrived. He ordered that the man should be brought before him and asked where he came from. "From the desert." "Whither bound?" "To the court of the Caliph." "What gift have you brought?" "Water of Paradise." Ma'mun, whose sagacity was unfailing, perceived what actually had occurred, and replied, "Let me taste it." When the water-skin was presented to him, he ordered that it should be emptied into a bottle, and having graciously sipped a small quantity of the water, exclaimed, "You have spoken the truth, O Bedouin: what is your request?" He answered, "O Prince, famine and poverty drove me away from my native land, and I knew not where to seek help but at the gate of the palace." "I will grant your request," said the Caliph, "on condition that you at once turn back and go no further." The Bedouin agreed, whereupon the Caliph commanded them to fill the water-skin with pieces of gold and charged one of his officers to accompany the Bedouin and see that he took the road to the desert. In reply to the courtiers, who were curious to know his reason for acting thus, Ma'mun explained that if the Bedouin had gone a little further and seen the Euphrates, he would have been ashamed of his paltry gift. "And I," he added, "am ashamed that any one who brings me a gift should leave my presence abashed and stricken with shame".' The foregoing abridgement indicates the changes which Rumi effected in using the story as an allegory. He uses the Bedouin as a symbol of the rational soul, invents the character of the Bedouin's wife to stand for the appetitive soul, and identifies the caliph with God. Rumi also makes the Bedouin 'see the great river, embark on it, and be borne to his everlasting home.' The saying 'I take pride in poverty' is attributed to the Prophet and was taken by the Sufis as their watchword. The 'Sura of the Forenoon' is Sura XCIII of the Koran.

(11) Rumi uses the lion, the fox and the wolf in this old folk-tale as symbols of 'the spiritual, intellectual and sensual

faculties of the mystic who is seeking God'. The command 'Take counsel with them' is a quotation from Koran III 153.

(12) Nicholson VII p.186 suggests sources for this famous apologue, which is a parable of the Sufi's absorption into the attributes of God.

(13) To bring cumin-seed to Kirman is the Persian equivalent of the English 'bring coals to Newcastle.'

(14) 'When the angels in Heaven boasted of their superiority to the wicked children of Adam, God made two of their number, Harut and Marut, subject to lust and passion and sent them down to earth, where they fell in love with a beautiful woman and tried to seduce her. She would not, however, yield to their desire till they taught her the word of power that enabled them to ascend to Heaven. Having learned it, she ascended, and God transformed her into Zuhrah (the planet Venus). Harut and Marut were imprisoned in a pit at Babylon, choosing to expiate their sin in this world rather than suffer everlasting torment hereafter.' Koran II 96 refers to the two fallen angels of Babylon.

(15) A. Christensen, *Contes persans*, p.88 cites modern versions of this amusing tale and adduces parallels from Scandinavian folklore.

(16) The source of this story was al-Ghazali, *Ihya'*, chapter 'On the wonderful qualities of the heart'; it was also used by the poet Nizami in his *Romance of Alexander*. For a verse-translation by Sir James Redhouse, see my *Persian Poems*, pp.124-5.

(17) Zaid ibn Haritha, freedman and adopted son of Muhammad, mentioned by name in the Koran (Sura XXXIII 37), was claimed by the Sufis as an early prototype of Muslim mystic. The 'vision of Zaid' is very frequently cited by Sufi writers; see for instance my *Doctrine of the Sufis*, p.111. 'God is not ashamed before the truth' is a quotation from Koran XXXIII 53.

(19) Nicholson quotes from the history of Ibn al-Tiqtaqa the following version of this well-known anecdote. 'Ali, having overthrown a man in combat, sat down on his breast in order to behead him. The man spat in his face. Ali immediately rose and left him. On being asked why he had spared the life of his enemy, he replied, "When he spat in my face

I was angered by him, and I feared that if I killed him my anger would have some part in killing him. I did not wish to kill him save for God's sake alone".' The quotation 'When thou threwest' is from Koran VIII 17. 'Father of Dust': Ali's nickname was Abu Turab.

(23) The source of this story was 'Attar's *Ilahi-nama*.

(24) *The Opener* is Sura I and *The Clatterer* is Sura CI of the Koran.

(25) Nicholson points to possible sources of this story in 'Attar and Muhammad 'Aufi.

(26) In the rubric the hero of this anecdote is named as Ahmad ibn Khizruya, an eminent Sufi who died in 854. The episode of the boy who sold halwa seems to be taken from Muhammad ibn al-Munawwar's biography of the poet and mystic Abu Sa'id ibn Abi 'l-Khair; see Nicholson VII, p.252.

(27) This lively story gives an excellent description of the dervish 'concert'; the phrase 'The ass is gone' parodies the opening of a typical mystical ode.

(28) The phrase 'Children of Adam, eat!' is suggested by Koran VII 29 and similar contexts.

(31) Nicholson could not suggest any source for this remarkable tale. Reference is made in the course of it to the following Sufis: Junaid of Baghdad (d.910), Bayazid (Abu Yazid) of Bistam (d.877), Ma'ruf al-Karkhi of Baghdad (d.815), Ibrahim ibn Adham 'Prince of Khurasan' (d.777) and Shaqiq of Balkh (d.810). The phrase 'Whoso brings a good deed' is quoted from Koran VI 161.

(32) The command 'Return!' is a quotation from Koran LXXXIX 28.

(33) 'This Story is an allegory of the spirit that would fain demolish the "wall" of bodily senses and affections by which it is shut off from the contemplation of God.' The quotation 'And bow thyself and draw nigh' is from Koran XCVI 19.

(34) The quotation 'a rope of palm-fibre' is from Koran CXI 5, where the reference is to the wife of Muhammad's enemy Abu Lahab.

(35) The phrase 'baptism of God' is taken from Koran II 132.

(36) Dhu 'l-Nun the Egyptian, who died in 859 and whose

gravestone is still extant, was one of the greatest of the early Sufis. The anecdote is related elsewhere not of Dhu 'l-Nun but of Abu Bakr al-Shibli (d.945). Nicholson quotes from 'Attar how 'Shibli fell into such an ecstasy that, after he had several times tried in vain to kill himself, he was put in chains and carried to a madhouse. "In your opinion," he said, "I am mad and you are sane: may God increase my madness and your sanity, so that I may become nearer and nearer to God, and you farther and farther from Him!" When they were about to force medicine down his throat, he exclaimed, "Don't trouble yourselves, for this is not a malady that any medicine can cure." Some persons came to see him "Who are you?" he asked. They replied, "Your friends." He began to throw stones at them, and they all ran away. "O you liars," he cried, "do friends run away from their friend because of a few stones? I see you are friends to yourselves but not to to me".' The reference to striking 'with the tail of the cow' echoes Koran II 67.

(37) Luqman, proverbial for his wisdom, gave his name to Sura XXXI of the Koran. The short anecdote inserted in parenthesis occurs in Hujviri (transl. Nicholson), p.20: 'A dervish met a king. The king said: "Ask a boon of me." The dervish replied: "I will not ask a boon from one of my slaves." "How is that?" said the king. The dervish said: "I have two slaves who are thy masters: covetousness and worldly expectation".'

(38) The Koranic quotation is from Sura LXVII 30.

(40) Nicholson could not trace the source of this story. The 'Lote-tree of the Boundary' is mentioned in Koran LIII 14 in a description of a mysterious vision vouchsafed to Muhammad.

(41) The snake is often used to symbolize the appetitive soul. The prince stands for the spiritual preceptor.

(43) An elaborate version of this folk-tale is quoted in E. G. Browne, A Year amongst the Persians, p.198. The 'dog of the Men of the Cave' is a reference to Koran XVIII 17. 'Turn thou away from them' is a quotation from Koran XXXII 30.

(44) A version of this story, with the Persian physician Rhazes substituted for Galen, occurs in Kai Ka'us, Qabus-nama (transl. R. Levy), p.31: 'Once when Muhammad son of Zakariya al-Razi entered a certain place with a group of

disciples, a lunatic presented himself and smiled in his face. Immediately on his reaching home he ordered an infusion of epithymon, which he drank. When his disciples asked why he took this infusion, he replied, "It is because of that lunatic's smile. If he had not perceived some of his own dementia in me, he would not have smiled in my face. There is a proverb that birds of a feather flock together".'

(45) St Matthew xxv 43-45 immediately springs to mind, but a well-known Tradition of Muhammad runs as follows. 'On the Day of Resurrection God most High will say: "O son of Adam, I was sick and thou didst not visit Me." He will reply: "O Lord, how should I visit Thee, who art the Lord of all created beings?" God will say: "Didst thou not know that such and such a one, My servant, was sick, and thou didst not visit him? Didst thou not know that if thou hadst visited him thou wouldst have found Me beside him?" ' For the full text of the Tradition see Nicholson VII, p.303.

(46) Nicholson quotes the following closely similar story from 'Aufi. 'Four persons—a doctor of divinity and canon law, a descendant of Ali, a soldier, and a bazaar dealer—went into an orchard and were still enjoying the fruit when the owner appeared. Finding they had consumed a large amount, he resolved to punish them; but considering that he was one against four, he first addressed the doctor of divinity in complimentary terms. "You," he said, "are a divine and a model to us all; for our temporal and spiritual welfare depends on the learning of the divines. And this man (he continued) is an eminent Sayyid of the Prophet's Family, to which we all are devoted and which it is our duty to love. And here is a soldier: they wield the sword and through their exertions our homes are preserved from ruin. Now, if you gentlemen come into my orchard and unlawfully eat all my fruit, I bear you no grudge. But this fellow is a dealer in the market: what merit has he? What excuse can he have for robbing my orchard?" Thereupon he seized the *bazari* by his collar and handled him so roughly that at last he lay helpless on the ground. Then, turning to the soldier, he said: "I am the most humble servant of divines and Sayyids, but you—don't you know that I have paid the tax on this orchard to the Government and that not a penny has been kept back? I will bow to

the judgment of religious authorities and confess my fault; but who are you? What right have you to come to my orchard?" So saying, he fell upon the soldier, gave him a good drubbing, and bound him fast. After that, he turned to the doctor of canon law. "All the world," he said, "shows reverence to Sayyids; but you, who pretend to knowledge, don't you even know that orchards should not be entered without the owner's permission? For Sayyids I would sacrifice myself and all I possess, but an ignoramus like you, who is called a *danishmand* and deems the property of Moslems free for any one to take, deserves an exemplary chastisement." He suited the action to the word, and having tied up the divine, faced the Sayyid alone. "O rascally impostor," he cried, "with your long hair and crass ignorance! Won't you tell me why you have come to my orchard without my leave and wasted my property, though the Prophet never said that the wealth of his people is a lawful perquisite for the descendants of Ali?" He tied him up on the spot, and in this way obtained from all four the full value of the fruit which they had stolen.' Rumi has greatly improved upon his model and given more verisimilitude to the story. The *Intermediate* and the *Comprehensive* are the titles of two lawbooks by Muhammand al-Ghazali.

(47) The source is evidently the following anecdote related by 'Attar in his *Biographies of the Saints*, the narrator being Bayazid. 'A man met me on the road and asked me whither I was going. I said, "To make the Pilgrimage." He asked me what money I had with me. "Two hundred dirhems," I replied. "Give them to me," he said, "for I have a wife and children, and walk round me seven times: this will be your Pilgrimage." I did so, and returned home.' For a full account of Bayazid (Abu Yazid al-Bistami) see my *Revelation and Reason in Islam*, pp.89-103.

(49) For the sources of this story, the oldest of which is Abu 'l-Laith al-Samarqandi (who died about the year 1000), see Nicholson VII, p.322.

(50) The point of the 'drunkard' saying 'Hu, hu' is that 'Hu' is the shortened form of 'Huwa' which signifies 'He' i.e. 'God.' The cry 'Hu, hu' is often put in the mouths of God-intoxicated Sufis.

(52) Nicholson comments on this story. 'In my opinion chase of the thief symbolizes the mystic's quest for union with God, which cannot succeed if self-consciousness intervenes at the last moment.'

(53) Moawiya, who ousted Ali from the caliphate and ruled from 661 to 680, is usually portrayed as the worldly man who organized the Arab empire by a combination of ruthlessness and statesmanship. It is curious that he should have been chosen as the protagonist in this remarkable debate, for which Nicholson could not suggest any source. Bu Lahab was the Prophet's uncle and bitter enemy and was cursed in Sura CXI of the Koran. Bu 'l-Hakam was also an opponent of the Prophet and was given the nickname Bu 'l-Jahl, meaning 'Father of Ignorance'. His proper name is derived from the same root as the Arabic for 'wisdom'.

(54) The 'Mosque of Opposition' is mentioned in Koran IX 108, the supposed historical background to which is summarized in Nicholson VII, p.337.

(55) Muhammad, or according to other opinion Ali, is credited with the well-known saying, 'Wisdom is the believer's stray camel,' the subject of Tale 39 above.

(57) Goha, or Juhi (Juha), 'is the hero of many drolleries like those attributed to Khoja Nasru'ddin, Eulenspiegel, and Joe Miller.' The substance of this story occurs in al-Baihaqi, though there it is assigned to a certain Ibn Rawah who, on being asked about his son, replied: 'There is nothing like him in the world. He saw a mourning-woman following a bier and heard her crying, "Alas, master, thou art being taken to a house wherein is neither water nor food nor bed nor mattress nor coverlet nor lamp nor light!" "O father," says he, "they are taking him to our house".'

(59) The source was 'Attar, Biographies of the Saints. 'One day whilst Ibrahim was seated on the bank of the Tigris, stitching his tattered dervish robe, the needle fell into the river. Some one said to him, "You gave up such a splendid kingdom: what have you gained?" Ibrahim signified to the river that his needle should be given back. Immediately a thousand fishes rose from the water, each carrying in its mouth a needle of gold. He said to them, "I want my needle," whereupon a poor little fish came to the surface with the

needle in its mouth. "This," said Ibrahim, "is the least thing I have gained by giving up the kingdom of Balkh: the other things you cannot know".'

(61) Nicholson commented: 'This apologue conveys a warning to novices who from ignorance and self-conceit behave disrespectfully towards their spiritual guides.'

(62) For the sources see above, p.16. The Sura 'He Frowned' is Koran LXXX.

(64) This miracle is attributed to the Sufi saint Ibn Khafif of Shiraz, who died in 943. This is Ibn Battuta's version, as summarized by Nicholson: 'The Shaykh was travelling in Ceylon with a party of dervishes. They lost their way among the mountains and were in danger of starving, so they asked the Shaykh's permission to catch one of the young elephants which frequented that district. He forbade them, but being overcome by hunger they seized a fat young beast, slaughtered it, and made a hearty meal. On that night the old elephants assembled, marched to the place where the dervishes were lying asleep, smelt each man, and killed the whole party except the Shaykh. Him too they smelt, but did no harm to him; for he had refused to eat. One of the elephants, curling its trunk round him, lifted him on to its back and carried him to a place inhabited by infidels who, when they saw him, touched the skirt of his mantle (in token of veneration) and conducted him to their king.' The citation 'Slink you into Hell' is from Koran XXIII 110.

(65) Khazir was a mysterious guide who first appears in Koran XVIII 64 (not named, but identified by the commentators as 'one of Our servants unto whom We had given mercy from Us, and We had taught him knowledge proceeding from Us') as accompanying Moses and doing strange things. The Sufis took him as the exemplar of the Shaikh who requires absolute and unquestioning obedience of the disciple.

(66) Nicholson could not trace any source for this amusing and well told story.

(67) Aesop has a similar story about a jackdaw. 'The streets of Mina' refer to Mina, a town nearby Mecca which is the terminal point of the Muslim pilgrimage.

(68) The following is Nicholson's abridgment of a version of the story of the birth of Moses given in the Persian *Tales of*

the Prophets. 'Pharaoh said to the astrologers, "How can it be averted?" They answered, "On the Friday night when the conception of this boy is to happen, order a throne to be set up for you outside the city and mount it and proclaim that the Israelites shall come and behold you." Pharaoh never showed himself in public, especially amongst the Israelites: when he rode in the city, the people went into their houses, and any one who met him of a sudden would fall flat on the ground lest he might see Pharaoh's face. According to Wahb ibn Munabbih, when Pharaoh heard this proposal, he said, "That they should see my face is the worst crime of all"; but he gave the command. Having mounted a throne, he spoke kindly to the Israelites and bestowed on them much wealth, so that they rejoiced. At nightfall he said to them: "I desire that ye stay with me in this plain the whole night; tomorrow morning we shall return together to the city." So the Israelites stayed there all night under strict guard, for fear any man should go home. Pharaoh, it is said, had made Heliopolis his capital. The keys of the city were in the hands of Imran, who knew about the prediction. His wife was an Israelite woman, and he lay with her that night, saying to himself, "If it happen as the astrologers predict, the boy may be my son." Some relate that during the night Pharaoh summoned Imran and demanded the keys, that he might enter the city; but Imran said, "The King ought not to go alone: the King has many enemies, and I fear an attempt may be made on his life." Pharaoh said, "Thou hast spoken well, O Imran: come, then, with me to the city." When they entered the city, Pharaoh said to Imran, "I have preferred thee to all others. Now, tonight thou must not take off thy shirt but remain in attendance at the palace-gate." Imran said, "I obey." The city being emptied of men, the women were going about in the streets, for they did not know that Pharaoh had returned. Imran's wife saw her husband at the gate of the palace. They lay together and she became pregnant with Moses. Imran said to his wife, "It is in my mind that the boy for whom the King is searching will be the child thou hast conceived tonight. Beware! Do not acquaint any one with thy condition, for Pharaoh has forbidden the Israelites to lie with their wives this night." Ibn Abbas says: "No prophet was ever born without his star appearing in the sky."

297

When the mother of Moses became pregnant, his star appeared. The astrologers, seeing a star brighter than all the rest and knowing that the child whose birth it presaged was the one sought by Pharaoh and that he would be victorious over all, rent their garments and shrieked and cast earth on their heads. The noise reached Pharaoh in his palace: he came forth and asked Imran what was the matter. "Possibly," said Imran, "the Israelites are making merry because they have seen the face of the King and enjoyed his munificence." Pharaoh re-entered the palace, but he had no sleep that night. Then the astrologers came to Imran, saying, "What was dreaded has come to pass: the person against whom the King seeks protection is begotten." Imran replied: "Ye are to blame: ye proposed that he should show his face to the Israelites and distribute his wealth among them and then failed to take precautions." He brought them before Pharaoh, who swore he would put them to death, and only reprieved them when they promised to deliver the child into his hands as soon as it was born. When they announced to him the birth of Moses, he was terrified and asked what could be done. They told him he must again set up a throne outside the city and proclaim that every Israelite woman who had borne a child during the month should come thither, bringing her child with her, so that the mothers might receive the same bounty as the King had formerly bestowed on the fathers; then he must give orders to kill every male child and spare the females. Wahb ibn Munabbih says that Pharaoh in searching for Moses killed seventy thousand children.' The story of Moses is related most fully in Sura XXVIII of the Koran.

(69) A story about a frozen snake reviving is told in Vara-vini's *Tales of Marzuban*, p.36 of the translation by R. Levy.

(70) The incident of the rod of Moses and the panic which followed its metamorphosis into a snake forms the background to this story. Sura XX of the Koran contains another account of Moses before Pharaoh.

(71) For the source of this story see above, p.16.

(72) The background to this story is Koran XI 47-49

(73) The Zaid of this anecdote is no particular historical person.

(75) The Persian *Tales of the Prophets* supplied Rumi with

the material for this story. 'A certain Israelite committed a wrong against one of their great men. When the two met before David, the wrong-doer said (by way of exculpation), "This man had taken my cow from me unjustly." The rich man denied that he had done so, and the other could produce no evidence. David bade them withdraw, saying, "I will look into the matter." Afterwards God revealed to him in a dream that he must slay the guilty man. David said to himself, "It is only a dream: I will wait to make sure." He dreamed the same dream twice and thrice. Then he sent for the rich man and told him that he was commanded by God to slay him. "What!" he exclaimed, "will you slay me without proof when I am innocent?" David answered, "Yes, by God, I will carry out God's command." Knowing that David would slay him, the man said, "Give me time enough to tell you that I am not punished on account of the present offence, but because I murdered this man's son." David gave the order that he should be put to death, whereupon the Israelites regarded David with exceeding reverence, and his kingdom was firmly established.'

(76) This international folk-tale occurs in many places, including the *Thousand and One Nights* (transl. R. Burton, 'Supplementary Nights' IV, p.90).

(78) The name of the hermit is given as Abu 'l-Khair al-Aqta' ('the Maimed') al-Tinati, who died about 950. To the biographical references given by Nicholson may now be added al-Sulami, *Tabaqat al-Sufiya* (ed. J. Pedersen), pp.382-5).

(81) Buhlul was a famous dervish who lived in the time of Harun al-Rashid and became the hero of many folk-stories.

(82) Nicholson could not trace any other reference to this Daquqi. 'No indeed, not a refuge!' is a quotation from Koran LXXV 11. The Ox and the Fish are the mythical monsters upon which the earth was supposed to rest.

(83) No source for this story was traced by Nicholson. Jesus is said to have created birds out of clay in Koran III 43.

(84) The background to this narrative is Koran XXXIV 14-18. The story of the Hare occurs, among other places, in the *Kalila wa-Dimna*; see Nicholson VIII, p.72.

(86) Anas ibn Malik was a famous transmitter of Traditions

of Muhàmmad who died towards the beginning of the eighth century.

(88) The sources of these two stories are given in Nicholson VIII, p. 83. 'Uzza was an idol worshipped by the pagan Arabs.

(89) Nicholson could not trace the source of this story.

(91) Hamza, uncle of the Prophet Muhammad and one of his earliest followers, after many heroic exploits was killed at the Battle of Uhud in 625.

(92) Bilal the negro was Muhammad's muezzin; he is buried near Damascus.

(93) The source is Koran XIX 16-18.

(94) Nicholson could not trace the source of this story which he considered to have some historical foundation. 'All things perish' is a quotation from Koran XXVIII 88. 'Surely to Him we return' is Koran II 151. 'God is the third of three' is Koran V 77, a refutation of the Trinity.

(95) The background is Koran VIII 50, referring to the events of the Battle of Badr. 'The Quraysh had marched out from Mecca in order to defend their caravan, which Mohammed threatened to waylay and capture. Having learned that it was safe, they debated whether they should return home or advance on Badr, where the Moslem army was encamped. The danger of leaving Mecca open to an attack by the Banu Kinanah, with whom they were then at feud, might have turned the scale, if Iblis, assuming the form of Suraqah ibn Malik the Kinanite, had not risen to the occasion and pledged his word that they had nothing to fear.'

(96) Nicholson could not trace the source of this story.

(98) Karbala was the scene of the martyrdom in 680 of Husain. By Mansur, Hallaj is intended, the martyr-mystic executed in 922.

(100) 'Attar, Asrar-nama, p. 58 suggested this story.